Atlantic Ocean

N

CAPE CHARLES

CAPE HENRY

Tangier Sound

Crisfield

Pocomoke Sound

TANGIER I.

SMITH I.

apcake Bay

Newport News

Norfolk

Potomac R.

Mobjack Bay

Hampton

Piankatank R.

Hampton Roads

James R.

York R.

Rappahannock R.

A CRUISING GUIDE
To
THE CHESAPEAKE

*Including the Passages from
Long Island Sound along the
New Jersey Coast and Inland Waterway*

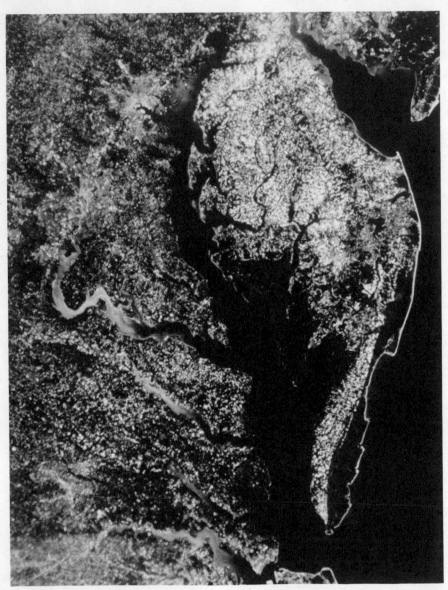

Chesapeake Bay—a high-flying view! (Photo courtesy of the Chesapeake Bay Foundation.)

A CRUISING GUIDE
To
THE CHESAPEAKE

Including the Passages from
Long Island Sound along the
New Jersey Coast and Inland Waterway

WILLIAM T. STONE
FESSENDEN S. BLANCHARD
AND
ANNE M. HAYS

WITH PHOTOGRAPHS AND CHARTS

G. P. PUTNAM'S SONS ⚓ *New York*

G. P. Putnam's Sons
Publishers Since 1838
200 Madison Avenue
New York, NY 10016

Library of Congress Cataloging-in-Publication Data

Stone, William T.
  A cruising guide to the Chesapeake.

  Bibliography: p.
  Includes index.
    1. Boats and boating—Chesapeake Bay (Md. and Va.)—
Guide-books.   2. Marinas—Chesapeake Bay (Md. and Va.)
3. Chesapeake Bay (Md. and Va.)—Description and travel—
Guide-books.   4. Chesapeake Bay (Md. and Va.)—Navigation.
I. Blanchard, Fessenden Seaver, 1888–1963.   II. Hays,
Anne M., date.   III. Title.
ISBN 0-399-15003-X
GV776.C47S76   1989   917.55′18′0443   88-30536

Printed in the United States of America

1   2   3   4   5   6   7   8   9   10

CONTENTS

FOREWORD

This seventh edition of *A Cruising Guide to the Chesapeake* appears after almost four decades of continual use as a guide to exploring the largest and one of the most remarkable estuaries in the continental United States. Since the first edition was published in 1950, each decade has brought significant changes to the Chesapeake, not only in cruising conditions but also in the Bay itself and the people who share the use of its bountiful resources in so many different ways.

In this seventh edition, significantly revised and updated, we take note of such major changes as the rapid increase in the boating population and the accompanying growth in boating facilities all around the Bay. It is interesting to recall that there was no uniform federal numbering system covering recreational boats at the time of our first edition, and it was not until 1960 that the Coast Guard first published its nationwide compilation of boating statistics. According to those figures, the total boat population on the Chesapeake increased approximately 300 percent between 1960 and 1986, from just over 88,000 in 1960 to more than 300,000 in 1986. Divided almost equally between Virginia and Maryland, the largest concentrations of pleasure boats have developed around Annapolis, Baltimore, St. Michaels, and Oxford in the Upper Bay, and Norfolk, Newport News, and Portsmouth in the Lower Bay.

Perhaps the most pervasive overall change we have found since the last edition is the growing public awareness of environmental threats to the Bay. Even as recently as 20 years ago, when we were researching the 1968 edition, conservation problems rarely seemed to intrude into the consciousness of those who used the Bay for their livelihood or recreation. Pollution and erosion had begun to cause concern in areas of rapid urban growth and industrial expansion, but it was not until the late 1960's that critical trouble spots began to surface as matters of immediate political and economic concern. Now we find the Chesapeake region, along with most of the nation, troubled about oil spills, thermal pollution, eutrophication, shoreline erosion, dredging and soil disposal, municipal waste disposal, pollution from vessels, and conflicting federal and state marine sanitation laws. There are political conflicts over regulation of shorefront property and agricultural usage in waterfront locations, port development and bulk cargo terminals, maritime zoning and marina construction, and protection of wetlands and fisheries.

A cruising guide is not the appropriate place to deal with environmental problems, and we are not qualified to evaluate the impact of natural and man-made changes on the ecology of the Chesapeake. Yet it is fitting that boatmen who use the Bay and observe its changing character are among the first to be concerned. Many yachtsmen belong to groups such as the Chesapeake Bay Foundation, which are seeking better understanding of the Bay and its environmental problems. We include in the appendix of this edition an updated evaluation of major environmental threats to the Bay, written by William C. Baker, President of the Chesapeake Bay Foundation, based on findings of a 6-year scientific survey conducted by the Environmental Protection Agency.

Despite the many changes recorded in the present edition, the distinctive characteristics of the Chesapeake remain, and most of the unique qualities which make this extraordinary tidal estuary such a rewarding cruising ground are still largely untarnished. Parts of the Chesapeake are still isolated from the mainstream of economic development around the Bay, although this whole great tidal basin is close to major centers of population. Modern transportation has brought all of the Chesapeake country closer to these population centers and within easy range of recreational boatmen in any part of the country. You can quickly reach the friendly shores of the Chesapeake, whether you fly in by jet from the Pacific Coast to pick up a charter yacht at Annapolis or whether you trailer your outboard cruiser from the Midwest to a quiet launching ramp on the Piankatank. However you may come—or whether you are only planning a future cruise—this guide is designed to aid you in the discovery and safe enjoyment of some of the nation's finest cruising waters.

There was no guide to the Chesapeake when Fessenden Blanchard first came down from New England, where he had co-authored *A Cruising Guide to the New England Coast* with Roger Duncan. Recognizing the need for a guide to the Chesapeake, Blanchard set out to produce one. When he met Bill Stone in a quiet anchorage in Rhode River in the fall of 1948, he outlined his plans. Although Stone had been sailing the Chesapeake since the early 1930's, he felt he didn't know enough about the many creeks and coves to join Blanchard for that first edition. However, Blanchard and Stone began collaborating before the next, revised edition in 1962, continuing until Blanchard's death in 1963. For the 25 years and five editions since then, Stone has continued to cruise the Bay extensively in his own boats (most recently a Nevins 40, *Brer Fox*) and to update *A Cruising Guide to the Chesapeake* with the valuable assistance of many other Chesapeake sailors who have contributed their local knowledge over the years. In this edition, he is joined by Anne M. Hays, who has been sailing on and writing about the Chesapeake for nearly 20 years.

We continue to adhere to the original purpose of the Guide, as conceived by Blanchard: to obtain and then put into convenient form the sort of information not ordinarily provided on charts or in the *U.S. Coast Pilot;* to discuss cruising conditions on the Chesapeake from the boatman's viewpoint; to describe what you may expect to find on the Bay, on each of its 40 rivers, in as many as possible of its creeks and harbors. Our continuing aim is to keep alive the art and practice of leisurely cruising; to include such practical items as uncharted channel markers or hidden obstructions—and what to do about them; to indicate snug anchorages and the nature of the holding ground; to suggest places to tie up and the location of yacht clubs, marinas, and repair yards (where such are still to be found); and to indicate points of scenic or historic interest which may be within hailing distance. If we reveal a bias, we confess to favoring sail to power as a way of cruising; we admit a preference for anchoring out to tying up at a marina slip, and a prejudice against unseamanlike handling of any vessel, whether sail or power.

In preparation for this new edition we have re-explored the Chesapeake once again, poking into rivers, creeks, and inlets we haven't seen for several years, revisiting favorite anchorages, and searching for new snug harbors that have escaped the boat population explosion on the Bay. The list of snug harbors and quiet gunkholes is shrinking, inevitably, with the rising boating population, but the configuration of the Chesapeake, with its several thousands of miles of tidewater shoreline, is such that a knowledgeable cruising skipper can still find a quiet anchorage around the bend in a river or creek undiscovered by others. In remote parts of the Bay we have actually found choice little hideaways often unsuspected by local boatmen and not easily identified on the charts. The "we" is more than editorial, for we have continued the practice of drawing upon the local knowledge of many other Chesapeake sailors—several hundred of them who know their own rivers, creeks, and harbors more intimately than any single cruising sailor could ever hope to know them.

Several contributors to earlier editions deserve continuing recognition for their valuable assistance in covering areas they knew intimately. Some of them have passed on, but their names will long be remembered and honored on the Bay: Frederick M. Gardiner, John A. Meigs, Kenneth B. Millett, Linton and "Bunny" Rigg, Sam Foster, C. Lowndes Johnson, F. Slade Dale, Howard I. Chapelle, David J. Dunigan, Jr., and Dr. Walter C. Tilden.

Some who knew and wrote about the prewar Chesapeake were: Alfred F. Loomis, Robert N. Bavier, Sr., George and Robert Barrie, Roland Birnn, Frederick Tilp, Robert H. Burgess, and M. V. Brewington.

Still other Bay skippers have contributed to recent editions by sharing their "favorite anchorages" in rivers, creeks, and coves of the Chesapeake. These include Thomas H. Closs, George F. Johnson, John Miles, Dick Hutchings, Kenneth D. Saylor, Burke (Joe) Lucas, Ralph Wiley, and Arnold C. Gay. Reeves "Skip" Taylor, an experienced coastwise sailor, has supplemented our information about the passage from the Chesapeake to New York.

A number of other contributors have helped us to keep abreast of changes occurring in areas of the Bay where they have lived and sailed. This group includes Albert S. Polk, Don Nunes, George W. Noblett, Jr., Robert E. Hale, Jr., R. Latane Waring, and James M. Patterson III.

Special thanks must go to several institutions and agencies whose help has been appreciated: The Chesapeake Bay Foundation, the Mariners Museum at Newport News, Va.; the Chesapeake Bay Maritime Museum at St. Michaels, Md.; and the Chesapeake Bay Institute have been particularly helpful in giving us access to research or historical data on the Bay. The late William B. Mathews, Jr., formerly of the Maryland Department of Natural Resources, provided much useful information on boating facilities in that state.

We continue to be deeply indebted to "Fess" Blanchard, whose original contributions and enthusiasm for the Chesapeake are reflected throughout this new edition.

The present editors assume responsibility for changes and new material added to keep abreast of changing conditions. We have made every effort to check out facts and be as accurate as possible;

but we must warn readers, as we have in previous editions, that *the information contained herein cannot be guaranteed and must be used with caution.* Sections of government charts reproduced as illustrations are *not to be used for navigation purposes.* We are indebted to the National Ocean Service for permitting their use as aids in following the text, and for allowing us to reproduce some of their air photos of river and harbor entrances.

For the convenience of readers we include in Appendix A a chart summary showing the basic chart coverage for the Chesapeake and Delaware Bay areas. The summary includes the five-digit number, scale, and area covered, for both bays and the ocean and coastal sections between the Delaware and Chesapeake Bay entrance, plus coastal areas of New Jersey, Delaware, Maryland, and Virginia.

With each edition of the Guide we have continued to receive valuable information from cruising yachtsmen and readers who have noted changes we may have overlooked. We welcome receiving your comments and suggestions, which may be of value in future editions.

William T. Stone
Anne M. Hays
Annapolis, Maryland

Woodcut of John Smith, Chapin Library, Williams College. (Photograph courtesy of the Mariners Museum, Newport News, Virginia)

The country is not mountainous not yet low but such pleasant plaine, hils and fertile valleyes, one prettily crossing on other, and watered so conveniently with their sweete brooks and cristall springs, as if art itselfe had devised them . . .

The mildness of the aire, the fertilitie of the soile, and the situation of the rivers are so propitious to the nature and use of man as no place is more convenient for pleasure, profit, and man's sustenance . . .

The waters, Isles, and shoales are full of safe harbours for ships of warre or marchandize, for boats of all sortes, for transportation or fishing.

Captain John Smith in 1608. From *Travels and Works of Captain John Smith*, edited by Edward Arber, F.S.A. (John Grant, Edinburgh, Scotland)

Part One

INTRODUCTORY

CHAPTER ONE

INTRODUCTION TO CHESAPEAKE BAY

No cruising waters in the United States have more to offer the boatman than Chesapeake Bay. Whether you do your cruising by sail or power, in a large yacht or small trailer-cruiser, this historic tidewater area of Maryland and Virginia provides distinctive attractions that you are unlikely to find in any other coastal waters.

The Chesapeake is unique in many ways. It is the nation's largest bay, with a shoreline of close to 6,000 miles at tidewater (including tributaries) that exceeds the entire general coastline of the continental United States. It lies close to major population centers on the Eastern Seaboard, yet large parts of the Bay remain isolated and virtually unknown.

One early colonist called the Chesapeake "the noblest Bay in the Universe," and succeeding generations down to present-day boatmen have echoed their praise of this inland sea and its surrounding shores. "No body of water in the country has cast such a spell over those who have had the opportunity to spend some time in the area," said Robert H. Burgess in *This Was Chesapeake Bay*. But its greatest attraction to the cruising boatman lies in the charm and variety of its innumerable snug harbors.

When we were children, we used to enjoy fooling each other by putting small Christmas presents into large boxes. Opening a large box hopefully, we would find a smaller one inside. Inside the second box would be a still smaller one. Finally, after this had gone on for some time, cozily tucked away in a tiny box would be the present— usually all the better because it was small, all the more appealing because of the delay in finding it.

Finding a harbor in the Chesapeake resembles that experience. First there is a bay or a river—or both—then a large creek, then a small creek, and then tucked away inside the small creek in a little cove around the bend will be one of the snuggest anchorages in the world. You will probably have this cruising present all to yourself. The Long Island Sound yachtsman who is enthusiastic, and rightfully, about Hamburg Cove, or the Buzzards Bay sailor who talks of the snugness and beauty of Hadley Harbor, ought to visit the Chesapeake. There are literally hundreds of Hamburg Coves and Hadley Harbors here, some not even named.

These harbors aren't so hard to reach as might be thought from our description. Sometimes you find a good anchorage in a river or a large creek. More often you find it in a small creek, and usually you don't have to go too far upriver to get there. Writing about the harbors on Long Island Sound is easy. Except for those on one or two rivers like the Connecticut, most of the harbors lead directly off the Sound. It isn't difficult to define what is a harbor and what is not, where one begins and where it ends. When we get through, we can count the harbors and tell you, for example, that there are 60 in the 90 miles of Long Island Sound and perhaps no one will argue with us. Not so on the Chesapeake. When does the inside of a bend in a river or the little cove or creek still farther inside become small enough, or snug enough, or clearly enough defined, to count as a harbor? Several times we spread out chart 12263, which includes Annapolis, Oxford, and many other anchorages in the Upper Chesapeake, and tried to count the harbors on it. We are sure that no one else would get the same results. There may be 100 or there may be 150. We counted 89 good anchorages with at least 6 feet in depth showing on that chart. Over the years, as we have come to know the Bay more intimately, we have found more than 100 protected anchorages by poking into creeks and coves in our own boat and checking out the contours shown on the larger-scale charts (12268, 12270, 12266) that cover this same relatively small segment of the Chesapeake and its tributaries. We know we haven't yet found them all, but we'll tell you about some of our favorite gunkholes in the chapters that follow. We don't know any other coastal region in the country—including Penobscot Bay and along the coast of Maine— that has as many sheltered harbors in so small an area.

"It's like the deck plan of an octopus," said a Chesapeake sailor of an earlier era in describing the configuration of the Eastern Shore. "The coastlines resemble filigree, rather than solid littoral," says Varley Lang in *Follow the Water*.

"Cruising has two main pleasures," Howard Bloomfield wrote in *Sailing to the Sun*. "One is to go out into wider waters from a sheltered place. The other is to go into a sheltered place from wide waters." You have plenty of opportunity to do both on the Chesapeake. For you are not always following the arms of the octopus. You have plenty of chance to take it like any blue-water sailor—on some wide waters, when the Bay decides to kick up.

The Chesapeake is the largest saltwater estuary in the continental United States. Approximately 187 nautical miles (200 statute miles) long from the Chesapeake and Delaware Canal, its northern entrance, to the southern entrance between Cape Charles and Cape Henry, its width ranges from 3 ½ to 10 miles north of the Potomac to from 10 to 25 miles in its lower reaches. Directly into the Bay flow nearly 40 rivers, not counting literally hundreds of tributary rivers and creeks—all really estuaries, for they are tidal for all or most of their navigable length. With salt near the entrance, the water in the longer rivers grows less and less brackish as you near the head of navigation. Except for the Susquehanna at the upper part of the Bay, all of these rivers are navigable for considerable distances, the deepest being those on the Lower Western Shore, like the York and the James, where battleships can—and do—anchor.

Chesapeake Bay is the approach to such important seaports as Baltimore, Newport News, and Norfolk. On its rivers are other cities and many towns, some large and some very small. Ninety-five miles up the Potomac is the capital of the United States. Yet, despite its many cities and towns, most of the Bay country is a land where the tall chimneys of factories are seldom seen, a land of fields and farms, of tree-fringed shores, with occasional mounds of oyster shells to remind the cruising man that here also are a people who live by and from the sea.

Fessenden Blanchard's description of his first bird's-eye view of the Chesapeake from a small plane in the summer of 1948 is almost as applicable to the Bay country of the 1980's. The mazelike pattern of rivers and creeks spreads out as far as the eye can see, and the same snug harbors are spotted below. More pleasure boats of all kinds are to be seen on the Bay and in the harbors now, and there are more houses along the waterfront. Although undeveloped waterfront land is fast disappearing near the big urban population centers, and wetlands are being threatened in many parts of the Bay, most of the 6,000 miles of tidewater shoreline around the Chesapeake and its tributaries remain very much as Blanchard described it.

"After following the Chesapeake and Delaware Canal," Blanchard wrote, "we flew first down the Eastern Shore. We saw a pleasant, cultivated land, with many well-kept farmhouses, large and small. The shores were not high, but still high enough to appeal to us, and with their border of trees, in many places steep enough to offer good protection against strong winds. Here and there we could see some of the famous houses of colonial and later times, overlooking majestically the creeks and rivers which used to be their highway, or tucked away among tall trees and box hedges. The number of abandoned and often dilapidated steamboat wharves which we saw was astonishing. They are to be found on every important river and creek, relics of the nostalgic days when travel was largely by water. The quantity of private docks made us envious. The writer's long-cherished ambition for a private harbor of his own seemed not such

This group of people on a Chesapeake Bay Foundation trip are hauling a net to learn about Bay life. The boat is the Wood Duck, *a Chesapeake Bay workboat owned by the CBF. (Photo courtesy of the Chesapeake Bay Foundation.)*

a wild dream after all." There are more private docks today, and more yachtsmen who have found their own protected coves.

Much of what Blanchard had to say about the Lower Eastern Shore holds true today. "As we crossed the broad mouth of the Choptank," he wrote, "about 70 miles down the Bay from the Chesapeake and Delaware Canal, the land became low and frequently marshy, with many islands and shoals, sometimes extending far offshore. We caught a glimpse of what looked like the recent track of a keel on one of them. Snug harbors were much fewer and with some notable exceptions, less appealing than farther up the Bay. We flew over the Little Choptank and its creeks, saw Deal Island and Crisfield, circled Smith Island several times, while Tangier showed dimly through the haze. These, we decided, were the exceptions; these, with their fishermen, oystermen, and crabbers, we wanted to see again at close quarters."

The entrance to Chesapeake Bay and the busy commercial harbors of Hampton Roads, Norfolk, and Newport News have seen many changes since the first edition of this guide, but Blanchard's first air-view impressions of the Western Shore starting at York River are still valid today. "Here the land is generally steeper, the water much deeper in the rivers and close to the shore. Islands here are less frequent. With some exceptions, like the Severn in Maryland, we found the rivers more attractive near their mouths than farther up, where the shores are apt to become low and marshy and the creeks shoaler. This is good news for the yachtsman whose time is limited, though to some cruising men there is a special appeal in upriver exploration. Except for one long stretch of cliff-studded coast below Herring Bay, there are good harbors every few miles for the entire length of the Western Shore, and history is around every bend on its rivers."

Except near the mouth of the Susquehanna and on breakwaters, you'll see few rocks in the Chesapeake. No big surf rolls in and crashes among rocky ledges, as it does on the coast of Maine; yet the seas can be steep and high enough to be a challenge. The contrasts in scenery are fewer and less striking than on the more rugged and varied New England Coast; for instance, you can't sail in a day from the sand dunes of a Provincetown to the rocky shores of a Cape Anne. Nor can you cruise among the high cliffs and hills of a Penobscot Bay or a Mount Desert. Yet you will find on the Chesapeake enough variety to interest you, a great deal of charm, and much security, ease, and comfort. If you want privacy and a snug anchorage all to yourself, yet within easy reach of civilization, you are much more apt to find it on the Chesapeake than farther north.

Chesapeake Bay is virtually tideless, so that tying up overnight at dock or slip is an easy matter. There are far more attractive facilities of this kind on the Bay than on Long Island Sound or the New England Coast. Until we cruised there, we never appreciated how pleasant it could be to tie up in a slip, as at Oxford or Solomons Island, step ashore for a walk and nearby supplies, fill our water tanks from a convenient hose, perhaps have a shower before supper, and plug in our electric cord for the evening.

There are limitations to this slip business, however, which become more serious every year as the larger Chesapeake ports get more crowded and marina facilities become more congested. You'll be lucky to find any kind of transient slip at Annapolis, St. Michaels, or even Oxford during the summer season, and if you are running the Waterway route on a schedule it's advisable to phone ahead for reservations. But anchorages are still to be found in or near all of the Bay ports, and we have plenty of suggestions in Part Three for finding a quiet spot where the water is cleaner and the surroundings become more peaceful and attractive only a little way farther up a creek or in a quiet cove without any of the facilities that are sometimes so convenient.

The Chesapeake is part of the great inland waterway to Florida. It is too often a "blue-flag country," as Fred Gardiner has called it, through which yachts pass hastily on their way north or south with their blue flags flying at the cross trees to indicate the absence of the owner. But every year more and more yachtsmen stop over for cruising or racing in the Bay. Racing skippers from Long Island Sound and New England bring their boats down for the popular

Fall Series of the Annapolis Yacht Club, held during the first three weekends of October, and the 100-mile Skipper race in late October. Powerboat owners, too, are discovering the pleasures of fall and spring cruising on the Bay, and are spending a week or two in these waters on their way north or south.

Chesapeake cruising has some drawbacks. But so has cruising everywhere else. The Maine Coast, while very beautiful, is apt to have long spells of thick fog in summer; the water is cold and frequently calm. In the spring and fall the air is apt to be very cold. The Buzzards Bay and Cape Cod areas may be hot and too crowded for privacy in summer, though a breeze can usually be counted on. Long Island Sound calms are proverbial and the opportunities for privacy limited. In all these places, the season of pleasant cruising weather is apt to start late in May and end in late September. On the Chesapeake there is at least an extra month of good cruising at each end of the season.

The chief drawbacks to the enjoyment of Chesapeake cruising are the hot weather in July and August, and the summer calms. But even the frequent warm weather is no serious handicap to those who know the game, to the old Chesapeake hands who cruise constantly in summer and enjoy it. They know enough always to have an awning, and where to anchor, so that they will be cooler than if they had stayed at home. To them, coolness is as important as snugness in the choice of a summer anchorage.

They will find a place where the evening breezes, usually from the southerly quadrant, have a chance to reach them across the water, unobstructed by high land or high trees. If possible, they will anchor where the wind draws up a river or creek, or across a low point or bar which protects them from the seas. Or they will find shelter opposite a creek or stretch of a river to the south or southwest.

Summer calms don't bother Chesapeake cruising skippers too much, or keep them in port in hot weather. The Sailing Club of the Chesapeake, with a roster of several hundred cruising boats, schedules its weekend rendezvous right through the summer months and holds its annual cruise week in August. Actually, there are relatively few days without a breeze of some sort during the morning or afternoon hours, and the Chesapeake has its fair share of cool fronts moving in from the northwest even during July and August. The Chesapeake Bay Yacht Racing Association (CBYRA) has a sanctioned regatta somewhere on the Bay virtually every week from May through October, and seldom is a race called off for lack of wind.

For the yachtsmen who live in Philadelphia and its suburbs, in Wilmington, Lancaster, Baltimore, or Washington, or anywhere else within easy reach of the Bay, summer cruising on the Chesapeake has much to offer. For those who come from the New England Coast or Long Island Sound, it is in the spring and fall that the Chesapeake is the cruising country par excellence. Then, the water and the air are usually delightful; the mosquitoes and the flies are seldom in evidence, and the poisonous sea nettles have not yet appeared, or have gone.

In the fall, particularly, squalls are infrequent, and the changing color of the leaves adds a new beauty. We will not soon forget some of the autumn sunsets, with skies and shores of red and orange, with blue above and around us, while our sloop lay peacefully at anchor in a quiet creek.

The number of cruising yachts based on the Chesapeake has increased enormously during the last two decades, with both sail- and powerboats represented in the marine population explosion. More than 10,000 pleasure boats from other states are registered in Maryland and berthed or used in the upper part of the Bay. We used to say that the sailing population was small compared to Long Island Sound and parts of New England, but that's no longer the case. Visitors from northern yachting centers in the eighties are astonished at the change. On any good weekend you are likely to see more sails off Annapolis, St. Michaels, and Oxford than you will on the Sound or Narragansett Bay. There is less sailing on the Lower Bay, although Hampton and Fishing Bay have become active yachting centers.

Sailing has gained rapidly since the 1960's, as more and more people who like cruising under sail are beginning to appreciate what the Chesapeake has to offer. Already at the above ports and elsewhere are to be found splendid fleets of seagoing sloops, cutters, yawls, ketches, and schooners, as well as converted bugeyes and skipjacks which would be a credit to the sport at Larchmont or Marblehead.

The Chesapeake is a paradise for motor cruisers and the new cruising houseboats which are seen on the Bay in increasing numbers. Much of the Bay's cruising is done in power craft, large and small. For them the Chesapeake is especially ideal, with its multiplicity of estuaries, rivers, and narrow creeks to explore and the attractive and interesting places to visit—even larger in number than those accessible to sailing yachts, because of the characteristic shoal draft of motor cruisers. Convenient slips, with their many facilities already described, add to the ease and pleasure of power cruising on the Chesapeake.

The number of yacht clubs and marinas is growing rapidly. Many of these are discussed later in connection with our descriptions of individual harbors.

The most highly publicized of the yachting events is the Annapolis to Newport race, held in June, on the alternate "odd" years between Bermuda races. Other important races include the Governor's Cup, from Annapolis to St. Marys City, those from Annapolis to Oxford, from Annapolis to Hampton, from Annapolis to Bermuda, and many others. Unfortunately, space does not permit our doing justice to the many regattas which fill the long and busy Chesapeake yachting season under the aegis of the CBYRA.

No cruising guide would be complete without some mention of the distinctive craft which do so much to enhance the appeal of the Chesapeake. Besides the log sailing canoes—in evidence chiefly at regattas—bugeyes, buy-boats, deadrise fishing boats and clam rigs, skipjacks, bateaux, and the unique and omnipresent crabbing skiff are still to be seen on the Chesapeake. Even if you don't like oysters or crabs, you will be glad of the contribution which oystering and crabbing have made to keeping most of these boats in circulation.

We almost forgot the push boats, or yawl boats, as they are called in most parts of the Bay. The skipjacks may use them as a source of power while dredging two days a week (Monday and Tuesday) or to propel them any other time when the dredges are not overboard. At the end of a day of dredging under sail alone, when the evening calm descends upon the Bay, it is the push boats which are launched to do the job for which they are named: get out and push.

Once on a crisp evening on the day after Thanksgiving, as we were leaving Smith Island by the back channel and heading for Crisfield, one by one the oyster fleet passed us by; skipjacks or bateaux, low in the water with their catch, running into port at sundown under full sail with a stiff breeze on their quarter. On another fall day, this time in the early morning, we sailed from Queenstown to the mouth of Chester River among a fleet of oyster tongers, their muscular figures silhouetted against the sunrise, working their tongs back and forth with their powerful shoulders gleaming in the early morning light. Such sights are long remembered. They are among the charms of the Chesapeake.

Each year since 1965 a fine fleet of these ancient Bay skipjacks has raced off Sandy Point near Annapolis in an annual workboat race originally sponsored jointly by the Windjammers Club of Baltimore and the Maryland Department of Natural Resources. Held during the last week in October in connection with Chesapeake Appreciation Days, the competition for cash prizes has attracted the best oyster boat skippers from Tangier Sound, Smith Island, Tilghman's, and the Choptank. A large spectator fleet has followed the skipjacks around the course, while several thousand additional spectators have watched the action from Sandy Point State Park. If you are in the area at Halloween time, this colorful event is well worth watching ashore or afloat.

The Chesapeake skipjacks constitute the only remaining commercial sailing fleet in the United States. Half a century ago the oyster fleet numbered some 1,500 vessels, but today their number has dwindled to fewer than 40. Although no new skipjacks are being

Only a few skipjacks still dredge for oysters. The best opportunity to see them under sail is at the annual Chesapeake Appreciation Days, held at Sandy Point State Park just north of Annapolis in late October.

built for commercial use, some of the older vessels, dating from 1888 to 1910, have been preserved and are still sailed as yachts or charter boats. The design of these distinctive Bay craft, with their clipper bows and sharply raked masts, is kept alive in a smaller, modern version of cruising yacht often seen in these waters.

There are many appealing features to cruising the Chesapeake. One is the friendly character of the people who run the small boatyards and waterfront services in many parts of the Bay which have not yet felt the encroaching pressures of urban development. You'll find interesting tidewater communities all along the Eastern Shore of Maryland and Virginia, especially in the Lower Bay, where most of the shoremen gain their livelihood from salt water. Many of the Eastern Shore families have lived in the same tidewater counties for generations, extending back to the first English settlements in America. A shoreman, more often than not, is part-time farmer and waterman, working his fields in between busy seasons of crabbing, oystering, clamming, and fishing. They are a unique breed, independent and self-contained, yet friendly to strangers so long as you don't try to tell them how to run their business. Above everything else, it is the people of the Chesapeake who make cruising there such an enjoyable experience.

Another distinctive characteristic of the Chesapeake is the large number of historic rivers and bays leading to towns and shoreside sites that are famous for their roles in the colonial era and through the first century of our history as a nation.

Virtually all of the 40 rivers tributary to the Chesapeake have some direct association with historic events before or after the American Revolution, so that any cruise offers the opportunity of "cruising into history." In Chapter Three we list rivers and towns with special historic attractions within easy access of cruising ports on both sides of the Bay. A sampling of these historic rivers follows.

RIVERS OF THE WESTERN SHORE

Susquehanna River, Havre de Grace, at the entrance is worth exploring. Bridges and dams prevent upriver navigation beyond Port Deposit.

An osprey returns with its prey to its nest on a navigation mark. Osprey have made a strong comeback on the Chesapeake since DDT has been banned.

Patapsco River takes you to Fort McHenry and Baltimore Inner Harbor.

Severn River, with the U. S. Naval Academy at the mouth, offers more than a dozen protected creeks and coves.

South River, West River, Rhode River are steeped in history and provide a score of choice anchorages.

Patuxent River, with Solomons Island, and the U. S. Naval training base at the mouth, and St. Leonards Creek and Sotterley upriver.

Potomac River is navigable for 96 miles to Washington along historic riverfronts.

Rappahannock River, navigable to head of tidewater at Fredericksburg, offers many fine cruising ports in lower reaches.

York River provides deep-draft anchorage off historic Yorktown and 26 miles upstream to West Point.

James River, which carried the first English settlers to Jamestown, winds its way on through Virginia history to Richmond 90 miles upstream.

RIVERS OF THE EASTERN SHORE

Bohemia River, near the Chesapeake and Delaware Canal at the head of the Bay, offers snug anchorages in a historic setting.

Sassafras River winds through historic countryside to the colonial towns of Georgetown and Fredericktown, now leading yachting centers.

Chester River, one of the finest rivers on the Upper Bay, leads 26 miles upstream to Chestertown, where George Washington helped establish Washington College.

Miles River flows into Eastern Bay through St. Michaels and the historic Wye River.

Choptank River rises in Delaware and flows past Oxford and Cambridge to reach the main Bay.

Nanticoke River, largest of the rivers on the Lower Eastern Shore, winds its way from Seaford, Del., past Vienna to empty into Tangier Sound above Crisfield.

Pocomoke River, one of the most fascinating streams on the Eastern Shore, carries a deep channel through a cypress forest to Pocomoke City, 14 miles above the mouth, and Snow Hill, 26 miles above the entrance.

This is only a sampling of the historic rivers of the Chesapeake; we include many others in the chapters ahead that cover each of the major cruising areas in depth.

Other attractive aspects of Chesapeake cruising are the historic towns and the old houses you are constantly running across if you know where to look. You can take a rewarding walking tour through historic Annapolis, which was called "the Ancient City" back when the Continental Congress met there in 1784. Almost every historic town on the Eastern Shore is located on navigable water, and you will find Chestertown, St. Michaels, Easton, and Oxford well worth a leisurely visit. Tidewater Virginia has much to offer the history-minded yachtsman, with Yorktown, Jamestown, and colonial Williamsburg all within easy reach of pleasant harbors.

We have several suggestions for books that may enhance your pleasure of rediscovering these historic waterways. At the top of our list are two classics, *Rivers of the Eastern Shore,* by Hulbert Footner, and *The Potomac,* by Frederick Gutheim, both in the "Rivers of America" series.

There are many other good books about the Chesapeake that we know would enhance the pleasure of cruising and help you to link the present-day Bay with its colorful maritime past. We haven't room to list them all, and some of the best are older books that are now out of print. You might still find Norman Hill's *Chesapeake Cruise* at your public library or a secondhand book store. Swepson Earle's *Chesapeake Bay Country,* long out of print, has been reissued and is generally available again. Our ship's library includes M. V. Brewington's *Chesapeake Bay, A Pictorial Maritime History* and Robert

Thousands of geese spend the winter on the Eastern Shore. Late-fall cruisers will see them flying by day and share an anchorage with them at night.

H. Burgess' *This Was Chesapeake Bay,* both published by Cornell Maritime Press. If you are interested in the Chesapeake watermen, you will enjoy Varley Lang's *Follow the Water,* William I. Tawes' *God, Man, Salt Water and the Eastern Shore* and Gilbert Byron's *The Lord's Oysters,* which give authentic accounts of tongers, draggers, and crabbers who work the Bay for a livelihood. *The Outlaw Gunner,* by Harry M. Walsh, published by Cornell's Tidewater Publishers, is the classic book on the days of market gunning on the Chesapeake.

The many moods of the Chesapeake and Maryland's half of the Bay country are captured in A. Aubrey Bodine's *The Face of Maryland,* a superb photographic study published by the author and distributed by Viking Press. Also, for those interested in the marine life of Chesapeake Bay, William W. Warner's 1976 best seller *Beautiful Swimmers,* published by Little, Brown and Company, belongs on your library shelf. You may want to plan a cruise in the waters covered by James A. Michener's *Chesapeake,* in which case you would

sail to the Choptank, where you would not have much trouble identifying Michener's fictional towns and creeks. *Regatta*, by Douglass Wallop, author of *The Year the Yankees Lost the Pennant*, takes you down the Bay from Annapolis to Oxford and brings alive that popular racing event.

We list other recent books in the bibliography.

Many years ago Frederick Gardiner summed up the delights of cruising the Chesapeake in a few sentences which hold true today: "You will not find here the rocks and pines of Maine, nor, except in small degree, its fog. You will not find the clear, blue sparkle of New England water—nor its chill. To sail, to fish, to swim when northern neighbors are building fires; to shoot, to bask in the sunshine of a particularly soothing climate; to watch the flicker of the white sails of the oyster fleet—if these are to be numbered among the delights of cruising, they are all present."

CHAPTER TWO

CRUISING CONDITIONS
ON THE CHESAPEAKE

I. WEATHER.

The best times for cruising on the Chesapeake are in the spring and fall, particularly from April 15 to June 15, and again from September 15 to November 15.

1. Temperature. Weather statistics are always disappointing. It is never quite as hot or as cold as you think it has been; the wind doesn't blow nearly as hard in the statistics as it did on the deck of your boat. Nevertheless, even the statistics back up the idea of Chesapeake cruises in the spring and fall. According to the climatological tables based on many years of observation at Baltimore and Norfolk, the two principal Chesapeake ports covered in the *Coast Pilot* figures, Chesapeake mean monthly air temperature in Fahrenheit compared to those of New York in the vicinity of Long Island Sound and the coast waters of New Jersey are as given in the table below. We have also shown the Chesapeake normal maximum and normal minimum temperatures, which refer to the highest or lowest daily temperatures during the month, the highest usually being daytime, and the lowest at night.

Mean Temp. for Month	Apr.	May	June	July	Aug.	Sept.	Oct.	Nov.
Baltimore, Md.	53.8	63.7	72.4	76.6	74.9	68.5	57.4	46.1
Norfolk, Va.	57.8	66.7	74.5	78.2	76.9	71.8	61.7	51.6
New York, N.Y.	49.4	59.8	69.5	75.1	73.6	67.0	57.8	46.5

Daily Max. Temp.								
Baltimore, Md.	65.2	76.8	83.2	86.7	85.1	79.0	68.2	56.1
Norfolk, Va.	67.7	76.2	84.9	87.9	86.2	80.9	70.1	60.5

Daily Min. Temp.								
Baltimore, Md.	42.7	52.8	61.6	66.5	68.7	57.9	46.4	36.0
Norfolk, Va.	47.9	57.2	65.5	69.9	68.9	63.9	53.3	42.6

You can choose your own season for Chesapeake cruising from the above, but remember that these temperatures were not taken in the sun, and that the mean maximum temperatures are what you will feel most in the daytime, and the mean minimum most at night.

"The sommer is hot as in Spaine," said Captain John Smith, "the winter colde as in France or England. The heat of sommer is in June July and August, but commonly the coole breeses assuage the vehemencie of the heat."

2. *Rainfall.* It rains a good deal more on the Chesapeake in the summer than it does in the spring and fall, or during summers on Long Island Sound or the Coast of Maine. This is due largely to the thunderstorms. But in April and May, and particularly in October and November, the rainfall is relatively low.

This is what the *Coast Pilot* quotes from Weather Service statistics:

Precipitation Mean Amount (Inches)	Apr.	May	June	July	Aug.	Sept.	Oct.	Nov.
Baltimore, Md.	3.07	3.61	3.77	4.07	4.21	3.12	2.81	3.13
Norfolk, Va.	2.71	3.34	3.62	5.70	5.92	4.20	3.06	2.94

Precipitation

Average Inches	*Apr.*	*May*	*June*	*July*	*Aug.*	*Sept.*	*Oct.*	*Nov.*
Baltimore, Md.	3.07	3.61	3.77	4.07	4.21	3.12	3.31	3.13
Norfolk, Va.	3.71	3.34	3.62	3.70	4.92	3.20	3.01	2.94

3. Winds. In June, July, and August, the prevailing winds are from the southerly quadrant, and calms are frequent, especially at night and in the morning; in April and May, and again in September and October, there is a fairly even balance between winds blowing down the Bay and up the Bay, with breezes from a northerly direction prevailing in November. Despite the frequency of thunderstorms in the hot months, the mean wind velocity is slightly higher in the spring and fall than in summer. It is also higher in the southern part of the Bay than in the northern.

One of the very satisfactory phases of Chesapeake cruising from the point of view of the sailboat cruiser who is not in a hurry to get to a particular spot is the fact that there are so many good harbors on both sides of the Bay and so many directions in which one may cruise pleasantly, that it is often possible to adapt your course to the winds. For instance, if you are at Annapolis with your wife for a quiet weekend cruise and it is blowing hard from the northeast you may find it easier to keep her as a regular member of your crew if you don't try to go to Gibson Island but take a trip up the Severn instead. Or, if it isn't blowing too badly, you can run down the Bay comfortably to Rhode River or across to Oxford.

A veteran Chesapeake Bay sailor tells us:

> The winds are more apt to "hack off" the shore when you are close up under it. Many times, when beating up the Bay, against a north-westerly or northerly wind, I have found that the wind is more westerly close to the western Shore and I have been able to follow a course alongshore without tacking.

4. Storms. Until recently hurricanes rarely entered the Bay. During the past several decades, however, severe hurricanes have swept through the Chesapeake. Hurricanes Hazel (1954) and Diane (1955) caused extensive damage to small craft and low-lying waterfront areas around the Bay. Hurricane Agnes (1972) brought devastating floods on its route between Florida and New York, leaving many lasting scars in the Chesapeake.

Some Chesapeake thunderstorms give a good imitation of hurricanes, producing hurricane-force winds in violent squalls. People started talking about these thundersqualls a long time ago. Captain John Smith had this to say:

> Seeing many Isles in the midst of the Bay [Tangier and Smith islands] we bore up for them, but ere we could attaine them, such an extreme gust of wind, raine, thunder and lightning happened that with great danger we escaped the unmercifull raging of that oceanlike water.

This was in June 1608. Later we hear that

> . . . our mast and sayle blew overboard and such mighty waves over acked us in that small barge, that with great danger we kept her from sinking by freeing out the water.
> The winds are variable, but the like thunder and lightning to purifie the aire, I have seldome either seene or heard in Europe.

Three hundred and fifty years after John Smith, an experienced cruising man voiced the same healthy respect for Bay squalls:

> And now a few words of advice about the Chesapeake. First is, don't sniff or feel superior or doubting when someone tells you about those "Chesapeake Bay squalls." We want to tell you that they are mighty violent and narrow-minded things which pounce down on you quick as a wink. Sometimes they are preceded by coppery haze. Sometimes (in our case round about 4:00 P.M. when plugging up Baltimore Harbor off Fort Carroll) just ordinary gray-black thunderheads rise first. We'd heard that old coppery-haze theory and viewed the approaching rain-

squall with no great alarm. We merely doused the main and sailed on under two small lowers. Then, suddenly, one blue-white fork of light-ning split the swirling murky mass directly over the center of town. A dark line of wind struck the water dead ahead which quickly turned to white. Raindrops the size of grapes stung our faces and rattled on deck and canvas like flung shot. Then, quicker than it takes to tell it, a Force 9 wind grabbed us, spun us around and sent us sky-shooting back southeast past the great Bethlehem Steel plant on Sparrows point. That squall gave us a nerve racking hour and had not a big anchor held the first time it was let go, it might have caused consider-able damage.

Twenty-two sailing vessels were once driven ashore on Kent Island in one of these severe squalls from the northwest. Some never got off.

But don't be too alarmed about these accounts. If you keep your eyes open and watch for the signs of a squall, which experienced sailors can detect, you will have plenty of time to prepare for it. If you have the chance to get into a snug harbor, do so. If you plan your cruise so as to be in a harbor about 4 P.M., you will usually, but not always, reach port before a squall strikes. If you don't have time to get into port and are cruising under sail, get your sails down and be prepared to run under bare poles unless under a lee to the west or northwest, when you can often anchor safely. If necessary, and you have a good anchor with plenty of scope, you can often anchor almost anywhere along the shores of the Bay. With a good motor cruiser, or a powerful enough auxiliary, you can usually run slowly into it.

An outstanding Chesapeake sailor who is also an author advised us that:

If a squall bears south of southwest, or north of northwest, it is apt to miss you altogether, passing, respectively, south or north of you. If it is between southwest and northwest, look out. Squalls are most frequent in the summer months.

Another experienced Chesapeake cruising man gave us some more very good advice on squalls:

Signs are to be found three to five hours beforehand. These signs are murky gray, cumulus clouds in the west and northwest, which usually come up against south or southwest winds. If there is a lot of lightning in the evening, you will usually get a squall during the night. This may be serious, because you will be asleep. When you see signs of a squall, get into a good shelter early, or hug the western shore. Never trust these squalls, so take your sails down, tie them up securely, and be prepared to scud before it, or anchor. They seldom last long and usually come from between west and north.

Very seldom do they come before 3:00 to 4:00 P.M. The most common time is at sundown. They often cut a very narrow path, but can be devastating in that path. They are most frequent from June 15th to September 15th and are more apt to occur if there is much moisture around.

The late Frederick Tilp used to enjoy telling his "tidewater tale" of a British frigate on Potomac River in the War of 1812, which had her jib blown away while the quarterdeck was in complete calm. So say the British Admiralty files.

Here is another, told us from personal experience by our friend Mr. Tilp. We thought at first that he was speaking figuratively, like "raining buckets," for example. But he wasn't. He was a reliable man, and he said it actually happened to him. What is more, a weather official backs him up. It sometimes *rains frogs on the Chesapeake*—little ones, picked up and whirled aloft by a northwest squall, and then deposited on the deck of a yacht, or in the water alongside. You can believe it or not.

According to climatological tables formerly published in the *Coast Pilot,* the average days per month with thunderstorms in Baltimore and Norfolk are as follows. Possibly, thunderstorms may be more frequent in other places between, but these figures clearly indicate that the fall months and early spring are the best times in which to avoid thunderstorms during the cruising season.

Average Days with Thunderstorms	Apr.	May	June	July	Aug.	Sept.	Oct.	Nov.
Baltimore, Md.	2	4	6	6	5	2	1	0
Norfolk, Va.	3	5	6	8	8	3	2	0

It is usually impossible to tell in advance how severe a thunderstorm will be. Our own first encounter with a Chesapeake thunder squall was in Rock Hall Harbor in early May. There was no room in a slip, so we anchored our sloop *Sea Fever* as near the center of the small dredged basin as possible, still not having room for as much scope as we like to put out.

At about 3:30 P.M., we had noticed a graying-up haze to the northwest. By 4:15 P.M., it had become black and ominous with frequent flashes of lightning. At about 4:30 P.M., the first rain came, followed by strong puffs of wind from the northwest, which swung us around in the opposite direction, within a boat's length or two of where some boys had been wading. A low stone wall to windward protected us from any seas but not from the wind. Soon the gusts became more frequent and stronger, swinging the boat violently from side to side on her anchor rode and heeling her over as the wind swept against her mast. Fortunately, our plow anchor held.

After about 15 minutes of the squall, furious gusts blew the top off the water, creating a foglike mist though we were only 100 feet or so from the windward wall. Then what felt like hail blew horizontally in our faces so strongly that we were glad to duck behind the cabin top. We had no way of estimating the strength of these gusts but we have been out several times in storms later reported as blowing from 50 to 60 miles per hour, and these gusts seemed at least as strong as the winds were then.

At the end of an hour from the time when the storm first struck it was over, though it took a half hour or so more before it really cleared.

Our next experience with a Chesapeake thunderstorm was at a Cruising Club rendezvous in Whitehall Creek, near Annapolis on the northwest side of Severn River. The preliminary signs of this squall were visible much more quickly than they had been to us off Rock Hall. The sky looked about as wicked. Yet the squall didn't amount to much—chiefly rain and very little wind. Later we experienced a series of squalls on another weekend in May at Gibson Island beginning in the later afternoon, continuing several times during the night, with another the following afternoon. In none of these was the wind very strong. So we agree with the veteran George Barrie, Jr., one of the authors of the classic *Cruising, Mainly in the Bay of Chesapeake*, when he said: "One can never tell what a squall will amount to."

The fishermen spin yarns about a squall which rolled up a concrete road like a carpet and another which unraveled a man's trousers while he streamed out like a flag with his arms embracing a tree. It wouldn't do to doubt the tales told by the fishermen of the Eastern Shore.

Keep your weather eye open, watch for sudden drops in your barometer, or for static on your radio. Marine weather reporting is far better today than it was when the first edition of this guide was published. If your boat is equipped to receive VHF radio transmissions you can get the continuous marine broadcasts direct from the National Weather Service in Washington, carried 24 hours daily on frequency 162.55. Your small-craft charts also list National Weather Service broadcasts from other cities around the Bay, and weather information which may be obtained by marine radiotelephone. The charts include all storm warning display locations in the area. As these and other navigational aids are constantly changing, it's important for boats cruising the Chesapeake to keep their charts up to date.

5. *Fog.* There is very little fog on the Chesapeake, especially in summer, when it is most common on the New England Coast. The

average hours of operation of fog signals on the Chesapeake are generally about one-fifth of the average hours reported by light stations in eastern Long Island Sound and southern New England coastal waters, during the six months from May through October. For example, records compiled by the Coast Guard show that Point Lookout at the entrance to Potomac River averaged only 88 hours of fog signal operation during that six-month period over the past 20 years, compared with more than 600 hours at Montauk Point, Long Island. New England stations between Boston and Portland, Me., reported up to 10 times as many hours of fog as those on the Chesapeake in the summer cruising months.

June, July, and August are virtually free of fog on the Chesapeake, except for occasional early morning mist. The foghorn at Point Lookout has averaged only 4 hours of use in the month of July and 8 hours in August since 1950, according to tables published in the *Coast Pilot*. You are likely to encounter more fog in the spring and fall (42 hours in April, 22 in October, and 37 in November at Point Lookout).

But occasionally the weather fools all of the statistical averages. A dozen years ago we had a foggy weekend in October that blanketed the entire Upper Bay and kept a Cruising Club rendezvous fog-bound for more hours than the whole monthly average. In Annapolis you couldn't see the Spa Creek Bridge from Arnie Gay's docks at Shipwright Street. This was something "beyond the memory of the oldest inhabitants" and caused so much surprised comment that we are inclined to believe the statistics, after all. But most of the time you'll find the lack of fog one of the Chesapeake's greatest cruising assets.

II. DEPTHS OF WATER.

There has been so much conversation, verbal and written, about running aground on the Chesapeake that some Long Island Sound and Yankee yachtsmen think that cruising there is an intermittent process of bumping from shoal to shoal, and no place for a draft of over three or four feet. We had this idea ourselves until we began cruising on the Bay, studying the Chesapeake charts, and noting to our surprise the enormous number of rivers, each with many miles of deep water as well as the tiny creeks which a deep draft yacht can follow nearly to the head. Like many incorrect beliefs, the idea of the Chesapeake as suited only for shoal draft yachts has become so firmly imbedded in some minds that it may take an explosion to break it loose. We'll try to provide the explosion.

There are at least 232 harbors along the two shores of the Chesapeake's 170 miles—north and south—with depths of 6 feet or more. This includes only harbors leading directly off the main part of the Bay, or small creeks offering snug anchorages off the larger rivers and creeks, usually not over 5 or 6 miles at most from the mouths. It omits hundreds of good and deep anchorages in bends of the various rivers and larger creeks. As already pointed out, the determination of when a harbor is a harbor is often a matter of judgment on the Chesapeake and subject to various interpretations. But we are sure that our numbers are conservative and that old Chesapeake hands will tell us that there are many more. The rivers have cut deep into the sandy soil of the Bay.

For yachts drawing 5 feet or less the number of available harbors would increase, but not so much as you might suppose until depths get down to the usual motorboat drafts, 3 or 4 feet. Then the number of harbors takes another big jump. Even craft drawing over 6 feet have available all of the harbors they are likely to need for safe cruising.

Some present-day boat owners will go aground with ease and frequency anywhere, even on the coast of Maine. Armed with a few "maps," and without the intelligent use of a chart, they land on the bottom.

It is true, however, that even experienced yachtsmen are apt to go aground more often on the Chesapeake than they do on the New England Coast. This is due, we believe, largely to the following factors:

(1) There are many outlying shoals, particularly along the Lower Eastern Shore, some of which are inadequately marked. For instance, it is often impossible to follow a straight line between two buoys and the extent of the shoals projection outside of the straight line is often not easy to gauge.

(2) There are many tempting creeks to explore, often with unmarked shoals. These shoals are easy to hit without the greatest care in following the chart, and sometimes even when care is exercised. Frequently when the shoals are privately marked it takes a mind reader to know on which side the private stakes are to be left. We have tried to indicate this in some cases in this guide, but after 30 years we haven't yet had time to explore to the headwaters of every creek!

Once, for example, we found an uncharted red, white, and black buoy in the middle of the entrance of a tempting creek. It was not clear on the chart on which side of the middle the water was deeper. And we weren't smart enough to select the right colors on the buoy. We left the buoy close to port and grounded—very briefly.

If we had known then about the rule of the "Ebb Tide Bends" we'd have left the buoy to starboard instead of to port and would have found the deep water, for the creek was to our port as we proceeded up the river. Usually, and despite many exceptions, the deeper water is to be found on the downriver side or "pint" of a creek opening into a river. Look, for example, at a chart of South River for evidence of this. As the ebb tide is usually stronger than the flood, the upriver side of a creek entering a river is more likely to have a shoal, created by the downriver wash of the current.

(3) There are many dredged channels, into harbors or connecting bays and rivers, which are constantly filling in and being dredged again. Frequently, the charts are not up to date on the latest depths.

(4) The penalty of going aground on the Chesapeake is usually so slight that there is a temptation to be careless. As the late Kenneth Mellett once said: ". . . grounding in search of a new gunk hole is an incident, not a crisis." The bottom and shores are all sandy or muddy, sometimes so hard that it is easy to jump overboard and push off, or to use a pole. On the Chesapeake, there are no "cruel rocks to gore her sides like the horns of an angry bull," as there are at Gloucester on the Reef of Norman's Woe.

The fact that, normally, the rise and fall of tide is only from 1 to 2 feet on the Chesapeake is both an asset and a liability, if you go aground. It is an asset because the low tide is not apt to leave you heeled over very far on your side, perhaps out of water altogether. It is a liability because you may have to wait a long time for the tide to rise enough to get you off.

After his first three seasons of cruising on the Chesapeake, Fess Blanchard had to admit he had been aground more often than in over forty years of cruising on the New England and Canadian coasts—all for one or more of the reasons given above. Yet, we never have had any trouble in getting off promptly from our Chesapeake groundings, which is more than we can say of our mishaps else-where. So far, we have found that heeling our sloop over—by wind or 199 3/4 pounds of weight at the shrouds—has done the trick very easily and successfully.

The temptation to explore tiny creeks, to venture into places which we would not attempt on the rocky shores of Maine, is so great that it is always well to use your depth finder or carry a 12-foot sounding pole on the Chesapeake, marked with the depth of your own boat and various depths beyond that. Sounding is more accu-rate with the pole than it is with a mechanical depth finder or lead line, and you can sometimes pole your way into a little creek, using first one end of the pole and then the other like a double-bladed canoe paddle. Even though most new cruising boats are equipped with electronic depth finders, a few old-time Chesapeake skippers prefer the "feel" of poking up a creek with pole or lead line. We have often thus poked our way into many a fascinating little creek on Chesapeake Bay.

III. TIDES AND CURRENTS.

Under normal conditions, the tidal range in the Chesapeake is from 1 to 2 1/2 feet. In the northern end of the Bay, from Baltimore to the mouth of Patuxent River, it runs from 1 to 1 1/2 feet. Only when you get as far south as Mobjack Bay does the tidal range along the Bay proper get as high as 2 1/2 feet.

As you go up some of the larger rivers, the tidal changes increase in some cases to $2\frac{1}{2}$ or 3 feet. For instance, they are $1\frac{1}{2}$ feet in the lower part of the Potomac and 3 feet at Washington.

More important than the normal tide range in determining the rise and fall of water in the Bay is the effect of strong winds. For instance, several days of northwesters may drive a good deal of water from the northern part of the Bay and out of the creeks and rivers, so that you may get an extreme low tide of minus 2 or 3 feet, or 3 or 4 feet below the normal high. Strong southerly winds may have the reverse effect.

Swift currents, compared to those, for example, at the eastern end of Long Island Sound, are unknown on Chesapeake Bay, though strong northerly winds may increase the velocity of the ebb current in the Bay enough to make the current a real obstacle or a help according to the direction in which you are going. Similarly, strong southerly winds increase the velocity of the flood and decrease the velocity of the ebb.

As a rule, the flood currents in the Bay run from a half knot to a knot; ebb currents, aided by the fresh water behind them flowing out of the rivers, run up to a knot and a half.

As the *Coast Pilot* points out, full tidal information is given for Chesapeake Bay in the yearly issue of *Tide Tables, Atlantic Ocean.* Similarly, *Current Tables, Atlantic Coast* gives data on the currents in the Bay and also contains a current diagram for the Chesapeake. Moreover, the National Ocean Service now publishes *Tidal Current Charts* for Upper Chesapeake Bay. With these charts and the tide tables, which should be aboard every cruising boat, it's an easy matter to determine the hourly speed and direction of currents at various points in the Bay, as well as the times of high and low water.

It should be noted that the effect of flood and ebb currents are marked at the entrances of the principal tributaries and may sometimes be felt at a considerable distance from these entrances. Off the mouths of the York, Rappahannock, and especially the Potomac, eastward-setting ebb currents or westward-setting flood currents are often experienced.

It is frequently possible in going north up the Bay against an ebb current to avoid the strongest part of this current, by working the slack waters close along Kent Island or other parts of the Eastern Shore, taking advantage of the various hollows in the coastline.

IV. OBSTACLES TO NAVIGATION.

1. Fish Traps. These are no longer as much of a hazard as they were a few years ago, but they still require a sharp lookout in some parts of the Bay. Along the Western Shore, fish traps and abandoned stakes may be encountered several miles from shore all the way from Annapolis to Hampton. The most troublesome areas are south of Patuxent River, and between the Potomac and York, with a heavy concentration of stakes off Mobjack Bay. The boundaries of fish trap areas are plainly marked with bright yellow buoys on National Ocean Service charts, with fairways in river channels and entrances into harbors and bays.

These fish traps can be easily avoided in daytime, but in a fog (fortunately infrequently) or at night they may be a menace that must be carefully watched for and avoided. They are poorly lit at best and frequently not lit at all.

2. Crab Pot Buoys. During summer months it is often difficult to avoid tangling with crab-pot lines that lead to literally thousands of floats and buoys close to entrance channels on both sides of the Bay. According to local navigation regulations, these are supposed to be kept clear of the main channels on both shores of the Bay and into major rivers and creeks, with special markers at the outer boundaries. But in recent years the boundaries often seem to be disregarded with the result that a good many boats run afoul of buoys and crab-pot lines in waters they thought were clear of such hazards. Particular caution should be taken at night.

3. Duck Blinds. These are frequently found along shore and at a distance are sometimes confused with day beacons or other navigational aids. Watch for them and don't get fooled. They are usually located in depths of 6 feet or less.

4. Restricted Areas. There are many of these on the Chesapeake which are designated for the use of the Army and Navy. However, except for the section near Aberdeen Proving Grounds on the Upper Bay, the Naval firing range on the lower Potomac, and the Bloodsworth Island area off the Lower Eastern Shore, they don't interfere seriously with the use of the Bay and its tributaries by cruising boats. The danger zones in the vicinity of Bloodsworth and Tangier islands should be avoided when the Navy is conducting rocket and guided missiles operations, but these areas are remote and relatively isolated.

A study of the charts and *Coast Pilot* will usually show where the restricted areas are and indicate the restrictions. Or you will be warned by the Coast Guard if you happen to stray into an area where target practice is going on.

V. Pests.

1. Sea Nettles, or Poisonous Jellyfish. This pest is on everyone's list of obstacles to the pleasure of summer cruising on the Chesapeake. The touch of one of these jellyfish causes a rash which is almost unbearably irritating for a while, though we understand that the effects may be minimized after a short time by washing in household ammonia or mud, or applying meat tenderizer.

Nettles and squalls have about the same season, from June to mid-September, though the nettles are usually at their worst in July and August. They are uncommon in the spring and fall seasons.

Nettles don't like fresh water. Thus, in a moist summer, when fresh water is flowing freely in the springs and rivers, the nettles are less in evidence. The spring of 1972 was a wet one, followed by tropical storm Agnes which poured so much fresh water into the Chesapeake that almost no nettles appeared north of the Patuxent all summer. The spring of 1980 was a dry one and they appeared early. Thus the number of these stinging jellyfish varies from year to year. Few of them are found near the head of the Bay, above the line of the oyster limit, which is about at Pooles Island and Fairlee Creek. The amount of salt content in the water is a measure to a considerable extent of their number. Thus, in rivers, both because of the direction of the current and the larger salt content of the water, there will be more nettles on a flood than on an ebb tide. Where oysters thrive, you are apt to find them more frequent.

The combination of nettles and a water temperature which is sometimes too warm for enjoyment is a serious handicap to the pleasure of bathing in summer, though it is often possible to avoid the nettles by picking your bathing spots carefully, or by swimming at places where nets are used as a protection from them. On hot sunny days you'll find cool water, and fewer nettles, in mid-Bay or deep river channels where the swimming is good.

2. Mosquitoes. These can be very bad where the land is marshy, and especially in wet seasons. Mosquitoes like moisture, just as nettles prefer the lack of it. So you are apt to be lucky about nettles, when you are unlucky about mosquitoes, or if you are a pessimist, put it the other way. Mosquitoes are likely to be at their worst in early summer and vary according to the harbor and where you anchor. Don't anchor to leeward of a marsh if you can help it. Below the Choptank, on the Eastern Shore, the mosquitoes are especially bad, since a large part of the whole area is marshland.

If you cruise on the Chesapeake—or anywhere else—during the summer months, make sure that your boat is well screened.

3. Flies. These can be a nuisance at some times of the year, as they are in most other places along the Atlantic Coast. Flies are at their worst from about mid-June to mid-September, with spring and fall relatively free of this pest. Fortunately they are less of a problem than they used to be. No properly outfitted boat should be lacking an aerosol bomb. However, to look on the bright side, flies are no worse here than on Long Island Sound, nor are mosquitoes as bad as on some parts of the Maine Coast, or farther south along the coastal waterway.

4. Pollution. This is one of the major environmental problems confronting the Chesapeake as well as most other inland and coastal waters of the United States. Industrial and municipal pollution have seriously affected the public use of water areas near the three principal population centers in the Chesapeake Basin: Baltimore and parts of the Patapsco River; Washington and the upper tidewater Potomac; Norfolk–Newport News and the Hampton Roads, Nansemond, Elizabeth, and Lafayette rivers. Some progress has been made in cleaning up each of these critical areas.

Apart from these three areas, the Chesapeake is remarkably free from the kind of pollution that could affect the use of the Bay for recreation, including fishing, swimming, and cruising. Tropical storm Agnes inundated the Bay with polluted flood waters from Susquehanna, Potomac, and James rivers in June 1972, providing costly evidence of the delicate ecological balance which was upset by changes in the freshwater-saline content in clam-bed and oyster-bar areas of the Upper Bay. Swimming was prohibited for a time by health authorities in the Upper Bay during that disaster period, and clamming was suspended for an indefinite time; but oyster dredging continued in the fall and natural healing processes had apparently cleansed most of the damaged areas by the end of that year.

Pollution from private vessels was not regarded as a serious problem and not regulated until the mid-seventies.

Yachts entering the Bay from other cruising areas should be aware of state and local requirements covering the use of marine heads (which generally, as of this writing, means no discharge of untreated material overboard), as well as federal standards applicable to marine sanitation equipment. Those complying with the regulations should be aware that not all marinas are equipped with pump-out facilities. An informal survey of marinas in 1988 found 40 to 50 marinas in Virginia, and approximately the same number in Maryland, with pump-out facilities for transient boats.

CHAPTER THREE

PLANNING A CRUISE
ON THE CHESAPEAKE

If you are planning to cruise the Chesapeake, the chances are you belong to one of three categories of boatmen who come to the Bay by various routes and modes of transportation. First, if you are lucky enough to have your own vessel in commission on or within reach of the Atlantic Coast, you belong in the boat-owning contingent that may be concerned with the logistics of coming down from New England, or Long Island Sound, or even from the Great Lakes. Part Two, which covers the passage from Long Island Sound to the Chesapeake, is designed to help those of you who are coming, perhaps for the first time, from northern or western waters and are unfamiliar with this coastal section. Those entering the Chesapeake from the south are likely to be yachtsmen returning from winter cruising or racing in southern waters, or annual visitors who are familiar with the Intracoastal Waterway route via Norfolk.

The second category includes the growing number of mobile boatmen who trail their craft to the Chesapeake from other localities. In recent years more and more trailer cruisers have been coming to the Bay from nearby states which lack the tidewater resources of Maryland and Virginia, and from distant landlocked regions of the Middle West or the South. Some come for a weekend, others for a vacation cruise of a week or more. Members of the trailer fraternity need special guidance on facilities which may be available in different parts of the Chesapeake, and we mention several marinas and small towns which have launching ramps at convenient points of access around the Bay.

The third group embraces all those cruising enthusiasts who may or may not have sampled the delights of this historic tidewater area. It includes veteran boat owners who keep their craft in one section of the Bay and seldom venture into unfamiliar waters of another section; it includes new boat owners planning their first cruise, and even those who may be temporarily without a boat.

Regardless of which category you may be in, you will find it helpful to look over some of the charts and books that may be needed for navigation or may add to the enjoyment of your Chesapeake cruise. A complete list of National Ocean Service Charts covering the Chesapeake and the passage from Long Island Sound will be found in the Appendix, along with other government publications, such as the *Coast Pilot*.

We also list in the appendix several supplementary navigational materials, including chart kits, chart books, and marine atlas sets covering the cruising area of this guide. These are privately published, conveniently packaged folios of reproductions of government charts, some of which include additional information on courses, marine facilities, or air photographs of river and harbor entrances. One of these is the *Chart Kit* series, published by the Better Boating Association (BBA). The Chesapeake and Delaware Bay area is covered by reproductions of government charts, with navigational courses superimposed for ease in planning a Chesapeake cruise. Another is the *Charts* folio published by the Waterway Guide, providing extensive coverage of the Chesapeake and Delaware bays. This collection includes reproductions of government charts from New York to Norfolk, with numerous air photos of river harbor entrances as well as coastal inlets.

Still another chart book and marine atlas is the *Guide for Cruising Maryland Waters*, published by the Maryland Department of Natural Resources. This chart book includes courses and distances for cruisers traveling in Maryland waters, along with other useful information on marine facilities.

These chart kits and marine atlas folios provide the convenience of compact size, making them handy to stow below and easier to use in the cockpit of a small cruising boat than the full-size government charts. But they should not be regarded as completely adequate substitutes for National Ocean Service charts in areas where large scale is an important factor. All of the privately produced chart folios are compelled to reduce the size of government charts, in greater or lesser degree, in order to meet their respective book or folio size limitations. As a result, the wise skipper will want to supplement his chart kit with selected government charts providing the largest scale for critical navigation areas.

Two other useful aids are Chesapeake Bay Magazine's *Guide to Cruising the Chesapeake Bay*, published by the Chesapeake Bay Magazine, and *Boating Almanac*, Volumes 3 and 4, listing boatyards, marinas, launching ramps, and other boat facilities on the Chesapeake and Delaware bays and the New Jersey Coast.

For background reading we mention several books on the history of Chesapeake Bay, the titles of which are listed in the bibliography.

A number of books which have been especially helpful to us in preparing this guide should also be mentioned here and include: the Mid-Atlantic edition of the *Waterway Guide; Tidewater Maryland* and *Tidewater Virginia*, by Paul Wilstach; *The Potomac*, by Frederick Gutheim; and *Tobacco Coast*, by Arthur Pierce Middleton. Accounts of cruising the Bay in earlier days add to the enjoyment of our own present-day explorations, and two volumes are always at hand: the classic *Cruises, Mainly on the Bay of the Chesapeake*, by Robert Barrie and George Barrie, Jr., and *Sailing to the Sun*, by Howard Bloomfield. Although some of these books are out of print, you will find most of them available in leading libraries.

Other books that we have found both useful and enjoyable are *Chesapeake Circle,* by Robert H. Burgess; *The Bay,* by Gilbert Klingel; and *Chesapeake Bay and Tidewater,* by A. Aubrey Bodine. We could add many more titles to this list, but if you are ready to plan your cruise, it's time to get down to such practical questions as where to cruise on the Chesapeake in the time you may have available.

Let us suppose that you have come from Long Island Sound through Hell Gate and along the Jersey Coast (inside or outside) until you have arrived via Delaware Bay and the Chesapeake and Delaware Canal. Or you may have come to the Canal from Philadelphia or Wilmington. After a snug anchorage for the night in the basin at Chesapeake City, you are now ready for a cruise on the Chesapeake. Where shall you go? Where are the best harbors, the most attractive and interesting places? How far can you get in the time available—without hurrying too much?

One thing we are sure of; no two people will agree on where to go. If you ask too many of your friends you may—with apologies—be like the mule who died of starvation between two bales of hay because he couldn't make up his mind which one to tackle first.

While we have tried to answer these questions in some detail in the chapters which come next, on the rivers, creeks, and harbors of the Chesapeake, we shall attempt here to furnish an idea of what is to be found in each part of the Bay, and what seems to us especially worthwhile. It will simplify our discussion if we divide the Chesapeake into five major cruising areas, as we have divided the chapters which follow, and then take a quick look at the Bay as a whole. These areas are:

    I. *The Upper Eastern Shore,* from the Chesapeake and Delaware Canal to and including Choptank River.
    II. *The Upper Western Shore,* above Potomac River.
    III. *Potomac River to Washington.*
    IV. *The Lower Eastern Shore,* below Choptank River to Cape Charles.
    V. *The Lower Western Shore,* below Potomac River to Cape Henry.
    VI. The Chesapeake as a whole.

I. The Upper Eastern Shore, from the Chesapeake and Delaware Canal to and Including Choptank River.

In this section is found some of the best cruising on the Bay. The shores, while not as high as some of those across on the other side, are high enough to be very attractive, fringed as they are with trees and vistas of green fields behind. Mosquito-breeding marshes are not common here, as they are on the Lower Eastern Shore. Beautiful rivers and creeks with many snug harbors; glimpses of famous old houses among tall trees, gardens, and box hedges; sheltered or open waters—all of these are there for the seeking.

An easy first day's run from Chesapeake City along the Eastern Shore might well involve a trip up the lovely Sassafras River to Georgetown, one of the Bay's leading yachting centers. If you are in a hurry to get farther south, Worton Creek, also about 25 miles

from the canal, has plenty of water—if you pick the right places—and one of the most perfectly protected anchorages on the Bay. Still Pond and Fairlee, near Worton, appeal to many yachtsmen. Farther on are Rock Hall, for supplies, and Gratitude—intriguing in actuality as well as in name—for a quiet night.

Just below is the entrance of Chester River, at Love Point, with a good harbor at Queenstown about 7 or 8 miles up and plenty of fine inland cruising on Grays Inn or Langford creeks, on Corsica River, or up the Chester itself to Chestertown, an attractive and interesting port.

Between Chester River and the Choptank, and divided by Eastern Bay, two great eagles' wings seem to project out into the Bay. The upper one is sandy-shored Kent Island, cut off from the mainland by a narrow dredged channel of uncertain depth. The lower one is the peninsula of about the same size between Eastern Bay and Miles River to the north and the broad waters of the great Choptank River below. Only the southern tip of the peninsula is separated from the mainland, leaving Tilghman Island as the wing tip.

Rock Hall Harbor. (Photo courtesy of BaySailor.)

These two wings look surprisingly alike on the chart (and from outer space as shown on NASA photographs). The chief difference between them from a cruising man's standpoint is the shortcut inside of Kent Island, from Chester River into Eastern Bay. This shortcut is known as Kent Island Narrows, but should be entered with considerable caution by boats drawing over 5 feet; for, despite frequent dredging, Chester River side shows a constant tendency to fill up.

Don't skip Eastern Bay, whether you can make it through the Narrows or have to go around Kent Island. No cruise along the Eastern Shore is complete without a trip up the narrow and winding branches of Wye River, where you will find plenty of deep water and snug anchorages in tiny creeks around every bend. Here and there some of the Chesapeake's most famous old houses come into sight. Miles River runs into Eastern Bay opposite the entrance to the Wye. St. Michaels is a splendid port for stocking up or spending the night, and there are some fine creeks on the river. Before rounding Tilghman Point on your way out of Eastern Bay, you may want to spend the night in Tilghman Creek, just inside of the point and one of the best harbors on the Chesapeake.

Continuing south inside of Poplar Island—perhaps stopping in the "Poplar Pot"—and through Knapps Narrows (which is deeper and easier to navigate than Kent Island Narrows) you will be entering the wide and sometimes stormy mouth of Choptank River, largest on the Eastern Shore. A short distance ahead of you, 9 miles from Knapps Narrows, will be Oxford, which, with Georgetown, is to yachting on the Eastern Shore what Annapolis and Galesville are to yachting on the Western Shore. Plan to spend at least a couple of days with Oxford as your base, taking a trip up the lovely and historic Tred Avon with its many sheltered creeks. In the lower Choptank, Island Creek is especially attractive but be sure to take a swim on the inside of the perfect sandy beach which forms a miniature Sandy Hook in La Trappe Creek.

Although we recommend a trip to Cambridge, one of the most important ports on the Eastern Shore, the Choptank above Cambridge is far less appealing than it is below.

In a week or ten days of unhurried cruising you have now had an opportunity to see the best of the Upper Eastern Shore. And that means you have visited some of the finest cruising waters on Chesapeake Bay—or anywhere else, for that matter.

II. THE UPPER WESTERN SHORE, ABOVE POTOMAC RIVER.

In this part of the Bay, you will find the highest land, some of the most beautiful rivers and creeks, and, in our opinion, the most interesting harbor on the Chesapeake: Annapolis. Except in the restricted area around the Aberdeen Proving Grounds, where there is a Mosquito Creek, marshes are relatively few.

While there are several very good anchorages on Patapsco River, just outside of Baltimore, as shown in Chapter Six, and another one behind Sue Island on Middle River, the best cruising waters on the Western Shore begin for the southward-bound yachtsman with Magothy River—about 43 miles from Chesapeake City.

On the Magothy and within the 15-mile distance from its mouth to the entrance of Rhode and West rivers to the south—and all within an easy day's sail of each other—are some of the most perfectly sheltered and loveliest harbors on the Bay. In fact, we'd have to go a long way—outside of the Chesapeake, at any rate—to find their equal within such a small area. Over half of the good harbors on the Western Shore between the Canal and the Potomac are here.

Beginning with Gibson Island and some tempting creeks on the Magothy, the cruising skipper could well spend a week without getting over 15 miles farther south and still leave much to be explored. Here is Whitehall Bay, leading into Whitehall Creek, a favorite rendezvous area and a convenient anchorage for yachts visiting Annapolis. Beyond Whitehall Creek is the Severn, considered by many to be the most beautiful river on the Bay and certainly one of the most interesting. At its entrance is Annapolis and the

United States Naval Academy. The Severn is well worth at least a day's exploration, even in only a week's cruise. Don't fail to go up as far as Round Bay, 5 or 6 miles above the entrance and into Forked Creek, just beyond, poking into several other landlocked creeks on the way.

South River is also attractive and has several creeks, such as Church, Crab, and Harness, which are equal to the best on the Bay. Still farther south and just around the corner are Rhode and West rivers, each a well-known and deservedly popular rendezvous for cruising boats.

About 7 miles south of the West River entrance, at the upper end of Herring Bay, is Deale, on Rockhall Creek, last port with at least 5 feet of water before you come to the longest stretch of coastline on the Bay without a natural harbor. Except for some privately dredged marinas with channels of varying and uncertain depths (described later), there is no good harbor on the Western Shore between Herring Bay and Solomons Island on Patuxent River—a distance of 31 miles. An unbroken shoreline with many of the highest cliffs on the Bay, fossil laden and rising from 100 to 190 feet in some places, makes the outlook imposing, if not hospitable. Yachtsmen seeking shelter halfway down are apt to run across into Little Choptank River on the Eastern Shore, 5 or 6 miles from their course, where several creeks offer good anchorages.

Patuxent River is worth the trip southward, for near its mouth is Solomons Island, with some of the best harbors on the Bay, and one creek in particular, Mill Creek, which is a longtime favorite of Chesapeake cruising skippers. Across and farther up the river are several other attractive creeks with sheltered anchorages.

Allowing a day for the 43-mile run from Chesapeake City to Gibson Island, three or four days for exploration between Magothy and West rivers, and a couple of days for the trip to Patuxent and on it, it is possible to cover the Upper Western Shore very well (one way) in about a week's cruise. In two weeks, up one shore and down the other, or by the zigzag process, a large part of the best of the Upper Eastern Shore and Upper Western Shore can be well covered, though many a good creek will have to be passed by.

III. POTOMAC RIVER TO WASHINGTON.

The Potomac, which forms the boundary between Maryland and Virginia, is a cruising area all itself, with nearly 50 good harbors with 6 feet or more between its 10-mile-wide mouth and Washington, 95 miles upriver. While the trip up the Potomac is very interesting, especially if you want to visit Washington, fortunately for the cruising yachtsmen whose time is limited, most of the best harbors are within about 30 miles of the entrance.

The river is 4 or 5 miles wide, for most of the 30 miles, so if you are on a sailing yacht, you will have plenty of room for tacking, if you have to, though we wouldn't recommend the Potomac without power.

Be sure to examine the *Coast Pilot* and learn of the danger zones and prohibited areas mentioned. The Army, Navy, and Marines are much in evidence on the Potomac. Not enough, however, to keep you out of the best harbors, or enough to get you into any difficulty if you watch the chart, read the *Coast Pilot,* and follow the regulations—all of which are second nature to good yachtsmen.

If you do this, and if you look out for the red flags, and don't discharge into the range areas "phosphorus and other dangerous chemicals injurious to wild fowl, fish or other sea food," you will keep nicely out of trouble.

Some of the highest and most impressive cliffs on the Bay rise steeply from the Potomac just above Nomini Bay. Nomini, Stratford, and Horsehead Cliffs, with lovely Westmoreland State Park, offer some of the finest scenery on the Chesapeake—about 25 or 30 miles from the entrance of the river. From Colonial Beach or Mattox Creek, about 33 miles up the river, one may easily visit Washington's birthplace at Wakefield, Virginia, or take a trip to Stratford, the famous homestead of the "Lees of Virginia," a truly unique plantation in its own right.

The trip upriver might well start from the town of Wynne as a base, on Smith Creek, 7 1/2 miles above the bell off Point Lookout at the entrance to the river. From Wynne it is a run of about 9 miles up

63

the St. Marys River to St. Marys City, where high above the river the first settlement in Maryland was located. After exploring the site of the colonial capital and the campus of St. Mary's College, you'll enjoy running up the river another 2 $1/2$ miles for a look at Tippity Wichity Island, perhaps because of its name, though the scenery is appealing too. (The upper river has shoaled too much to permit sailing around the northern tip of the island, so keep to the south.) On the way down the St. Marys you can anchor for the night, if you wish, in pretty St. Inigoes Creek, with Cross Manor, one of the oldest houses in Maryland, above you among the tall trees and box hedges.

Coan River, on the Virginia shore, or Yeocomico River just above have many good anchorages at which you may wish to stop, perhaps on your way downriver; for they are across the Potomac from Smith Creek and the St. Marys.

Nomini Bay, with Mount Holly at its head, 25 miles from the Point Lookout Bell on the Virginia shore, and Breton and St. Clement Bays on the Maryland shore about the same distance upriver, are good objectives for a second day's easy run from Smith Creek or St. Marys River.

We have already referred to the cliffs above Nomini Bay and to Colonial Beach as a base for some historical exploration. If you don't go beyond Colonial Beach, you can take in most of the best of the lower Potomac in four to five days up and back—or less if your time is short.

Yachtsmen going all the way to Washington will find a few good available harbors above Colonial Beach, on the Virginia shore, and Wicomico River on the Maryland shore. Among these are Port Tobacco River, Mattawoman Creek, and finally the harbor at Washington, itself known as Washington Channel.

IV. THE LOWER EASTERN SHORE, BELOW CHOPTANK TO CAPE CHARLES.

Most of the Lower Eastern Shore is less attractive to cruising boatmen than other parts of the Bay, with low and marshy shorelines guarded by outlying shoals; it often seems more hospitable to mosquitoes than to yachtsmen. It has plenty of safe harbors, but some have only the convenience of a dock to tie up to, and a few lack even that. A land of two dimensions, it has been called, much of it no more than 10 feet above the sea.

Yet it has its attractions and is well worth exploring. It is quiet, old-fashioned, and, at least on the surface, remote from urban tensions, and its harbors and towns are among the most interesting on the Bay. We got the idea from the late Alf Loomis that no one can pretend to know the Bay until he has visited either Smith or Tangier Island. We certainly agree, and we'd be inclined to include also Fishing Creek, back entrance to Honga River; Chance and Wenona, on Deal Island; Crisfield, sea-food metropolis; the Pocomoke, with its overhanging cypress trees; Chesconessex and Onancock, on Virginia's Eastern Shore and handy to Tangier; and Kings Creek, next to Cape Charles Harbor.

If you are looking for atmosphere, if you want to see oystermen and crabbers, fishermen and muskrat trappers, these are the places to go. Except at Crisfield and Tangier, you will probably not meet many other yachtsmen; but you will see a good deal of country which time seems to have passed by, and you will meet—at Chesconessex and on Smith and Tangier islands—some fine old-world people who have changed very little since their ancestors came over from the British Isles many generations ago.

In the area around Chance and Crisfield you are just across the peninsula from the place where the first white man landed on the Eastern Shore. This explorer was Giovanni da Verrazano, an Italian on a voyage of discovery for the king of France. Sailing north along the Atlantic Coast, he came ashore in Chincoteague Bay, not far from the headwaters of Pocomoke River. Verrazano and a party of Frenchmen marched 8 miles inland, encountering an Indian tribe but stopping short of discovering the Chesapeake. This was in 1524—almost 80 years before the Jamestown colony was established in 1607.

Fortunately for the yachtsman coming down the Bay, all these harbors are within 50 miles or so of the Choptank and can easily be visited in a cruise of four or five days, starting, say, from Oxford on the Tred Avon.

Between Onancock and Cape Charles the Lower Eastern Shore has little to offer but peace and quiet and country scenery. So if your time is limited and you have to choose between it and the Lower Western Shore, we recommend the latter. It has everything the former has plus greater variety and convenience in harbors. If you choose the Lower Eastern Shore be sure to bring a dinghy—otherwise you may have to wade ashore—and plenty of bug spray.

The water comes up almost to the back doors on Smith Island.

66

V. THE LOWER WESTERN SHORE, BELOW POTOMAC RIVER TO CAPE HENRY.

The land is not so high here as farther up, but many of the Bay's finest harbors and rivers and a number of its most cherished historical landmarks are on this part of the Bay. No cruise in this area can be complete without visits to Carter and Urbanna creeks on the long and deep Rappahannock River, to Jackson Creek, Fishing Bay,

Milford Haven, and Wilton Creek on the Piankatank, to Horn Harbor and Mobjack Bay, to Sarah Creek and Yorktown on York River, to Hampton Roads and Jamestown Island.

Leaving your boat at a snug anchorage or tie-up in Sarah Creek, you can get a rented car at the dock and run across the Gloucester Point bridge over York River to Yorktown; a tour to Williamsburg and Jamestown can be arranged. Since there is no good anchorage or adequate facilities for tying up at either Yorktown or Jamestown, the use of Sarah Creek as a base from which to visit this historic peninsula is in our opinion the best bet for the yachtsman who also has a feeling for historic places.

At Hampton Roads, there are very few good anchorages in the busy roadstead, but plenty of marinas to choose from in Hampton Creek, Willoughby Bay, and Norfolk harbor, or at several other places all described later in Chapter Nine. Don't miss the Mariners Museum on the James above Newport News. It can be reached easily by car from Newport News or Hampton, and still more quickly from Deep Creek a few miles up the James. Try telephoning the Museum. They may be able to arrange transportation for you. They are most hospitable and are particularly anxious to have visits from yachtsmen.

The Rappahannock, York, and James rivers, while deep enough for a long way upriver, are all, in our opinion, most attractive and interesting, as well as freer from marshes near their mouths. The shorter rivers, like the Great Wicomico, Piankatank, and those leading into Mobjack Bay can be easily explored without long trips from the main part of the Chesapeake.

From the Potomac to Cape Henry, there are many harbors deep enough for the largest yachts and attractive and snug enough to appeal to even the most confirmed Maine Coast enthusiast.

In a week of cruising and sightseeing along the Lower Western Shore, you can skim the cream off some very rich milk. Perhaps milk is the wrong word to use for cruising folk, but it won't do to mix our metaphors, and you get the idea.

At this point it may be helpful to take a closer look at distances

Little
Choplank R.

Cambridge

Patuxent R.

Solomons

Chesapeake

St. Marys City

Honga R.

Potomac R.

Tangier
Sound

SMITH I.

Crisfield

Pokomoke Sound

TANGIER I.

Atlantic
Ocean

k R.

Piankatank R.

N

York R.

Mobjack Bay

Bay

James R.

Hampton

CAPE
CHARLES

Newport News

Hampton
Roads

CAPE
HENRY

Norfolk

LOWER BAY DISTANCES
NAUTICAL MILES

From	To
Solomons	28 Deal Isl. (Chan)
	32 Smith Isl.
	54 Tangier Isl.
	42 Crisfield
	69 Onancock
	Windmill Pt.
	(Rappahannock R.)
	84 Mobjack Bay
	(East R.)
	Piankatank R.
	87 Yorktown
	(Sarah Creek)

From	To
Yorktown	
(Sarah Cr.)	12 Old Pt. Comfort
	19 Newport News
	Norfolk (Mile "O")
Norfolk	35 Cape Charles
(Mile "O")	29 Kiptopeke
	38 Jamestown
	90 Richmond
	25 Cape Henry

between popular cruising ports like Annapolis, on the Western Shore, and other appealing destinations on the same side of the Bay or on the Eastern Shore. In some parts of the Upper Bay, distances from one side to the other may be less than those between neighboring ports on the same side. Annapolis, for example, is closer to St. Michaels on the Eastern Shore than it is to the Inner Harbor of Baltimore or Solomons on the Western Shore. On the other hand, if you are starting a cruise from Oxford, you will be closer to Annapolis across the Bay than to Chestertown far up the winding Chester River on the Eastern Shore. A sampling of distances between ports on both sides of the Bay is shown on the accompanying sketch charts. In planning a weekend cruise, the prevailing wind and weather are likely to be controlling factors governing your destination. But, in any case, you have a wide choice of harbors from both sides of the Bay.

Cross-bay distances are considerably greater in the lower half of the Bay than in the Upper Bay area, as shown in the sketch chart on page 69. Nevertheless, you may have similar alternatives in the choice of interesting and attractive ports of call on both sides of the Bay. For example, starting from Yorktown, or Irvington on the Rappahannock, you may find it just as interesting and perhaps more comfortable in some weather to sail across the Bay to Tangier Island or Onancock than it would be to find a suitable port on a passage north or south along the Western Shore. We refer to this distinctive feature later in this chapter in discussing the Chesapeake as a whole, but it is worth keeping in mind the wide choice of options as we review the choice of harbors in each section of the Bay.

VI. THE CHESAPEAKE AS A WHOLE.

As noted above, one of the unique features of the Chesapeake Bay is the accessibility of its many fine harbors from almost any point of departure around its shores. The five cruising areas described briefly above (and in detail in the following chapters) are not separated by great distances, one from another, but in fact form parts of two larger maritime regions known as the Upper Bay and the Lower Bay. Thus the port of Annapolis on the Upper Western Shore is within easy reach of Oxford, Cambridge, and St. Michaels on the Eastern Shore, and a hundred or more harbors equally close by on both sides of the Bay. If you are cruising up or down the Chesapeake, you can add variety by zigzagging back and forth, with assurance that you will find a good harbor on the other shore. If you don't like to buck a stiff head wind, you can always ease off and find a sheltered anchorage on either shore by sundown. We once tested this theory in a two-week "downhill" cruise under sail, choosing our course each day to avoid head winds. The result was a succession of pleasant, off-the-wind sailing days with delightful and unexpected anchorages at night. We don't know anywhere else along the Atlantic Coast where you could quite match that kind of cruising, or find as many snug harbors within a comparable area.

These characteristics make the Bay far more interesting for cruising boats transiting the Chesapeake as part of a longer passage on the Intracoastal Waterway, if their owners are wise enough to take advantage of the many options of course and route that are open to them. As we noted in Chapter One, altogether too many transient yachts continue to dash hurriedly north or south without taking time to enjoy the Chesapeake. But if you are able to allow only an extra day or two in your cruise plan, you'll be rewarded with a choice of routes that can lead you to unexpected benefits in ports and anchorages along the way.

For too many boats in transit we fear the Chesapeake is coming to be looked upon as little more than another "hazard of the course" to be endured as a necessary evil in the annual migrations that send several thousand small craft south in the fall and bring them back in the spring. Some are discovering that even in transit, you can enjoy the Bay without penalties. The fastest cruising yachts usually plan at least one stopover, while the slower powerboats and auxiliaries generally allow two or three days with overnight stops. The route favored by most power yachts takes them straight up and down the

Bay not far off the ship channel, with an overnight stop at Annapolis, or either Solomons or Windmill Point in the mid-Bay area. The slower power contingent may make all three of these stops in transiting the Bay, often without variation from year to year, although in recent years more through-travelers vary the annual routine by visiting Oxford or another port on the Eastern Shore.

There's no need to confine your ship to the traditional routes and ports of call, even on a two- or three-day transit schedule between Annapolis and Norfolk, and there is much of interest just off the beaten path. Whether you are heading up or down the Bay, you can generally find an alternative course that may prove to be advantageous for the day's run and probably won't affect your estimated transit time for the whole Bay. The basic choices lie between following the main channel or favoring whichever shore seems to offer the most advantages under prevailing conditions. We have often encountered wind and sea conditions that make it easier and more comfortable for a sailboat (and sometimes a powerboat) to stand over to the Eastern Shore for an overnight stop than to fight head winds all day down the channel route to an anchorage after dark on the Western Shore. Here are a few examples.

If you are leaving Solomons heading south with a strong head wind building up steep seas that make it impossible for you to hold your course and speed, try running off to the east through Hooper Strait into Tangier Sound, where you will find protected waters and a choice of "different" harbors for the night. The harbors at Chance and Wenona, on Deal Island, offer good protection at the northern end of Tangier Sound; Crisfield has excellent marina facilities and its busy harbor is worth a visit at any time; Onancock, on the Virginia shore just beyond the southern entrance to the Sound, is a good overnight stopping place either entering or leaving Tangier Sound.

Boats traveling north in the spring may have the same kind of choices in reverse. If you encounter head winds and rough seas off the Rappahannock or the Potomac, your choice lies between ducking into any one of the protected creeks between these two rivers on the Western Shore, or standing off across the Bay to Onancock and the southern entrance to Tangier Sound. You'll be surprised to find that the total distance traveled (by the time you return to the main channel through Hooper Strait) is not very much more than it would have been had you followed the Western Shore. Under the conditions we describe, an auxiliary sailboat can actually make better time by running across the Bay on a reach and continuing up Tangier Sound under power, if necessary, than it could hope to make beating up the main Bay.

Similar choices may be made farther up the Bay, north of Cove Point, or south of Annapolis, where the long unbroken coastline of the Calvert Cliffs provides no shelter on the Western Shore, while the wide entrance to the Choptank only a few miles across the Bay beckons you to the Eastern Shore and convenient snug harbors like Dun Cove (on Harris Creek above Knapps Narrows) and Hudson Creek in the Little Choptank. In the chapters which follow we have many more suggestions. Add a day or two to your transit timetable to visit at least a few of our favorite gunkholes.

Part Two

LONG ISLAND SOUND
TO THE CHESAPEAKE

CHAPTER FOUR

CITY ISLAND TO SANDY HOOK, THE NEW JERSEY COAST AND WATERWAY, DELAWARE BAY, AND DELMARVA COASTAL ROUTE

This chapter is directed to that part of the cruising community which is concerned with the logistics of taking a boat to or from the Chesapeake, via Sandy Hook, the New Jersey Coast or Inland Waterway, and Delaware Bay. Our thoughts on making this passage have not changed very greatly since the first edition of this guide was written, although man-made changes have altered major sections of the waterway route, making it somewhat less attractive than we found it two or three decades ago. We have always favored the outside route for a well-found cruising vessel, chiefly to avoid the delays and inconveniences of traveling the circuitous waterway course with its tidal flats and shifting sandbars, its bridges, and its often heavy water traffic.

Today we are more emphatic about the advantages of running outside, and the disadvantages of cruising the inland route. For the truth of the matter is that the New Jersey link in the Intracoastal

Waterway system is not what it used to be. Fixed bridges now cross important sections of the waterway, preventing passage by vessels needing 35 feet or more clearance; channel depths are not always maintained in all parts of the system; and the controlling depth drops to 3 feet in some critical areas, such as just inside ocean inlets. Larger sailing vessels have no alternative to making the outside passage at least between Cape May and Atlantic City, and our advice to deep draft powerboats and motor sailors is to watch the weather bulletins and take the outside course between Sandy Hook and Delaware Bay, putting in at Manasquan Inlet or Atlantic City if convenient or necessary. Shoal draft powerboats and other small craft that may be unsuitable for open water passages should, of course, take full advantage of the protected waterway route, which they will find interesting and even attractive at many points along the way.

Distances are not very great, whichever route you plan to take, with less than 20 miles difference between the outside and inside passages. From Long Island Sound to the entrance of the Chesapeake and Delaware Canal is about 189 nautical miles by the offshore route, compared with approximately 206 miles via the waterway. Starting from City Island at the western end of the Sound, your course will take you through the East River and busy New York Harbor to Sandy Hook or Atlantic Highlands, where you can lie overnight before starting down the coast. From Sandy Hook to Manasquan Inlet you must go outside along the coast. There you will have a choice between continuing outside to Atlantic City or Cape May or taking the waterway route for the next 100 miles to Cape May and Delaware Bay. Distances in nautical miles are approximately as follows:

	Via East River and New York Harbor	Via Jersey Coast	Via Inland Waterway
City Island to Sandy Hook	31		
Sandy Hook to Manasquan Inlet		24	
Manasquan to Absecon Inlet (Atlantic City)		47 } 83	60 } 100
Absecon Inlet to Cape May Harbor		36	40
Cape May Canal to Delaware Bay		3	3
Delaware Bay and River to Chesapeake and Delaware Canal		48	48
Total nautical miles		189	206

Note that distances shown on NOS charts for the waterway route are in statute miles; all other distances are in nautical miles.

The time required to make this passage by either route will vary widely, of course, depending on the type of boat and the kind of weather you encounter along the way. Fast power cruisers make the outside passage between Sandy Hook and Cape May in a single daylight run, if weather and sea conditions are favorable. We have made the same passage under sail in a day-and-night run of less than 24 hours with an offshore breeze providing a beam reach and calm seas; but we have also taken twice that long under adverse wind and sea conditions.

Weather and sea conditions are always the controlling factors in making any coastwise passage, and the Jersey coast is no exception. Seasonal differences are considerable and should be taken into account in planning this part of your cruise. Fog is common in the spring and early summer, and strong frontal systems move across the coast regularly in both the spring and fall, bringing hard nor'westers that can hold you in port for a day or so. Summer weather is generally good for passage making on this section of the coast: the prevailing winds are from the south; early morning fog usually burns off by noon; and the high pressure systems bring generally moderate to light northerly winds and clear weather. Tropical storms and hurricanes reach this far north and should be looked for any time between June and November. Early fall is usually a good time to make the passage south; September and October are the best months. By October and November the cold fronts begin to come in regularly, often followed by easterly winds and high seas that make most of the inlets dangerous or impassable.

Conditions on Delaware Bay are discussed later in this chapter, but the passage from Cape May to the Chesapeake and Delaware Canal can usually be made in a single daylight run, even by 6-knot auxiliaries, if you are lucky enough to find the right combination of wind and tide. Don't count on finding the combination always in your favor, however, and always allow for a layover day somewhere along the route.

I. CITY ISLAND TO SANDY HOOK.

1. The Current. The important thing for auxiliaries going through East River and its famous Hell Gate is to pick the current right. Unlike Long Island Sound, the ebb current through here sets westward, the flood tide eastward.

A good plan is to start from City Island about an hour before the ebb current turns westward at Rikers Island (6 miles from City Island), and then carry the ebb through Hell Gate and the East River all the way down the Upper Bay, Narrows, and Lower Bay. The *Tide and Current Tables for the Atlantic Coast* will tell how to figure this out. Distances in nautical miles from City Island are approximately as follows:

To Rikers Island—east end	6	miles
" Hell Gate Bridge	10	"
" The Battery	16½	"
" The Narrows—Fort Lafayette	22½	"
" Gravesend Bay—Marine Basin	24½	"

To Sandy Hook   30½ miles
   " Atlantic Highlands—Yacht Basin   34   "

Currents through the East River passage (mean velocity at full strength) are 1 knot at Throgs Neck; 1½ knots from Whitestone Point to North Brother Island (just beyond Rikers Island); 2 to 5 knots from there to the Battery and Governors Island. The higher velocities occur at Hell Gate (4½ knots for the westward current and 3½ for the eastward), at Blackwells Island, and in the narrow parts of the channel east of Brooklyn Bridge. In the Narrows the speed is 2 knots on the ebb and 1½ knots on the flood. The direction and velocity of the current are affected by strong winds. In general, the current runs with the channel, though there are heavy swirls in Hell Gate, which sometimes sweep tugs and barges off their course, as well as yachts.

If the wind is against the tide at Hell Gate, there can be a nasty slop. Don't attempt the passage without power adequate to maintain full control and without a sharp lookout, not only for traffic but for floating driftwood.

2. *The Passage* (*12366, 12339, 12327, 12335, 12334, 12349*). While it is desirable to have all of the largest scale charts, it is possible to navigate safely with the first three in this series. The usual channel to follow runs north of Rikers and North Brother, west of Blackwells Island, and (unless you want to get a closer view of the Statue of Liberty), east of Governors Island. Minimum height of any bridge is 127 feet (Brooklyn).

This is a fascinating passage and it can be exciting when traffic, floating debris, and the current combine to make it so. Don't try it at night. The multiplicity of lights is confusing and the driftwood invisible.

Rikers and Ward islands are interesting, if not very inviting, for the former is occupied by the buildings of the New York Department of Correction and the latter by the old insane asylum and some hospitals. There are also hospitals on North Brother Island. On Blackwells Island (locally called Welfare Island) are some of the

Sandy Hook. (Photo courtesy of the U.S. Coast Pilot.)

New York municipal buildings. To the west is the island of Manhattan.

3. Anchorages. After passing between Throgs Neck and Willets Point, there are several places to anchor, of which we'll mention only a few of the most important. However, if the current is favorable, we don't recommend stopping at least until the Yacht Basin at Atlantic

Horseshoe Cove

Shrewsbury River
Entrance

Sandy Hook Bay

ndy Hook Point

September 1986

Highlands. If the current turns favorable too late for a daylight passage, it is possible to gain some time by spending a night in Flushing Bay.

a. Flushing Bay (12334). This is a moderately good anchorage, but it is exposed to the north and 2 miles from the main passage. The channel is well marked to the facilities on the west side. Slips or moorings are available to transients in 10 feet of water. Gas, diesel fuel, ice, water, some marine supplies, and quick service are all on hand. If you spend the night you may be kept awake by traffic to and from La Guardia Airport.

b. Sandy Hook (12324, 12326). While the anchorage under Sandy Hook is too exposed from northwest to south to be satisfactory for yachts, you can often find a comfortable overnight spot in settled weather southwest of Sandy Hook Light. Landing is prohibited, however, as Sandy Hook is a government reservation.

c. Atlantic Highlands (12328). Facilities here for yachtsmen have been greatly improved and there is anchorage or a tie-up behind the breakwater which is good in all but hard easterlies, when shelter may be obtained by running into Highlands Reach. The breakwater is hard to identify from the mouth of the Bay, but the end of it is about in line with the highest point on the long ridge behind it and slightly to the left (east) of a buff-colored cut in the cliffs.

Preparatory to a trip around Sandy Hook, the place to tie up is at the excellent Atlantic Highlands Yacht Harbor and Municipal Marina 3½ miles from the Hook's end. Report first at the easternmost gas pier, and obtain a slip assignment, with electric connections. The Harbor Master is on duty from 8 A.M. to 5 P.M. Besides gas and diesel fuel, water and ice are available and there are pay telephones. An attractive restaurant occupies part of the parking lot and the Atlantic Highlands Yacht Club is on the second floor of the building housing the restaurant. Supplies are a 5-minute walk up the street. Mechanics are on hand. Ask the Harbor Master for weather forecasts or call up the Coast Guard. Depths in the anchorage run to 14 feet. There is no charge for anchoring.

This is a good place for meeting or disembarking members of the crew, for it is less than 60 minutes from the heart of New York City by car. It is especially important as the last good port for those headed along the New Jersey Coast towards the Jersey Waterway entrance at Manasquan Inlet. The Leonardo State Marina, about a mile and a half west of the Yacht Harbor, also has facilities for transient yachts.

II. THE NEW JERSEY COAST.

1. Choice of Routes. As indicated above, there are three ways to get to Cape May Harbor, preparatory to the passage up Delaware Bay to the Chesapeake and Delaware Canal—northern gateway to the Chesapeake.

a. The outside passage along the Jersey Coast covers a distance of approximately 107 nautical miles from the end of Sandy Hook to the entrance of Cape May Harbor. Until Manasquan Inlet is reached, 24 miles from Sandy Hook, there is no choice. All vessels *must* take the open sea passage, with only one possible harbor on the way: Shark River Inlet, about 19 miles from the end of Sandy Hook.

Along this outer passage of 107 miles there are 12 inlets of sufficient importance to be worth mentioning. Some of them have been considerably improved and are safe to enter except during a strong onshore wind or heavy seas. Others should only be entered with local pilotage and under favorable conditions. All of these inlets will be described later. With careful attention to weather forecasts, and prompt action in getting into an inlet *before* the seas become dangerous, safe harbors are available to the careful long-shore cruiser.

The outer passage is shorter than the Inland Waterway, especially below Atlantic City. If you have a sailboat, the opportunity for using sails will be much greater. If you proceed under power, you can go faster unless the seas are rough, for there are no traffic speed restrictions to hamper you, and there are few shoals to require the caution so frequently necessary on the Waterway. This is particularly true if your yacht draws over 4 feet and much more so if she draws over 5 feet.

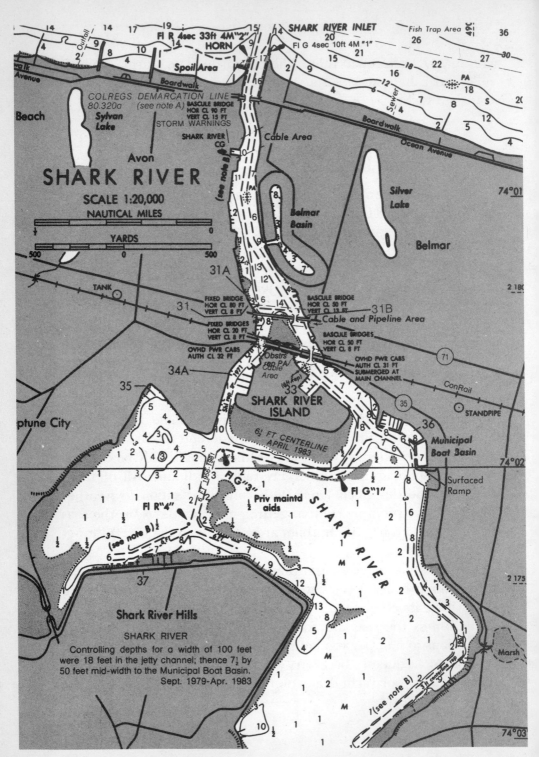

Shark River Inlet (from chart 12324).

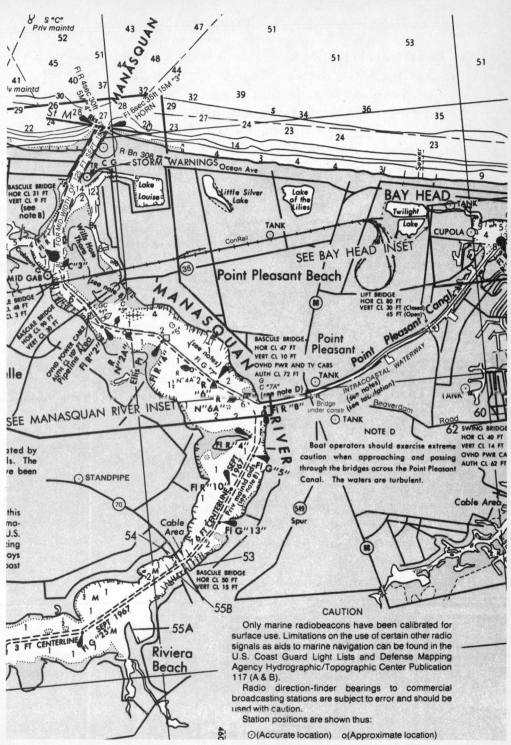

Manasquan Inlet and River and Point Pleasant Canal (from chart 12324).

b. The second alternative is the Inland Waterway from Manasquan Inlet to Cape May, a distance of about 100 miles via the Waterway, compared to about 83 miles for the outside passage between these two harbors. From Sandy Hook outside to Manasquan, and inside from there on to Cape May, the distance is about 124 miles, compared to 107 by the outside passage. We shall describe the Inland Waterway later. It is an interesting trip, worth trying for at least part of the way if your vessel doesn't have too tall a mast for the 35-foot bridge clearance below Atlantic City, or doesn't draw too much. Four feet is probably the limit for comfort, as we shall point out, though the difficulties for drafts of 5 feet or slightly more are not insurmountable.

c. The third way is to combine both routes, going outside when the weather is favorable. This plan is especially recommended for small sailboats and for motor cruisers in a hurry. By this method, one can enjoy the two great pleasures of cruising to which we have already referred: going out into wide waters from a sheltered place, and going into a sheltered place from wide waters.

2. *The Outer Passage (12323, 12324, 12316, 12318).*

a. Sandy Hook to Manasquan Inlet. In some ways, the most attractive part of the New Jersey coast is the stretch where an outer passage is required, from Sandy Hook to Manasquan Inlet, a distance of 24 nautical miles. Here the shore is relatively high; there are still a few reminders of the old beach front and less crowding than at many popular beach resorts along the coast.

In following this part of the coast it is usually possible to keep within a quarter of a mile of the shore or even closer for most of the way, after passing through False Hook Channel. The fish nets which once constituted such a hazard along this section of the Jersey shore have been removed, and even the stray pole stumps have been

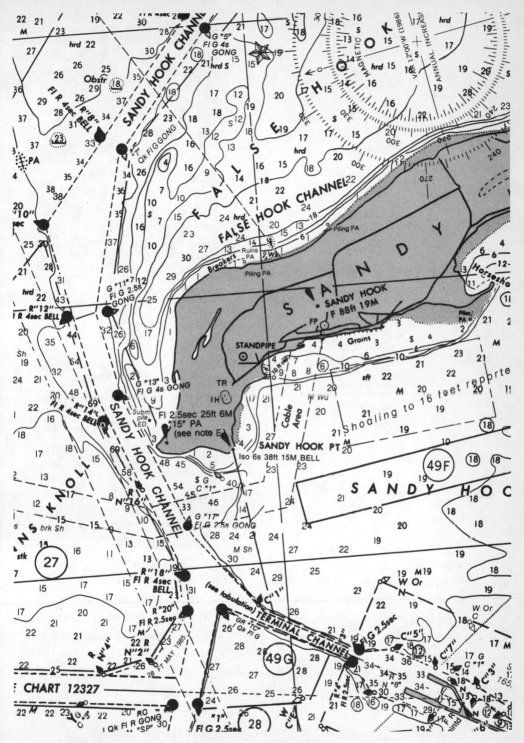

Sandy Hook Channel and anchorage (from chart 12324).

Manasquan Inlet. (Photo courtesy of the U.S. Coast Pilot.)

blasted out by the Army Engineers. You may still encounter a few fish nets inside Sandy Hook, and floating driftwood can be troublesome in the harbor entrance, especially on ebb tides. Otherwise, it's generally clear sailing close in along shore, provided you keep a sharp watch for shoals off the inlets. The charts cannot be depended on for the location of shifting inlet bars, but the increasing steepness of seas usually gives an indication of shoal water.

Stockton Lake

Watson Creek

Crabtown Creek

Manasquan

Manasquan River

Coast Guard Station

Manasquan Inlet

September 1986

b. Below Manasquan Inlet. Below Manasquan Inlet the shoals in many places tend to reach farther offshore than above, and it's advisable for deep-draft yachts to keep well off the beach. Small craft can usually run close alongshore without trouble, provided they keep well outside the inlets and be on guard against strong currents. At night, it's a good rule for all craft to stay well offshore in any case.

"Don't assume bold water spang up to the beach, just because the chart shows it so . . ." says one yachtsman. "We got careless toward evening of our second day and got bumped hard just above Brigantine Inlet, east of Pullen Island."

The importance of checking the weather frequently cannot be overemphasized, for unless you get through an inlet *before* the seas have built up, it may be too late.

3. *How to Negotiate an Inlet and How Not to.* While the inlets vary greatly in their value as harbors, certain things may be said which apply to all of them in greater or less degree.

(1) Their entrance channels are subject to frequent change, both in depth and position. Thus, the charts are unreliable on these points and any information may soon be out of date. Many of the entrance buoys are not charted, for they are moved frequently by the Coast Guard to be in accord with the latest depths.

(2) No inlet, even the best, may be safely entered in a strong onshore wind or high sea.

The Coast Guard Shows How. In the course of our early explorations along the Jersey Coast, we arrived one morning in September at the U.S. Coast Guard Station at Barnegat Inlet. The wind was not strong but fairly high seas caused by a distant tropical hurricane were breaking wickedly almost all the way across the entrance, despite a channel depth of almost 11 feet. Yachts and fishing craft had been advised a few hours before to stay inside.

We wanted to find out what it was like to go through the inlet under such conditions. After explaining to a most cooperative Coast Guard officer that we were working on a cruising guide, and hoped to be able to give some good advice to yachtsmen on how to negotiate an inlet, he offered to take us out on a patrol which was about to start, for an object lesson in what to do—and what *not* to do. We were glad when the latter part of the lesson was over.

As we went through the turbulent waters at the entrance our Coast Guard instructor pointed out that most boats that have difficulty entering an inlet come to grief not by hitting bottom, even when the waves are breaking, but by broaching to. What happens is usually this: A boat gets just in front of a steep breaking wave. This may throw her stern partly out of water, causing her to become out of control from the rudder. Then she is apt to swing sideways, roll over, and fill up, or perhaps be hurled out of the channel against a shoal or jetty.

"It isn't bad enough to tip us over or swamp us, just now," said the Coast Guard skipper, "so I'll show you how easy it is to broach to. Another boat tried it yesterday, accidentally, and had a bad time until we got there."

Whereupon, with a steep sea curling menacingly astern, he turned the rudder slightly. The stern was thrown off the course and as we began to heel over, another wave gave us a further roll and we landed sideways in the trough of the sea, with considerable water coming over the boat. The closed forward cabin saved us from a drenching but we wished we'd kept our hat on when we hit the cabin roof.

That was enough about what not to do. The writer hastily explained that he was convinced. While we pitched and rolled in the mouth of the inlet, the skipper gave some very good demonstrations and advice about what to do in approaching an inlet, when the seas were bad. Here is a summary of this advice and that of several other men of long experience in these inlets.

(1) In sizing up whether or not it is safe to attempt to go through an inlet, remember that conditions from the outside usually look better than they really are, for the waves of course break toward the shore. Conversely, the reverse is true, when on the inside, looking out.

(2) If the location of the channel and the meaning of the buoys are not easy to recognize, circle around outside until everything is clearly understood. If you do this a few times, so that it is obvious from the lookout tower that you don't know the way in or are doubtful about whether it is safe to attempt it, the Coast Guard boat may show you the way. If you want help, try to communicate with the Coast Guard by ship-to-shore telephone, or signal to attract attention.

(3) Go in under power, if you possibly can, since this enables a better control of speed. In fact, don't enter an inlet unless you have power, except under the best conditions.

(4) Cruise back and forth just outside of the place where the waves are steepest or breaking and wait for a favorable moment. This comes after a series of high rollers, when the waves are less steep. Then head in without delay.

(5) Don't let your boat get carried along just ahead of a steep one, or you run the risk of broaching to. The following paragraph suggests how to accomplish this.

(6) If your boat has considerable speed and you are an experienced inlet skipper, or if conditions are not bad, you can often enter an inlet successfully by riding the back of a cresting sea at a speedy gait, but it is a dangerous and tricky procedure at best and few experts would recommend it. The safer method, which is also the simpler—and has the added advantage of applying equally to fast boats, slow boats, sailboats, or motorboats—is to enter the inlet at very slow speed and let the seas overtake and pass you as you work your way in. Keep just enough speed through the water for steerageway, but be ready to cut down even more as a cresting sea overtakes you, even reversing if necessary, so that the sea will pass by you without carrying you along on its face. You will be relieved—after perhaps first having the thrill of your life—to discover how heavy a sea you can let overtake you in this manner without serious mishap. Spray may fly as the sea hits your stern, and you may take aboard a lot of broken water, but in a moment it is all over, and you'll have more confidence by the time the next sea catches up with you. An ebb current makes the seas break more steeply and accentuates the difficulties, so, if possible, always go in or out a bad inlet with a flood tide, preferably near high water.

(7) Be alert to steer a straight course and keep a firm grip on the helm.

(8) The following advice came from an experienced boatman who approached the entrance to Cape May Harbor when a fairly strong onshore wind was blowing diagonally against the jetties and piling up some steep and dangerous seas:

"Don't approach the passage between the jetties," he said, "from directly off shore. Come up on the entrance as much as possible from the downwind side, so that you are heading diagonally into the seas instead of having them on your quarter. Then, at the right moment, swing sharply around the leeward jetty and into the channel."

Conclusion. For most of the year and for most days, except in northeasters, there will be no difficulty in entering the better inlets. This of course is with the provision that the buoys are understood and reasonable caution is exercised.

An East Coast sailor who keeps his auxiliary cruising boat at Atlantic City re-explored most of the inlets between Manasquan and Cape May, reporting controlling depths in the entrance channels and other navigational hazards for us while we were updating this book. His findings, and information obtained from the New Jersey Department of Coastal Engineering, confirmed and strengthened our earlier reports and our own observations on the shoaling of several of the inlets, which are now considered unsafe for all but shoal-draft motorboats with local knowledge. Specifically, this applies to Beach Haven, Little Egg, Brigantine, Corson, and Hereford. A note on the chart, which applies to all of these and to Great Egg as well, issues this warning: "The entrance channels at the inlets not protected by jetties are subject to frequent changes. The buoys are not charted because they are frequently shifted in position. Buoys are removed if shoaling makes inlets unnavigable."

Barnegat, reputedly the worst inlet on the coast, was in the early stages of a lengthy program to upgrade it by repairing the jetties and dredging the channel in 1988. Get up-to-date local information before using it.

4. The Inlets and Their Harbors.

a. Shark River Inlet (12324). Rated one of the safest inlets, Shark River has two parallel jetties, with a lighted navigational aid on the end of each one, and an offshore buoy targeting the inlet. The controlling depth is 12 feet in past the four bridges over the main, or south, channel. All four bridges will open on request (vertical clearance 15 feet for the one closest to the ocean, 13 feet for the next

95

Barnegat Inlet. (Photo courtesy of the U.S. Coast Pilot.)

Clam Island

Tank

highway bridge, and 10 feet for the railroad and Highway 35 bridges). The bridges have approximately the same clearance when they cross the north channel, but those spans are fixed. Some skippers have reported that the Ocean Avenue bridge is slow to open, so take care if there is a strong offshore breeze blowing you into it or a strong current flowing in. The bridge was being rebuilt in the summer of 1988, and may subsequently be faster to open. The river

BARNEGAT BAY

The Dike

Sedge Islands

Abandoned Lighthouse

Barnegat Inlet

Light 4A

September 1986

is too crowded to anchor, but docking facilities are usually available. Many large commercial fishing boats routinely use this inlet.

b. Manasquan Inlet and River, Brielle (12234). This is a first-class inlet, easy to enter or leave except in an onshore blow or when a heavy sea breaks across the entrance. An offshore buoy and lighted navigational aids on the two stone jetties make the channel, controlling depth 12 feet, easy to negotiate. Inside, a channel leads off the south side with about 15 feet to the Coast Guard station and a restaurant which offers dockage to diners. There are a number of places to tie up farther in on the north shore toward the railroad bridge. The railroad bridge, vertical clearance 3 feet, may be open already unless there is a train coming. An experienced Bay Head yachtsman writes: "You should warn your people about the railroad bridge and its treacherous angle, narrowness and mean currents." The channel shallows to a minimum depth of 4 feet as you approach within 300 feet east of the railroad bridge.

c. Barnegat Inlet and City (12234). Barnegat Inlet (see photo, pages 96–97) is rated as one of the worst. Local boats use it, but authorities warn strangers not to enter; it certainly should not be used in bad weather. Until the Corps of Engineers finishes the extensive improvements already under way in 1988, this is the situation. The outer third of the north jetty is submerged at high water, when the extent of it can be identified only by the breaking water. The south jetty is completely submerged and very treacherous. The famous Barnegat Lighthouse, no longer lit, is preserved as a state historic monument, half red and half white.

d. Beach Haven Inlet (12316). This is a natural inlet, marked with navigational aids by the Coast Guard, which shifts them periodically as the channel shifts. The depths shown on your latest chart cannot be depended on. Coastal Resources says, "Use extreme caution." Little Egg is very close by and is better.

e. Little Egg Inlet (12316). This is another natural inlet, with constant changes going on among the sands and shoals. It is only another 10 miles to Absecon.

f. Brigantine (12316). This inlet should be avoided. When we were there, the depth on the bar was 3 feet and the seas were breaking heavily. They usually are.

g. Atlantic City (Absecon Inlet) (12316 and inset, chart 12318). A dredged channel with a depth of about 17 feet runs between two parallel jetties, lit with navigational lights, in a northwest direction leading to the deep water along the northeast shore of Atlantic City.

The passage, from its offshore green flashing gong 1, is wide, well buoyed and easy to follow. The tidal range is about 4 feet and the current at times is fairly strong.

There have been many changes in the Atlantic City harborfront since the first edition of the Guide appeared. Old landmarks, like the Tuna Club, have disappeared, to be replaced by modern boating facilities that are still expanding in all directions around the harbor.

The Coast Guard Station is housed in a large white building with a red roof and a tall flagpole. It is visible as you turn from the channel into the harbor on the point to starboard. Weather reports can be obtained there, and sea conditions checked for the nearby inlets.

Absecon Island, on which the city is located, extends west by south about 7 miles to Great Egg Inlet, with Atlantic City, Ventnor, Margate City, and Longport adjoining each other southward in that order. Together, they form one of the outstanding seaside resorts of the world. Unless you crave seclusion all of the time, don't miss it.

h. Great Egg Inlet (Ocean City) (12316). This is another natural inlet. It is marked with three mid-channel buoys. Watch for shoaling to a depth of only 4 feet, which has been reported at the middle channel marker. There is a tidal range of about 4 feet.

Once when we were there waves were breaking, it seemed, all the way across the bar. Yet boats were coming and going, always carefully watched by the Coast Guard. Our admiration for the Coast Guard rose to a new high after we had seen them in action along the Jersey Coast. There are facilities inside at Margate City, Somers Point, and Ocean City.

i. Corson Inlet, Strathmere (12316). This inlet was described by Coastal Resources personnel as "basically closed."

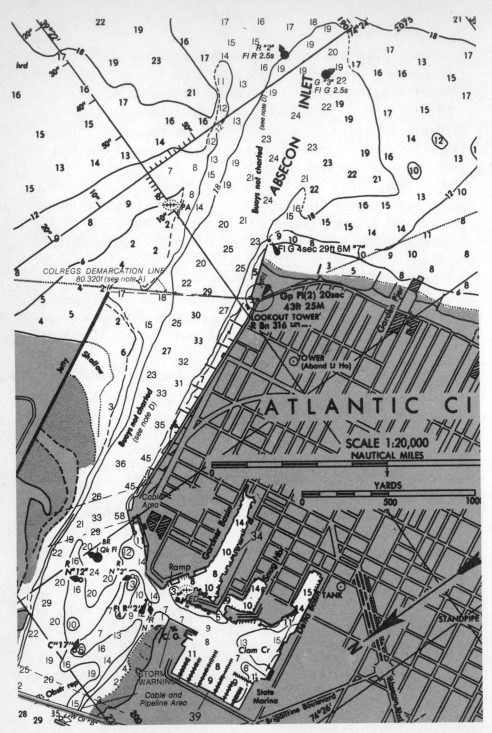

Absecon Inlet and Atlantic City (from chart 12316).

j. Townsend Inlet (12316). This is called a "natural" inlet, although there is an unmarked jetty on the south side. There are mid-channel buoys throughout the channel, which has a controlling depth of 12 to 15 feet. The Coast Guard moves the buoys to conform to the shifting channel, so they are not charted. Use caution if you use this inlet.

k. Hereford Inlet (12316). There are no jetties and the ocean approach to this inlet is very dangerous because there are a lot of offshore shoals. Although it is dredged periodically, a channel that is dredged today may be gone tomorrow. It is best to go to another inlet.

l. Cape May Inlet and Harbor (12316). This is the best of all the inlets along the New Jersey Coast. The entrance is protected by two jetties about a mile long, marked with navigational lights. Twenty-foot depths carry into the harbor, where the water level drops to about 8 feet, and possibly less when a storm blows the water out. A Coast Guard training base is located inside.

On entering, the New Jersey Waterway is to the starboard, or north. Cape May Harbor is westward to port. The main harbor is about 1 1/2 miles long and 1/4 to 1/3 mile wide—too large for comfort at times. On the port, or south shore, are some Coast Guard buildings and docks, not for public use, and the docks and moorings of the Cape May Yacht Club are next door. The north shore is chiefly marshland, intersected by marshy waterways and the southern terminus of the New Jersey section of the Intracoastal Waterway. Here you will find several well-equipped yacht basins and marinas, including the Bree-Zee-Lee Yacht Basin, Mill Creek Marina, McNeill's Marina, and South Jersey East. Other facilities on the north side of the harbor include Hinch Marina, McNeill's, and Mill Creek. While most of these places are less congested than the south end of the harbor, they are also somewhat more remote from shore-based supplies, restaurants, and services.

In Schellenger Creek at the south end of the harbor near the entrance of Cape Island Creek and the Cape May Canal you will find everything close at hand. The water is deep enough for most cruising yachts; it is usually 7 feet or more. Here is the fine South Jersey Marina, with slips with electricity, gas, diesel fuel, water, ice, hauling and repair service, showers, rest rooms, and a snack bar available.

At this end of Cape May Harbor there is also Utsch's Marina, with many slips and other services.

Swarms of transient boats stop yearly in Schellenger Creek. It isn't secluded and private but it is one of the most interesting places on the coast. There is an excellent restaurant called the Lobster House at the old Schellenger fish dock at the entrance to the creek, offering dockage to diners, and a large, well-stocked fish market is adjacent.

Anchorage space in Cape May is limited. You might squeeze into the mooring area off the Cape May Yacht Club next to the Coast Guard Station or into the small cove south of the entrance to Schellenger Creek. An alternative, if you want to anchor away from town, is to run north up the Intracoastal to Sunset Lake, where depths run from 9 to 29 feet.

III. The New Jersey Inland Waterway (*12324*, *12316*).

From Manasquan Inlet to Cape May Harbor, the New Jersey Inland Waterway winds its way for about 100 nautical miles through shallow bays and wide marshes, flanked on the seaward side by an almost ceaseless procession of seaside resorts. No high cliffs tower above the cruising yacht; in fact there is hardly a hill in sight—just an expanse of green and brown and gold marshland. Yet this is an interesting trip, at times fascinating, and always enlivened by the necessity of threading a winding way between endless buoys and stakes, here and there, perhaps pushing off a bottom of mud or sand—or being pulled off.

There are many good anchorages on the way and the passage is safe from the seas, which break almost unceasingly along the outer beach.

1. *Depths, Tides, and Currents Through the Waterway.* The first question to which all yachtsmen want an answer is: "What draft can be carried through the waterway?" Sailboats need to know additional information about bridge clearance, which is 35 feet in the section between Atlantic City and Cape May, and 60 feet north of Atlantic City.

As to draft, the answer depends partly upon how much of a hurry you are in, and partly on tidal conditions. The tidal range at and near the inlets, where the worst shallow spots are located, is from 3 to 4 feet, though in Barnegat Bay and between inlets it may be as little as 1/2 to 1 foot. If you have time to wait for the tide, at several of the shallow places a greater draft can be carried through them than if it is necessary to push right along, regardless of tide. Tide tables are thus almost a necessity, though information can be obtained along the way from Coast Guard stations.

The tide is also greatly affected by winds, both in time and height, with westerly winds causing low water and easterly winds high water in most of the Waterway. In Barnegat Bay, northerly and southerly winds drive the water to the leeward ends of the Bay. Current velocities may reach 3 knots near the inlets and adjacent channels.

Since our original edition, the dredging and maintenance of the New Jersey Intracoastal Waterway has been taken over from the State by the U.S. Army Corps of Engineers. We had hoped that considerable improvement would result, particularly in channel depths, and that the Jersey Waterway would compare favorably with the Intracoastal Waterway between Norfolk and Miami. Unfortunately that has not been the case and conditions appear to be very little improved from what they were. Lack of adequate funds for maintenance is the reason given. The New Jersey section of the Intracoastal Waterway used to have controlling depths of at least 6 feet in a 100-foot-wide channel from Manasquan Inlet to Hereford Inlet, with 10- and 12-foot depths to Cape May. However, depths of

4 feet are now reported in the initial section from the ConRail Bridge to Bay Head, from Absecon Inlet to Great Egg Harbor Inlet and from there on to Corson Inlet. Depths of 3.7 feet are reported between Corson Inlet and Townsends Inlet and only 3.2 feet between Little Egg Inlet and Absecon Inlet. Other sections have 5 feet or more, with the exception of the portion from Wildwood to Cape May Inlet, which has 10 feet. The depths are at mean low water (MLW).

The depth situation, plus the fact that several fixed bridges have been built across the waterway with a vertical clearance of 35 feet at high water, means that many auxiliary sailing vessels now have to follow the outside passage, depending for shelter mainly on the inlets at Manasquan, Atlantic City, and Cape May.

High northeast storm tides on the coast are usually felt on the inland waters, and tides running over the meadow banks frequently result. Under these conditions, and by taking advantage of the local tide, a boat probably could get through with a draft of 5 feet or more. But we don't advise trying it, unless you have lots of time and patience.

From Bay Head to Beach Haven, the tidal range is not great and is subject to wind conditions. From Beach Haven to Cape May the Waterway is subject to considerable rise and fall of tide, and hence if any difficulty is experienced at some spot due to local shoaling or a temporary condition, advantage can always be taken of the rise in tide to get out of trouble.

2. *The Principal Danger Spots (shoals or otherwise).* These and the channels vary from time to time, according to dredging activities and the effect of tide and wind. The charts may be outdated in reporting depths. A further difficulty is that Coast Guard reports are not always in accord with the figures given on the charts or by the Corps of Engineers (which is responsible for the Waterway). If a Coast Guard officer has recently hauled a boat off a shoal in a supposedly dredged channel, it is not easy to convince him that the channel is as deep as the office in Philadelphia says it is. On the

other hand, the Coast Guard may not always be kept up-to-date on dredging activities.

We advise yachtsmen planning to take boats through the Waterway with drafts of over 4 feet to get an up-to-date report on the shoal spots from the U.S. Army Engineer District (Custom House, Second and Chestnut streets, Philadelphia, Pa. 19106-2991 [215] 597-4802) and at the same time check frequently with the nearest Coast Guard station prior to reaching some of the reported shoal areas. This may save you and the Coast Guard considerable trouble in the end. Local authorities often can be helpful.

A local authority has the following comments about danger spots.

Regarding danger spots, we unfortunately have to start right at the beginning of the Waterway just after you come into Manasquan Inlet. The railroad bridge is the first bridge you come to going west in the Manasquan River. It seems to be much narrower than the 48-foot width claimed for it on the charts. Due to the angle on which it is set, the bridge, in crossing the river, creates a blind spot approaching it from either direction. This is because the machinery for the draw and the bridge tender's shanty are located on the south side of the bridge. Unfortunately, the channel changes direction right at the draw itself and it is therefore recommended that whether you are approaching this bridge from the east or from the west you swing to the north side of the river in order to get a look at traffic that may be approaching from the other side. The pilings of this bridge have deteriorated and the pilings themselves as well as the wailers have many treacherous spikes and bolts protruding from the Waterway. Due to treacherous current conditions right at the draw it is recommended that sufficient power be used going through this narrow opening to provide maximum control.

Going west from the railroad bridge the large highway bridge poses no problem; however, the channel turns south shortly after going west through the bridge. Unfortunately, many people miss this first change of direction and wind up on an involuntary clamming mission on the nearby flats.

About 2 miles west of the highway bridge is the entrance to the Bay Head-Manasquan Canal indicated by a channel junction marker in the river. Due to many factors this canal has rather violent currents at its bridges and should be used with caution. The canal is a safe and deep passage; however, during the season it is heavily traveled and is no place to be daydreaming.

The first bridge of the canal, when traveling in a southerly direction, is a secondary highway bridge over which travels a considerable amount of traffic on Route 88. Sufficient power should be applied when approaching and going through this bridge to maintain complete control of the vessel.

The next bridge reached, while proceeding south, is known locally as the Loveland Town Bridge and at certain tide conditions the approach and the passage through this bridge are quite treacherous. Here again, unfortunately, is a bridge located right at the point where the channel changes direction. Sufficient power must be applied to negotiate this bridge safely. We cannot point out too emphatically that both in the canal and in an approach to the railroad bridge at the Manasquan River the boat that has the current or tide running against it is the burdened vessel and consequently the privileged vessel is that one with the fair tide or current. Due to the velocities, which are attained during certain periods of the tide and certain phases of the moon, anything other than strict adherence to the burdened and privileged vessel formula can have some pretty disastrous results. These we have seen and certainly would like to see them diminish to nothing.

The above dangers are all in the area covered by charts 12324 and 12316. The worst danger spots on the Waterway shown on the latter chart are along the passage at the entrances of Beach Haven and Little Egg inlets. This section is often exposed to extremely rough water and the buoys are sometimes pulled under. Under such circumstances it is best to remain at Beach Haven and await more favorable conditions.

Another section where the chart indicates less than 5 feet and the depth may be less is at the southern end of Great Bay, south of Little Egg Inlet. Shoal spots sometimes develop on Main Marsh Thorofare farther south. Information as to conditions in this area may be obtained from the Little Egg Inlet Coast Guard Station.

3. Waterway Buoys and Markers. Going south, leave red to starboard and green to port. All Waterway markers have a yellow border and this helps to avoid confusion with markers indicating entrances to inlets of rivers which have precedence over the Waterway buoys, sometimes reversing the above colors. The red Waterway markers have even numbers with triangles on top, the green have odd numbers on square tops. Many have pointers indicating the Channel and some are lighted, red or green; others have reflectors. The fixed markers are on dolphins or single piles. If you stray off the main channel, note that side channel markings are maintained by the state and not the Coast Guard. State markers are usually slender stakes carrying a red triangle or green square.

Note also that distances shown on small-craft charts 12314 and 12316 are in statute miles, whereas charts 12323 and 12318 covering the outside route use nautical miles.

4. General Remarks on the Waterway.

a. By using your binoculars and care, the Inland Waterway is not difficult to follow. But go slowly when in doubt.

b. If the next buoy is not close and obvious, lay a compass course.

c. Check with the Coast Guard when in doubt about passages.

d. If you get up early, don't expect bridges to open promptly.

e. Keep your dinghy overboard in doubtful places, if your boat draft is on the borderline, with a kedge anchor ready for prompt kedging. But keep the painter short, so that backing won't cause it to foul the propeller.

f. If you run aground and can't get off on your own, and the tide is not low and rising, try to communicate with the nearest Coast Guard Station. If you don't have a radio telephone of your own, ask some passing yacht that has one to do it for you. You will find the Coast Guard on the job 24 hours a day.

The Coast Guard no longer assists grounded yachts unless the situation is life-threatening to those on board, but will help a stranded mariner contact a nearby commercial towing company. And they will stand by on the radio in case a dangerous situation develops. At this writing, the possibility of the Coast Guard Auxiliary resuming the service of towing is being discussed.

Here are a couple of old yarns spun by a Coast Guard officer, which may help you avoid making the same kinds of mistakes.

I pulled off a 54-foot schooner, one day, which had come roaring down the passage east of Devil's Island and Thorofare. This is a straight channel of about half a mile which then turns sharply to the right as you go south. The southerly end faces a marsh. The schooner, under both sail and power, didn't turn at the corner but sailed right up on the marsh. It was a job getting the sails down and pulling her off.

The owner, who was cruising alone with his wife, reported that he had gone below to the john and turned the wheel over to his wife. [We wonder if he came off the throne as quickly as the Queen did in a story by a certain famous yachtsman.]

Another fellow [said our Coast Guard friend, now warming to the story] also grounded at another time in the Waterway nearby, but refused Coast Guard help for three days. When he finally gave up and asked for aid, he began by giving a fictitious name and number, until the Coast Guard insisted on the right one. It turned out that he didn't want his name known since he was considered an authority on these waters.

5. Docks and Anchorages of the Inland Waterway. We can mention only a few of the best and most convenient docks and anchorages along the Waterway, for their number is myriad. They will be noted in geographical order, from north to south. Annual editions of the *Boating Almanac* and the *Waterway Guide* list all current facilities.

a. Manasquan River and Brielle (12324). The first good facilities in the Waterway are just inside the Inlet entrance at the mouth of the Manasquan River and about 3/4 miles upriver at Brielle.

Many yachts go up the main channel to the railroad bridge, where there are a number of tie-ups on the north shore, including:

(1) the Captain's Table, a restaurant which offers dockage while you are dining; (2) Hoffman's Anchorage, just beyond, with gas and other facilities, including hauling and repair; (3) Brielle Marine Basin, just above the bridge, with slips, gas, fuel oil, repairs, and other facilities, including electricity, showers, toilets, etc., and (4) the Brielle Yacht Club, which welcomes transients and can provide such necessities as gas, diesel fuel, electricity, and repairs.

b. Bay Head (12324). About 4 miles from the northern entrance of the Waterway, and at the southern end of the Bay Head–Manasquan Canal, is one of the finest stopping places on the New Jersey Waterway: Bay Head. Many yachts, reaching the northern end of the inland passage near nightfall, make this the first night's stop of their 100-mile voyage (or the last, if going north).

Just before you reach Bay Head, Johnson Brothers Boat Works on the canal is a large facility which can take care of most needs.

Bay Head is one of the most attractive communities on the Jersey Coast. On the north shore of the harbor is the Bay Head Yacht Club, housed in a large building with verandas. Across from the Yacht Club, on the east shore of the harbor, Dale Yacht Basin may have slips for transients, has gas and diesel fuel, ice, showers, laundry, etc.

There are other marine facilities a short way south in Point Pleasant on Beaverdam Creek.

If you are heading north for the outside passage toward Sandy Hook, be sure to check the weather report at Bay Head before leaving.

c. Toms River (12324). This old town, 17 miles from Manasquan Inlet, is the county seat and has stores and restaurants along its main street only a stone's throw from the waterfront. However, for Waterway cruisers it is too far away from the channel to be convenient, since it is over 4 miles up the river.

The trip up Toms River may be avoided by stopping at one of the excellent facilities just north and just south of the bridge at Bay

Shore. Slips, gas, a bar, a restaurant, and a motel are among the attractions.

d. Forked River (12324). A popular sport fishing rendezvous, Forked River has several marina facilities, including the Forked River State Marina on the south shore below the bridge.

About halfway upriver, on the north shore, is Captains Inn, once known as Eno's, long famous for its food and drink. Slips are usually available for tie-up during meals or overnight and protection is good.

e. Barnegat City (12324). This place, about 26 miles from Manasquan Inlet along the Waterway, including a side trip of about 4 miles along Oyster Creek Channel, has already been covered in the section "The Inlets and Their Harbors."

f. Waretown (12324). Sanborn Marine Center lies in a narrow basin south of Waretown Creek and is reportedly dredged to 5 feet. Stakes mark a channel to the perfectly protected lagoon. Here are gas, diesel fuel, water, ice, slips with electricity, rest rooms, marine supplies, a travel lift and ramp. Mort Sanborn is the owner.

g. Beach Haven (12316). This is preferable to Ship Bottom above it and is convenient to the Waterway. Among the many facilities are the following, from north to south:

(1) Southwick's Marina on the lagoon east of flasher 53, reached by dredged 4-foot channel with private markers (12324).
(2) Shelter Harbor Marina, opposite beacon 61, below stack. Facilities here are similar to the above.
(3) Morrison's Beach Haven Marine, opposite beacon 66 in dredged basin. Slips and other facilities.
(4) Beach Haven Yacht Club, opposite beacon 67 in deep water. Slips and usual facilities.
(5) Little Egg Harbor Yacht Club.
(6) Buoy 77 Marina, slips and most facilities.

Before proceeding farther south, check conditions across the sometimes dangerous Little Egg Inlet, already referred to.

h. Atlantic City (12316). This famous ocean resort is about 56 nautical miles from Manasquan via the Inland Waterway. Its harbor has already been covered in connection with "The Inlets and Their Harbors."

The Senator Frank S. Farley State Marina on the northwest shore of Clam Creek is managed now by Trump Castle Associates and the docks were completely rebuilt during the winter of 1987–88. When reopened in May, slips had been increased from 432 to 631 and all docks were floating instead of fixed. The basin was dredged to 12 feet before the new construction was done. The old rest-room facilities were slated to be replaced in 1989 and will be situated in the new three-story building which will also contain a restaurant, laundry, swimming pool, tennis courts, and health spa, all of which will be available to those renting space at the docks. There will be courtesy dockage for four hours available as a convenience to those who wish to eat at the restaurant, visit the casino, etc. The Harbor at Harrah's (off limits only to those who cannot get under the fixed bridge with 60-foot clearance) also has excellent facilities for transients. And we know personally of one couple who tied up there for ten days, winning enough in the casino to pay for dockage, meals, and shows for that time. But we don't guarantee that will happen to you.

i. Ventnor (12316). There are two good possibilities here, depending upon your taste. Tie up at Newport Marine in the angle north of flasher 29 at Ventnor Heights, or anchor where the deep water widens north of flasher #35.

j. Margate City and Longport (12316). A group of marinas with facilities line the east shore at Margate City and Longport Marine Co., south below the bridge at Longport, with gas and also other facilities.

k. Ocean City (*12316*). Already discussed with Great Egg Inlet (page 99). Several facilities are located about 1 ½ miles west of the ICW.

l. Sea Isle City (*12316*). Some of the docks here are not impressive but several have slips, hauling and repair facilities, gas, and other utilities, as well as head boats for fishing. They are located in the basins on both sides of the bridge.

m. Townsend Inlet and Avalon (12316). Some facilities noted previously in discussion of this inlet.

n. Stone Harbor (12316). Except for the fact that Stone Harbor is only 10 miles north of Cape May Harbor, this would rate as one of the best and most useful places on the Waterway for an overnight stop. It still offers a secure refuge with first-rate facilities for yachts

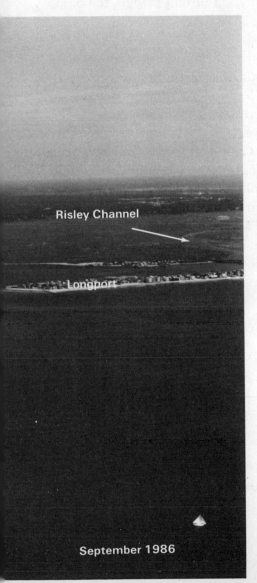

Risley Channel

Longport

September 1986

Great Egg (Ocean City) Inlet. (Photo courtesy of the U.S. Coast Pilot.*)*

headed south that can't comfortably make Cape May Harbor before dark, or for those heading north that make a late afternoon start.

Shelter Haven is the basin recommended by several experienced yachtsmen, though there are 7 basins in all; some, however, are too shoal at the entrance for many yachts.

At the Municipal Marina or Stone Harbor Marina one can obtain gas, oil, water, ice, marine hardware, and repair service just across the street. The normal tidal range is 4 1/2 feet.

In the Snug Harbor Basin, above the railroad bridge, the Stone Harbor Yacht Club is located.

o. Wildwood (12316). The Wildwood Yacht Basin can accommodate more than 200 yachts and has about everything besides slips with electricity: gas, diesel fuel, water, ice, toilets, showers, telephone, swimming pool, cocktail lounge, 3 restaurants, motel, etc.

We first visited Wildwood some years ago when we were looking for a safe and convenient place near Cape May to leave our boat for a week on a passage from the Chesapeake to New England. We found the well-kept marina there much quieter and safer than the facilities then available around Cape May Harbor, and only about 5 miles up the waterway from the inlet. It's still a good place to look for a berth if Cape May is overcrowded during the summer months. There is an anchorage in a natural basin about halfway between Wildwood and Cape May, where boats may find shelter when both main harbors are crowded.

Ottens Harbor is deep but mainly commercial.

p. Cape May Harbor (12317, 12316). This fine harbor is about 114 statute miles by the Waterway from Manasquan. The facilities here are reviewed in the section "The Inlets and Their Harbors" (page 97). Here yachts may wait for favorable conditions for a run up the often turbulent Delaware Bay.

q. The Cape May Canal (12316). Starting at the northwest corner of Cape May Harbor, this canal runs a fairly straight 3-mile course

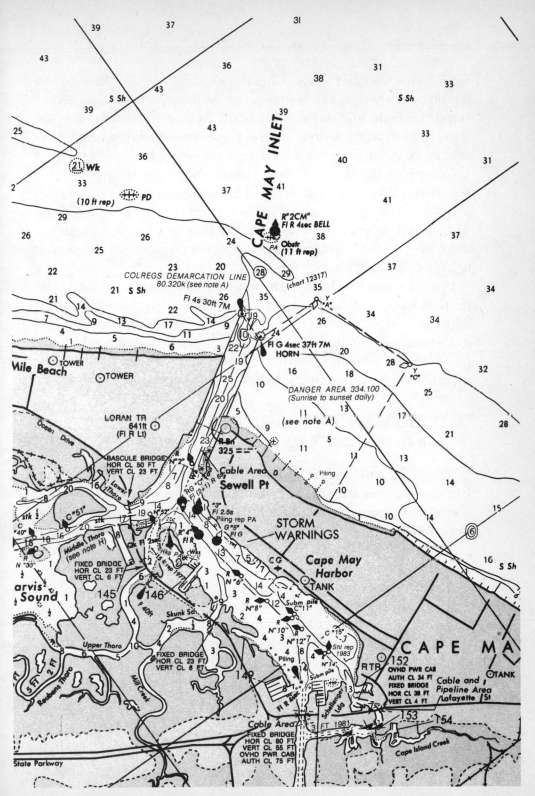

Cape May Inlet and Harbor (from chart 12316).

through lowland and salt marshes to Delaware Bay, enabling yachts bound up or down the Delaware to bypass the sometimes dangerous Cape May Point and save considerable distance at the same time. It also serves as a "back door" to the Cape May Harbor when heavy seas make the main entrance through the jetties impassable.

Current editions of Chart 12316 show controlling depths reported in latest surveys. There is a fixed bridge across the canal just west of the harbor with 55 feet vertical clearance at high tide. Tidal range is 4 feet; normal tidal current $2^1/2$ knots, sometimes more; speed limit $6^1/2$ mph. Enter canal only on green traffic control light at Cape May Harbor side.

In addition to that fixed highway bridge, the canal is crossed by a railroad bridge (swing, clearance 4 feet closed) and another fixed highway bridge (clearance 55 feet). When the old highway bridge was operating, the bridge tender said, "I wish people would read the clearance boards at the bridge. It would save me trouble and save them delay if opening the draw wasn't necessary."

IV. Delaware Bay and River—To the Chesapeake and Delaware Canal (*12304, 12311*).

Yachtsmen may argue violently about the relative merits of the Chesapeake and the Coast of Maine; they may differ eloquently about the cruising merits of Long Island Sound compared to Narragansett Bay. But there is one body of water on which there is complete agreement; we haven't heard one dissenting voice—they all dislike it with varying degrees of eloquence according to their gifts of self-expression. We are speaking of Delaware Bay.

It has one great asset for yachtsmen. It is a valuable connecting link in the Inland Waterway to and from the Chesapeake. Between the "back" entrance to Cape May Canal and the Delaware River entrance of the Chesapeake and Delaware Canal is about 48 miles of the "world's worst waterway," as one widely traveled cruising man has called it. On this stretch there is one convenient and good harbor, Cohansey River, 30 miles from the Cape May Canal.

Delaware Bay and River separate New Jersey from Delaware and Pennsylvania and are the sea approach to the important cities of Wilmington, Chester, Marcus Hook, Philadelphia, Camden, and Trenton. Perhaps we should add another asset from the yachtman's viewpoint. The River allows cruising skippers from these cities to bring their yachts to the Chesapeake or New England Coast.

The waters of the Bay are shallow and the seas are steep and short, as Kipling describes the Baltic in "The Feet of the Young Men." The shores of the Bay are generally low marshland. Harbors deep enough for most cruising yachts are very rare above the entrance; in fact there are only two worth mentioning, one so far out of the way as to be of little value as an emergency shelter. The mean range of tide is about 5 to 5½ feet at Brandywine Shoal Light and above. Normal velocity of current in Delaware Bay at full strength runs from 1.3 to 1.5 knots, with spring velocities of 1.6 to 1.8. See the Atlantic Coast Current Tables for full details and predictions. Cross currents in the Delaware need watching, as they sometimes drive yachts off their course.

Although much more frequent than on the Chesapeake, fog on the Delaware is not excessive, especially from April 1 to November 1. Hours of operation of fog signals at two points along the passage from Cape May Canal to the Chesapeake and Delaware Canal are no longer reported by the *Coast Pilot* as in earlier years, but conditions at the time of your passage can be obtained from the Coast Guard.

Fog is more prevalent at Brandywine Shoal, near the mouth of the Bay, than it is farther up at Ship John Shoal. Summer and early autumn fogs usually clear up by noon, but in the late fall dense fogs may last all day, or more than a day.

Sailors who know the Delaware well offer the following advice:

(1) Take advantage of the tidal current as best you can. It can save you hours if you play it right. Going north with a 6-knot vessel you can carry a fair current all the way to the Chesapeake and Delaware Canal. But you must start with the beginning of the flood (as it starts at Cape May entrance). Southbound, you should start with the first of the ebb after

leaving the canal. We used to think that only fast powerboats could carry the favorable ebb all the way to Cape May; but several able sailing skippers have reported making this run in 6 to 7 hours with a strong following breeze from the northwest.

(2) Don't go up the Delaware at night if you can avoid it, especially if you have to go up under sail. The traffic can be heavy and if it breezes up and you have to tack, there are many dangerous shoals and ledges on each side of the narrow main channel which you have to follow at night. You can get into a lot of trouble. In the upper part there is a confusion of flashing green lights and it is easy to get mixed up.

(3) If you go up by daylight, you can cut across from the exit of Cape May Canal to the east of Brandywine Shoal, or beyond. You have plenty of room and in daytime you can see the oyster stakes.

(4) Count the interesting light structures as you go, but don't get confused by the "Old Tower," as it is marked on chart 12304 between Miah Maull Light and Elbow Cross Light. Actually, the "Tower" is a foundation in ruins. Follow your compass course, keeping a careful log, and verify each channel marker you pass, because the swift current can play tricks with your D.R.

(5) Harbors are rare and out of the way, so fill up with needed gas and supplies before you leave Cape May.

(6) Keep a wary eye astern for overtaking vessels. In general, keep outside the main ship channel.

If the wind is against the tide, Delaware Bay can be choppy and wet, though unlikely to be dangerous if you are careful of your navigation. If the whole distance can't be made during the daylight hours, it is a good plan to put into Cohansey River for the night.

Anchorages on the Delaware. These are few and far between, except for the dredged channels into some marshy "rivers" along the western shore. These rivers are too shoal, unreliable in depth, and inadequate in buoys or charting to warrant consideration here. They should not be attempted without local knowledge.

The Harbor of Refuge and Breakwater Harbor inside of Cape

Henlopen are described briefly on pages 123 and 125 in relation to the Delmarva Coastal Route. There are two principal rivers on the Eastern Shore.

a. Maurice River, Bivalve, and Port Norris (12304). Maurice River on the east shore is too far out of the way to be of much value except as emergency shelter. It is a busy commercial waterway and one of the world's great oyster ports.

We were informed by the fishermen that a 7-foot draft could be carried in the dredged channel and much more inside. Cruising boats will find it most convenient to go upriver to Bivalve, where space for tying up at one of the docks is sometimes available along the west shore, or at small craft facilities on the east side of the river. Groceries and ship chandlery are available. Port Norris, farther up, has similar facilities. Storm warnings are displayed at Bivalve.

This is a rough and ready oyster town, with a rugged waterfront, colorful if not aesthetic, interesting if not yachty. The channel to Bivalve is easily followed, but you should keep a sharp lookout to avoid the stakes and dolphins that extend out into the river. Some of these are broken off and submerged at high water.

b. Cohansey River, Greenwich Pier (12304), East Shore of Delaware Bay. This river is about 30 miles up Delaware Bay from the Cape May Canal and is by far the most convenient and best harbor on the Delaware passage.

It is safest to enter through the dredged canal west of Cohansey Light, as the depth is 20 feet and it is well marked by range lights. Watch the current across the cut. You are only about a mile off the entrance to the Cohansey when you reach Ship John Shoal.

The quietest and most convenient anchorage, if no facilities or supplies are needed, is inside the marshy hook at the entrance, between the inside end of the cut and the light. Look out for old piles along this shore and keep outside of them. This anchorage is below most of the heavy traffic which runs between the Canal and Greenwich Pier.

If you want gas or supplies, go upriver to Greenwich Pier, which lies beyond a point with some trees—rare among these marshes. On the last bend in the river before Greenwich Pier you will see the docks of Hancock's Harbor on the west bank, where you can get fuel (gas and diesel), water, ice, and most other facilities. A little farther on is the Cohansey River Marina at Greenwich Pier, where slips and all marine facilities are available. The town is about a half mile from the dock. It is the seat of Cumberland County and has many beautiful, small early-American homes still occupied and kept in good repair.

Though depths are uncharted, the water is deep enough for fair-sized tankers all the way up.

This is an interesting river and it can be fascinating in the evening light. It can also be a very valuable one to yachtsmen as a stopping place along the often unpleasant passage through Delaware Bay.

c. Other Harbors of Refuge (12304, 12311), Delaware Bay and River.
Small-boat skippers making the Delaware passage may welcome a few tips from experienced yachtsmen on other harbors of refuge which can be used in emergency, or simply to break the long passage from Cape May to the Chesapeake and Delaware Canal.

Fortescue Creek is one such place. The creek is crowded during the summer with private fishing boats and headboats, but there may be room to tie up, though not to anchor out. Call the Harbormaster at the Fortescue State Marina, (609) 447-3115, for information. Though owned by the state, the marina is leased by the Captain's Association. Groceries are available but limited, and there are small, informal places to eat. The one large restaurant was for sale in 1988.

If it's late in the day as you approach Reedy Point at the entrance to the Chesapeake and Delaware Canal, and you don't think you will be able to reach Chesapeake City before dark, the same cruising man has two suggestions. One is south of the artificial island on the east side of the river. The anchorage lies in the shadow of the huge Salem Nuclear Power Plant. Be sure not to try to go between the flashing 4-second Hope Creek Jetty Light and the east bank. The jetty may be under water, but it is definitely there.

The second anchorage is west of Reedy Island and the dike

extending south of it. The entrance is about 3½ miles south of Reedy Point. You can anchor in 8 to 18 feet of water directly west of Reedy Island. The anchorage affords protection against anything except a northerly, and the current (while fairly strong) is less troublesome than it is in the channel.

A dredged channel leads to Salem River, northeast of the Chesapeake and Delaware Canal entrance, with controlling depths of 12 feet, but this river is out of the way for most pleasure boats making the passage to or from the Chesapeake.

V. DELMARVA COASTAL ROUTE (*12216, 12210, 12211, 12214, 12221*).

Although this is primarily a guide to the Chesapeake, we are including a section continuing the coastal route from Delaware Bay to the Virginia Capes at the southern entrance to Chesapeake Bay. Avoided by most small-boat skippers, the outside passage off the coast of Delaware, Maryland, and Virginia provides an alternative route for southbound yachts, approximately 112 nautical miles in length, or less than half the distance up Delaware Bay and down the Chesapeake to Norfolk.

There are good reasons, of course, for small yachts to favor the more protected waters of the two bays in passaging south, quite apart from bypassing a cruise on the Chesapeake. For the coastal route is not an easy one, and under adverse conditions it can present problems for boats that are not properly prepared. Unlike the New Jersey Coast, with its three good inlets, the Atlantic coast of the Delmarva Peninsula provides only one (Ocean City) which is good enough for most cruising skippers without local knowledge to enter comfortably. We don't recommend the outside passage for yachts which are not designed and fully equipped for ocean sailing, with an experienced skipper and crew prepared to stay offshore, if necessary, until they reach their destination on the Chesapeake. But under favorable weather conditions the coastal route offers an interesting alternative for seagoing boats.

There is an inside route that winds through bays and waterways behind the barrier beaches, and sometime in the future it may be navigable for cruising boats. For the present, however, it is too shallow and crossed by too many low fixed bridges to make a feasible alternative.

1. The Outside Passage (12216, 12210, 12211, 12214, 12221, 12304). If you intend to take the outside route, you should be prepared to make the entire passage offshore, even if weather conditions at the start seem to promise safe entry into one of the larger inlets. As we point out below, weather and sea conditions can change without warning, making all of the inlets impassable.

The distance from Cape Henlopen to Cape Charles is about 112 nautical miles measured along the coastline, only a few miles longer than the New Jersey Coast from Sandy Hook to Cape May, but much more than that if you are forced offshore by head winds or heavy seas. Ocean City, about 30 miles south of Cape Henlopen, is the only inlet we would consider entering without local knowledge. You can sail close along the beaches in 3 to 10 fathoms off the summer resorts of Rehoboth Beach, Bethany Beach, and Ocean City, and along the unspoiled coastline of Assateague Island. Beyond Assateague Light there are few distinguishing landmarks as the coast recedes to the southwest and shoals extend several miles offshore. Inshore navigation is hazardous from here to Cape Charles, with numerous fishtrap areas (limits of which are indicated on charts 12210, 12211, and 12221) and abandoned piles.

In normally good summer weather this passage is not especially difficult for able cruisers and auxiliaries. But even in summer you can't always count on good weather for the duration of an overnight passage, as many skippers who sailed the Annapolis-Newport race in 1967 can testify. That unpredicted June gale dismasted several yachts, disabled others, and resulted in the total loss of one contestant, who went aground in the dangerous shoals off Cape Charles.

The southern approaches to Chesapeake Bay have few outlying dangers, provided you keep well to seaward of Cape Charles, Fishermans Island, and the dangerous Nautilus Shoal, which extends 4 miles southeastward. It is well to establish your position precisely by rounding Chesapeake Light, as the ocean racing fleet does, or following one of the main ship channels into the Bay. The Light structure (which replaced the old Chesapeake lightship), 14 miles eastward of Cape Henry, is a blue tower with white superstructure on four piles rising 117 feet above the water. The name CHESAPEAKE is displayed on all sides. Take note that a traffic separation scheme has been established for the control of maritime traffic at the entrance of Chesapeake Bay (also Delaware Bay), designed to aid in prevention of collisions. The scheme provides for inbound-outbound traffic lanes marked by fairway buoys. The lanes are shown on Chart 12221, and the traffic rules are spelled out in the *Coast Pilot* chapters describing Chesapeake Bay and Delaware Bay entrances.

There are three channels through the Chesapeake Bridge–Tunnel:

(1) Thimble Shoal Channel northwest of Cape Henry.
(2) Chesapeake Channel, about 3 $^1/_2$ miles to the northeast.
(3) North Channel, leading close to Fishermans Island and Nautilus Shoal on the north side of the entrance.

All are clearly marked with lighted buoys, radar reflectors, and horns at the bridge or trestle passage points. The first two channels pass through 3/4-mile-wide openings between trestle islands, while the third, or North Channel, leads under a fixed bridge section with 75 feet vertical clearance and 300 feet horizontal clearance. The North Channel cannot be recommended in heavy weather, as it leads close to breaking seas on Nautilus Shoal, where more than one vessel has foundered.

2. Harbors of Refuge (*12216, 12210, 12211, 12214, 12221*). The only all-weather refuge harbor is behind the breakwaters north and west of Cape Henlopen at the entrance to Delaware Bay. Breakwater

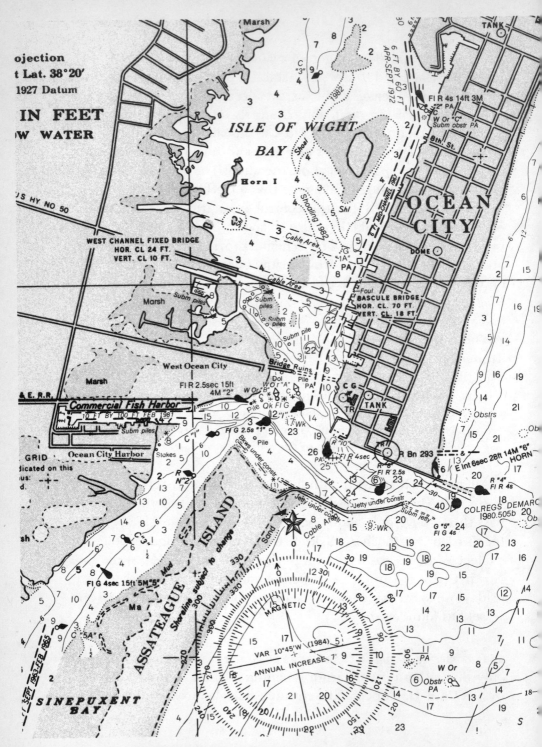

Ocean City Inlet (from chart 12211).

Harbor, behind the inner breakwater and the shore, is used by light draft vessels in all weather except heavy northwesterly gales. Even then, according to the *Coast Pilot,* it affords considerable protection. The Lewes terminal of the Cape May–Lewes ferry is in the basin at the southwest end of Breakwater Harbor. The deepest water is at the north end of the harbor behind the Harbor of Refuge Light, where depths of 15 to 70 feet are found. Smaller boats can anchor in 8 to 12 feet a mile to the southwest.

3. Delmarva Coastal Inlets.

a. Indian River Inlet (12216). This is the first opening in the barrier beach 12 miles south of Cape Henlopen. The channel entrance is marked by buoys, with lights on the jetties and a marker radio beacon on the north side of the entrance. Controlling depths were 15 feet in the dredged entrance channel between the jetties to the fixed highway bridge, with a vertical clearance of 35 feet, crossing the inlet, and 6 feet to the small-boat harbor west of the bridge. The harbor is used by local fishing boats and other small craft, but is seldom visited by cruising yachts. Larger auxiliaries, of course, are unable to clear the fixed bridge.

b. Ocean City Inlet (12211). This is the best and most easily negotiated inlet on the ocean side of the Maryland-Virginia peninsula. It is much used by commercial and sport fishing boats based at this resort city. Sport fishing enthusiasts from the Chesapeake often take their yachts from Annapolis to Ocean City, via the Chesapeake and Delaware Canal, for a week or more of ocean fishing off this port. Entry would be difficult in heavy onshore winds. An obstruction southeast of the inlet is marked by a white-orange buoy.

The Ocean City entrance runs between stone jetties, rebuilt so that they can be seen, even at high water. A long fishing pier is visible a short distance above the north jetty. Depths in the channel vary from year to year, and are subject to continuous change. Shoaling occurs on both sides of the channel at the inner end of the jetties, but 15 to 20 feet can usually be carried in mid-channel. A commercial fish harbor, reached by a dredged channel, lies directly west of the entrance and has some transient facilities in deep water, but many sport fishermen and pleasure boats swing north and follow another dredged channel along the inner side of Ocean City to Isle of Wight Bay. Be sure to follow the channel, as the water is very shoal outside of it.

A Coast Guard Station is just inside the entrance at the southwest end of Ocean City, and several marinas and charter-boat docks are just beyond on the city channel. Fuel, berths, and most marine supplies are available at the marinas.

Local knowledge rates the channel south behind Assateague Island as shallow and very changeable. The channel may follow the buoys—or a recent storm may have moved it.

c. Chincoteague Inlet (12211, 12210). This inlet 30 miles south of Ocean City is not jettied. The entrance channel is marked by buoys that are frequently shifted with changing conditions. Inside there are winding channels through marshes and shoals of Chincoteague Bay and Sinepuxent Bay behind Assateague Island, with depths of cons and a few lighted beacons provides a 30-mile inside route from Ocean City to Chincoteague Inlet, used by small fishing boats and pleasure craft drawing not over 4 feet. There's a fixed highway bridge with a clearance of 38 feet that prevents larger auxiliaries from making use of this waterway.

d. Wachapreague Inlet (12210). Although the entrance to this inlet, 20 miles southwest of Chincoteague, is marked by a lighted bell buoy and unlighted channel buoys, it is not recommended for cruising boats making the coastwise passage. The entrance channel shoals to 5 feet and can be dangerous in even moderate onshore winds with an ebb tide running. Only about 4 feet can be carried to the town of Wachapreague, an oystering and fishing village on the mainland about 4 miles west northwest of the inlet. Shoals and shifting channels make several other inlets unusable in the remaining stretch of Virginia's low-lying coastline between Wachapreague and Cape Charles. As suggested above, you will be well advised to give this coast a wide berth.

4. *Delmarva Inside Waterways* (*12216, 12210, 12211, 12214, 12224*). Eventually, there may be a section of the Atlantic Intracoastal Waterway system to provide an improved navigable route between Delaware Bay and the Chesapeake, linking the saltwater bays and sounds that extend all the way down behind the barrier beaches and sea islands. Such a route has been proposed, and Congress has even authorized initial steps toward its realization; but no federal funds have been committed and project costs have not yet been determined. So for the present, there is no navigable inside passage that offers a practical alternative to the offshore route.

It is true that today you can take a small boat from Lewes, Delaware, down the tidal waterway to Rehoboth Bay and Indian River Bay to Ocean City, and from Ocean City back of Assateague Island and through the inside Virginia Passage to Cape Charles and Chesapeake Bay. It could be an interesting trip in a canoe, or rowboat, or even a small outboard. But we don't recommend it for anything that draws over 2 feet, which is the controlling depth at several critical points along the route; and if you should attempt the passage in a cruising auxiliary you would be quickly stopped by fixed bridges with clearances of 7 feet as well as by 2-foot shoals.

Part Three

CHESAPEAKE HARBORS, RIVERS, AND CREEKS

CHAPTER FIVE

HARBORS OF THE UPPER EASTERN SHORE—FROM THE CHESAPEAKE AND DELAWARE CANAL TO CHOPTANK RIVER

I. THE CHESAPEAKE AND DELAWARE CANAL (*12277*).

From the low marshes of Reedy Point on the Delaware River to Chesapeake City at the head of Back Creek, on Chesapeake Bay, a deep, sea-level canal—government owned and toll free—connects the two bays and serves as an important link in the Intracoastal Waterway. From the Delaware entrance to Chesapeake City, where a fine anchorage and a multitude of supplies and facilities are available, is a distance of about 12 miles.

Since 1970 important changes have been made in the canal—and in rules governing its traffic—with the completion of a major federal project to widen and deepen the waterway. When dredging operations were completed in 1972, several bends had been straightened out, channel depths had been increased to 35 feet, and the width nearly doubled to 450 feet. This means that pleasure boats are now encountering more commercial traffic than in the past, with even larger seagoing vessels using the canal. It also means that small-craft skippers should know the latest traffic regulations issued by the Corps of Engineers. If you are in doubt about the rules, consult the latest *Coast Pilot*, Vol. 3, now published in annual editions. Passage through the widened waterway is easy enough in daylight, and not too difficult at night when you get used to the lights.

Traffic through the canal is now electronically controlled and monitored by the dispatcher at Chesapeake City. TV monitors have replaced the patrol boats formerly operated by the Corps of Engineers at Reedy Point, at the ConRail railroad bridge and Town Point, and vessels are checked through by remote control operating 24 hours a day. Small craft are not required to have special radio equipment (as large vessels are) for communication with the dispatcher, but all vessels which use the canal frequently are urged to install suitable ship-to-shore radiotelephones, capable of operating on 156.65 MHz (Channel 13), the frequency used for normal communications by the dispatch office. The dispatcher also monitors 156.80 MHz (Channel 16) for emergency calls.

1. Bridges and Clearance Levels. Five bridges now cross the canal, one of which is a vertical-lift bridge; four are high-level fixed spans with minimum clearance of 135 feet. Here's where the bridges are, traveling east to west: Mile 1.6—Route 9 highway bridge; Mile 5.0—St. George's Bridge; Mile 7.5—ConRail railroad bridge; Mile 9.2—Summit Bridge; Mile 13.0—Chesapeake City Bridge. The operator of the lift on the railroad bridge will respond to the usual signal used to request an opening—one prolonged and one short blast on your horn—and may answer with the same signal if ready to open immediately (or he may just open the bridge). If the bridge is not ready to open after a signal from your vessel, the bridge tender may sound five short blasts in rapid succession (or he may just not open the bridge).

Whistle or horn signals can be supplemented by lights, corresponding to the canal's traffic light system. An apparent failure in the automatic control system led to a costly accident on a foggy day in February 1973, when a large freighter crashed into the vertical lift span of the railroad bridge, causing both the bridge and the canal to be closed to traffic for many months. You can't be too cautious in approaching a lift bridge!

2. *Traffic Control Lights.* If you are entering the canal from the Delaware you will see the first traffic control lights at the Reedy Point jetties. Other control lights are at the railroad lift bridge and at Old Town Point Wharf at the entrance from the Chesapeake. Here's what the signals mean:

> *Fixed Red Light*—Waterway or bridge closed; vessel must stop, or be kept under control so it can be stopped if necessary.

> *Fixed Amber Light*—Caution; traffic restricted; or bridge being prepared for opening.

> *Fixed Green Light*—Waterway (or bridge) open to navigation. Vessel may proceed

> *Flashing Red Light*—Bridge opening to be delayed (used only on the lift bridge).

If you are entering the canal from the Chesapeake, look for the first fixed traffic lights at Old Town Point Wharf. Other fixed lights are on the Chesapeake City Bridge and the Summit Bridge.

Note that the system of lights and buoys marking the channel starts at each entrance, *and reverses at Chesapeake City.* Thus, when you enter at Old Town Point, flashing red lights and even numbers are on the south side of the canal; but from Chesapeake City to the Delaware River they are on the north side, with odd numbers and flashing white or green lights on the south side. If you are transiting the canal at night for the first time, you may find it hard to distinguish fixed navigation lights, flashing lights, and other vessels' running lights from the many bright lights along the banks.

3. Right-of-Way. All vessels proceeding with the current have right-of-way over those running against the current. Currents run strongly at times, ranging from 2 to 2½ knots but sometimes increasing to 3 knots or more in strong winds. Heavy tows sometimes have difficulty bucking a maximum 3-knot current, so it's well to allow plenty of room when passing. Small vessels (up to 150 feet) must be operated "so as not to interfere with vessels of greater length at bridges and bends."

4. Mooring Facilities. Tie-up facilities and anchorages are available in the canal, but they are intended primarily for commercial vessels rather than yachts. We spent an uncomfortable night tied to the dolphins on the north side of the canal west of Reedy Point, and we don't recommend using either of the two mooring basins, due to the wash and suction caused by passing ships. The anchorage basin at Chesapeake City, across the canal from Schaefer's, is much to be preferred. It is large enough to accommodate a number of cruising boats, but, unless it has been dredged recently, you will find only 4 feet of water in the middle of the entrance. If that is not enough for your boat, deeper water—possibly 5 or 6 feet—may be found near the bulkhead to the east.

A special small-vessel anchorage is located on the southeast side of the canal, off Courthouse Point (at Mile 16.3), but the water is too shoal for cruising boats which draw more than 3 or 4 feet. The Chesapeake City Basin is much to be preferred. And the commercial mooring facilities at Reedy Point are not recommended for small craft, as we noted above.

In view of the strong tides, be sure to run up to wharves, slips, or dolphins against the current; otherwise you can easily get into considerable trouble.

Some yachtsmen have found the combination of shore lights and those of the heavy traffic through the canal rather confusing at night. While it is undoubtedly easier to make the transit by daylight, if you have come up Delaware Bay during the day, you may have the choice between a night passage to Chesapeake City, spending the night somewhere in Delaware Bay, or rocking against some dolphin. Yachts going eastward as darkness approaches will be wise to await daylight at Chesapeake City.

The farther away you get from the Delaware on your way through the canal, the more attractive become the shores, with low swampy banks giving way to rolling hills and fields, separated by rows of trees. You are beginning to near the Chesapeake Bay country.

II. Chesapeake City (*12277*).

This interesting gateway to the Chesapeake came into existence with the canal. The main business, beside running the canal, is servicing the thousands of small craft which go through each year. Watching the passing show is one of the features of a stay at Chesapeake City.

A white building, the suboffice of the United States Engineers, on the southern shore of the canal, indicates for yachts going west the approach to the mooring basin around a point on the same shore just beyond. This basin provides a first-class, sheltered anchorage. When we were there, a good-looking yawl was riding peacefully at anchor with plenty of room for more.

There is an interesting old waterwheel in a pump house on the government reservation which used to run all the time refilling the lock after vessels passed through. The pump house is now a canal museum, containing excellent displays of C and D Canal memorabilia. You can visit Monday through Saturday, from 8 A.M. to 4:15 P.M., and Sunday 10 A.M. to 6 P.M.

On the north shore, across the canal from the basin, is Schaefer's, which has been operating at this spot for as long as most visiting boatmen can remember. There, at a landing, is a fine restaurant, bar, rest rooms, and one can obtain gas, oil, water, ice, groceries, liquor, marine supplies, and probably other things. Some dock space may be available if you get in early enough in the afternoon. You may have to double up, however, and would probably prefer the

Chesapeake and Delaware Canal and the Engineers' Basin anchorage.

anchorage basin; it is quieter there and the wash from passing ships is avoided.

Dockside Yacht Club, a commercial establishment in the anchorage basin, has 4 feet at the dock and may have a slip available. Dockside also has fuel and a restaurant.

As you leave Chesapeake City, the course into Chesapeake Bay leads 3½ miles westward to the point where Back Creek enters Elk River. On the southern shore, between Back and Herring creeks, is

the site of a great Indian trading field used by Chesapeake and Delaware tribes. Many darts and other Indian relics have been found there.

III. THE ELK RIVER (*12274*).

1. The Upper Elk. Elk River above Back Creek is more interesting historically than it is nautically. The channel to Elkton, the

"Head of the Elk" of colonial times, is narrow and winding, with extensive shoals on both sides and wide marshes above. "There is no reason to go up," as one old Chesapeake hand put it, "and plenty of reason to go the other way." The name of a cove on the chart just above Welch Point intrigues us. Nothing else does. Take a look at the chart to see what it is.

2. *The Lower Elk.* Between Back Creek and Bohemia River, none of the anchorages is very good, though they are at least out of the line of traffic to and from the canal.

One of these is just north of Courthouse Point on the east shore, where vessels drawing under 4 feet can anchor. In the bight east of Courthouse Point you will find a well-equipped yacht basin, "Harbour North," with transient slips for both power- and sailboats, and complete marina service.

At the entrance to Elk River you can still see the old dock formerly used by the Army Engineers, but the control vessels that operated off Old Town Point have been replaced by the automated canal signals mentioned in the section above.

3. *Bohemia River (12274).* Joining Elk River about 3 1/2 miles below the entrance to Back Creek, this wide river flows between wooded shores and a pleasant pastoral country. While the Bohemia lacks the high shores and snug anchorages of the Sassafras 8 or 9 miles farther south, it nevertheless provides a good opportunity to get off the beaten track.

About 3 miles up the river, on the south shore below the bridge, is the attractive Bohemia Anchorage, with 6 feet of water, slips, gas, repair service, water, marine supplies, and a lift. Although it is open for some distance to the northwest this is the first good port south of the Chesapeake and Delaware Canal. One experienced Chesapeake yachtsman advises going here instead of stopping at Chesapeake City. While most of the slips are rented for the season, transients can usually be given a spare one for the night. There are other new marinas in the area today, on both the north and south shores, that are used chiefly by powerboats and shallow-draft small craft, and the river is crowded with pleasure boats on summer weekends. The Bohemia River boat ramp is on the south side of the river just west of the bridge, and the Bohemia Yacht and Country Club is farther on in the bight near Long Point. If you enjoy exploring by dinghy, try running in Scotchman Creek past the fixed bridge at the entrance.

The anchorage here is open for some distance to the north and the outer boats are exposed to the northwest. Long Point offers some protection, but is low.

Provisions can be obtained at the village of Hack Point nearby; the Bohemia Grille and Market is just to the west of the bridge.

The channel at Long Point and beyond is narrow, with unbuoyed shoals on either side, so that care, plus a sounder, are desirable assets. It is of course possible to anchor in 7 feet at the mouth, but it is apt to be uncomfortable there. One experienced yachtsman writes that when he spent a night near the mouth, a northwest wind was blowing against an outgoing tide, so "we rolled a lot." Another calls it the best of anchorages and tells of a wonderful swim and bath in the cool, clean, and (believe it or not) "fresh" water of the river.

You are not apt to find sea nettles here. On the north bank, across from Hack Point, is the site of Bohemia Manor, built by Augustine Hermann, who was born at Prague in the kingdom of Bohemia, the first non-British person to achieve distinction and citizenship in Maryland. While only the outlines of the original manor house remain, a fine colonial brick residence, erected by the late Senator Bayard of Delaware, now occupies the spot; the senator was a direct descendant of Hermann.

4. *Cabin John Creek* (*12275*). Though wide open to the northwest and rolls from canal traffic on nearby Elk River, this creek provides a good anchorage a short distance up for boats drawing under 5 feet. Facilities, however, are lacking, and the shores are marshy—not a recommendation in summer.

5. *Rogues Harbor* (*12275*). This isn't much of a harbor, for it is protected only from north to west, and there is only 5 feet of water at the entrance. But it is located attractively, with some of the highest land on the Chesapeake close behind, and conveniently, for it is the last place which might be—and is—called a harbor along the main channel before the open Chesapeake is reached.

IV. SASSAFRAS RIVER (*12275*).

Many people consider this the loveliest river on the Eastern Shore. It also has one of the outstanding harbors and yachting centers: Georgetown.

The banks of the river are wooded and fairly high with fertile, cultivated fields behind; the channel is wide, deep, and well buoyed as far as the bridge between Georgetown and Fredericktown, almost 9 miles up from the Sassafras entrance at Grove Point. A trip up this river to Georgetown is one of the river voyages which should not be omitted, unless you are in a hurry to get down the Bay. If you are short of time, there are several good anchorages on the river only about 3 miles up.

1. Betterton (12275). Located on the south shore at the mouth of Sassafras River, this one-time summer resort is undergoing some major changes. When steamboat travel was popular, vacationers came here from Baltimore and Wilmington to spend a week or more at the Rigby Hotel or a smaller inn or tourist home. The beach was a popular place to spend the day, and the boardwalk and dance hall provided entertainment at night. Tourists continued to come to Betterton on Port Welcome into the 1970's, but fewer made the trip each year and the facilities languished. Now the town is gaining popularity again. The Rigby was torn down to make room for condominiums. A 250-foot stone fishing jetty replaces rotted piers. The beach has been cleaned up and a new bathhouse has been built for bathers nearby. A picnic pavilion on the bluff takes advantage of the stunning Bay view. And a 500-foot boardwalk, complete with benches and lighting, has been completed. A pier exists where small boats tie up during calm days. So far new construction and remodeling have not been able to provide two things that boaters need—deep and protected water. However, there is talk of breakwaters and restaurants and other attractions. So keep Betterton in mind as a place to stop sometime in the future.

2. Ordinary Point (12275). A popular anchorage in summer is behind this point, 3 or 4 miles upriver, northwest of the end in 5 to 9 feet. While not particularly snug, it is well protected from all but easterlies and no sea worth talking about ever gets there. However, according to one yachtsman, "Ordinary Point is very ordinary on Saturday and Sunday evenings during the yachting season. All Baltimore and Philadelphia are there, making whoopee." We might add that under usual (we won't say "ordinary") conditions, this place is a fairly good anchorage and you are more apt to get a breeze on a hot summer night than in some small landlocked creek. The holding ground is said to be good. There used to be a hotel there in early colonial days, hence the name "Ordinary."

3. Turner Creek (12275). Opposite Ordinary Point, and 3 or 4 miles upriver from the mouth, this attractive, landlocked creek gives perfect shelter from all winds. However, the narrow, winding entrance channel is not easy to follow and there are several unmarked shoal spots. So poke your way in cautiously using your sounder. Anchor just inside the long narrow point on your left as you enter, where the chart shows 11 to 15 feet. Shoal water has been reported off the long point. Favor the western side of the creek entering. On summer Friday and Saturday nights you may find Turner Creek chock-full of boats from the marinas at Georgetown and Fredericktown.

4. Knight Island (12274). One experienced cruising man recommends anchoring in 7 feet just west of the northern point of Knight

Island, where you will get no sea under ordinary conditions and a chance to get a "nice air from the southwest" on a hot night. It is open to the west, however, for nearly a mile and a half.

5. *Georgetown and Fredericktown* (*12274*). About 8 miles up Sassafras River, anchored or moored in a splendid natural harbor, just below the bridge, we found one of the largest fleets of attractive cruising yachts, chiefly sailing craft, to be seen anywhere on the Chesapeake. The convenience of this anchorage to Wilmington and Philadelphia, plus its many natural advantages, undoubtedly accounts for the size of the fleet—evidence of the influence on yachting of the proximity of large cities.

All services for boats are to be found here in one or the other of several large and well-run marinas, including the Georgetown Yacht Basin and the Sassafras Boat Company on the Georgetown side, and Skipjack Cove Marina, Duffy Creek Marina, the Granary Marina and Sailing Associates on the Fredericktown, or north, bank. The closest town for provisioning, Galena, is small and a considerable hike away. Because of this, some of the marinas offer a selection of staple food items.

The old Granary Restaurant at the Granary marina burned, but was rebuilt and reopened as a full-service restaurant. Dockage is available while dining. On the opposite side of the river, up a hill behind the Georgetown Yacht Basin, stands the Kitty Knight House, famous for its good food and views of the river. The house serves as a small inn as well as a restaurant. This house was built in 1775 and bears the name of a redoubtable lady, who, so the story goes, saved at least that one house from burning when a flotilla from the British fleet came up the Sassafras during the War of 1812. Young Kitty is reported to have kept beating out the fire with a broom until an admiring British officer ordered the house spared.

Across the bridge from the Kitty Knight House is a monument commemorating the exploration of the river in 1607–8 by Captain John Smith. The Captain certainly got around, and in this case, as in many others, we recommend following his example.

V. STILL POND (*12274*).

This cove is a convenient stopping place along the Upper Bay. We found it a comfortable and attractive anchorage in settled weather. No facilities or supplies are available. There are Indian shell mounds on Rocky Point.

The dredged channel to Still Pond Creek is advertised to carry 8 feet as far as the Coast Guard Station just inside the narrow entrance. The creek, however, has a tendency to shoal at the entrance. Dredging seems to occur fairly often, so if the serenity of the creek is appealing, give it a try, but proceed cautiously.

"At Sunset, we anchored in Still Pond Harbor," wrote two distinguished Chesapeake yachtsmen, George and Robert Barrie, whose book is one of the Chesapeake classics. "After dinner we rowed up to where Still Pond Creek should be, but in the twilight could not find it. Rowed along the beach, and as the moonlight became stronger, we finally did find the gap in the beach where the creek was pouring out at the rate of several miles an hour. We rowed in and found a weird, dismal place, that looked as though it might be full of alligators. The dead trees, the croaking of the frogs, and the shadows of the moonlight had a depressing effect, and we turned and fled. The place gets its name from the fact that the waters are so often still." That was written more than 75 years ago. Today the creek is an attractive place, still relatively unspoiled. The channel entrance is narrow, but clearly marked.

At the tower on Plum Point there is a house with four trees marking the site where, in 1849, the American Tom Hyer fought Yankee Sullivan of the British Isles with bare knuckles and won the heavyweight boxing championship of the United States.

VI. WORTON CREEK (*12278*).

This was one of the most attractive and convenient harbors on the Upper Eastern Shore until it became too crowded with moor-

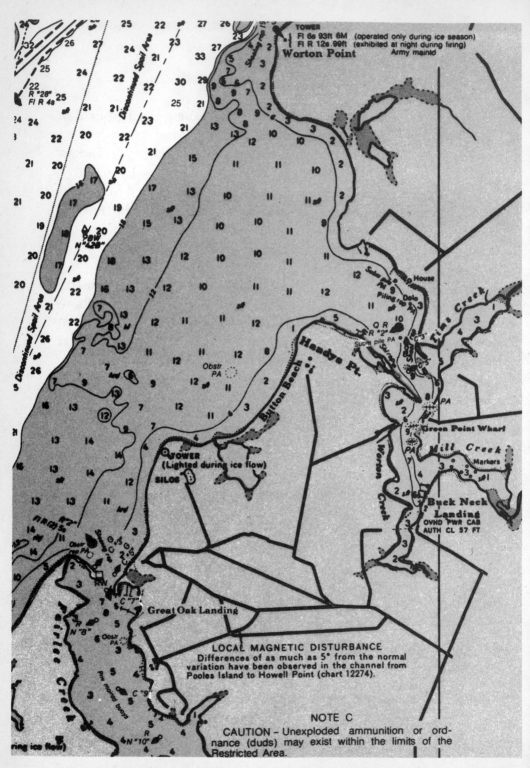

Worton and Fairlee creeks (from chart 12278).

ings for most transient boats to find anchorage room. However, it is still worth a visit because of its convenience of access from the Bay, its complete protection from all winds, its attractiveness, and the facilities available. But it is easy to go aground on the way in if you are not careful. One of the most experienced cruising men on the Chesapeake once landed his boat very hard on a shoal which still extends outside the first channel marker off the Handys Point pond.

If you keep in the channel, you can carry 6 or 7 feet draft into the creek. After giving Handys Point a good berth, follow the buoys in. A local authority advises leaving the flashing red buoy close to starboard but leaving black can 3 well to port. These buoys make getting into Worton Creek an easier job than it used to be—another indication of the ways in which cruising is becoming more fool-proof. Disregard private buoys to Tims Creek.

You can go close to the sand spit, which shelves so steeply that it is said you can dive off it. A good anchorage is in 9 feet off Green Point Wharf, though one authority recommends going farther up and anchoring opposite Mill Creek, where he has found it cooler. The shores are high and wooded.

When we first visited Worton Creek in the forties, we were told that white pine logs could still be found on Worton Point, left there by the Susquehanna Flood in the same year as the Johnstown Flood. More visible today is the debris left by Hurricane Agnes in 1972 and other more recent storms of lesser strength.

On that first trip, no facilities were available, but work had begun on the Worton Creek Marina. Developed by Bill Fairlee after World War II, it is now operated by Ken and Marian Roberts.

It is located at Buck Neck Landing, near the head of the creek in 5 feet at mean low water. At the time of our last visit the following commodities and services among others were available: gas, diesel oil, slips, moorings, a restaurant, groceries, ice, water, soft drinks, ice cream, notions, frozen food; also there is electricity at the slips, repairs, a railway, beer, showers, and marine hardware. The marina is used by many northern yachtsmen for winter storage, and Mr.

145

Roberts has increased the number of covered and open slips featuring de-iced wet storage. The marina at Green Point Landing has been upgraded recently and also offers many services. A third marina, The Wharf at Handy Point, was opened for business on Worton Creek in 1988.

VII. FAIRLEE CREEK (*12278*).

No longer does Fairlee Creek quite answer the description of the yachtsman quoted in the first printing of this guide, who said it gave him an "out of the world feeling." Now, thanks to the Mears Great Oak Landing, with its many facilities and promotion-minded management, Fairlee Creek has joined the so-called march of progress. Here you'll find docks and slips, showers and swimming pool, cocktail lounge and restaurant, and most of the other facilities and amenities that go with this kind of country-club setup and its not inexpensive luxury.

The channel into the creek has been dredged so that now the minimum reported depth is 7 feet at mean low water. Privately placed, uncharted buoys and range lights guide yachts in to well-equipped Mears marina, which is located on the southeast shore of the cove to port.

From a distance, Fairlee Creek can be identified by a low tower to the north. Watch for crab pot floats outside and for strong tidal currents in the entrance.

The creek is well protected from seas by a low bar and a hook at the entrance, where the strongest current is encountered. Inside, the creek opens up with the best anchorage along the wooded shore. It may be crowded in summer, but not more so than Worton Creek.

Don't try to take more than 4-feet draft to the south end of the creek, which has shoaled in recent years.

A veteran yachtsman who used to pilot his 65-foot pungy into Fairlee Creek, when it took some real know-how to make it in a boat

of that size, advised us to land with the dinghy on the long peninsula to starboard, which was once an island, and walk to the point
for a beach party. There is an Indian shell mound, he told us,
nearby. Today, unfortunately, you are likely to find only litter and
beer cans! Swimming is not recommended.

Many yachtsmen may enjoy the new Fairlee Creek and the splendid facilities now available. Others, particularly the old-timers, will
heave a nostalgic sigh.

VIII. Tolchester Beach (12279).

Proceeding south from Fairlee Creek toward Rock Hall and
Gratitude, the main ship channel runs close along the sandy beach
at Mitchell Bluff and Tolchester, once a popular Bay resort. In the
1920's and 1930's excursion steamers from Baltimore carried thousands of city dwellers to and from Tolchester Beach, where the long
steamboat wharf and turreted Victorian hotel were familiar landmarks. Don't look for the old hotel today; it's been razed for a new
development which includes a dredged yacht basin and marina that
provides a convenient harbor of refuge and stopover point for
vessels cruising the Bay. The entrance to Tolchester Marina leads
directly off the ship channel at marker 20 into a tight little harbor
protected by a breakwater and baffle bulkhead affording good
protection in all weather.

Tolchester Marina was opened in 1972. Then the docks were
expanded in the eighties by further dredging. Now their docks can
accommodate approximately 265 boats, up to 60 feet in length and
6 feet of draft. In addition to their other very complete services,
Tolchester Marina keeps a 40-foot powerboat on call for emergen-
cies. A sandy beach and tennis courts are on the premises. Light fare
is available at the snack bar, and a few groceries can be purchased.
There is no town within walking distance.

IX. ROCK HALL AND GRATITUDE (*12272, 12278*).

There have been a number of changes in these two popular Eastern Shore ports since our last edition, and an even greater transformation since our first visit to the area more than 30 years ago. The rapid growth of pleasure boating, and particularly sailing, in the Baltimore and Annapolis area has made Rock Hall, Gratitude, and Swan Creek popular rendezvous points for weekend cruising and brought many new marine and waterfront facilities to what had been quiet backwater communities.

1. Rock Hall (12279). As you progress southward in the ship channel your safest course is to keep well clear of the long shoal, Swan Point Bar, which extends for nearly 3 miles to the south, forming a sort of barrier reef, the outer limits of which are poorly marked on the charts. If you draw 4 feet or less there's a shortcut across the bar on a course of 125° magnetic from ship channel marker R-2 to the 30-foot lighted beacon about 1 mile west of the entrance to Rock Hall. We once sounded our way across at mean low water in calm weather, passing close to the lighted beacon (with ruins of the old beacon nearby), leaving C-5 and C-1 to port and then heading

On the Fourth of July, Rock Hall's watermen traditionally celebrate with a boat docking contest. (Photo courtesy of Austin Walmsley.)

between the two lights marking the jetty at the Rock Hall Harbor entrance. Although we found no depth under 5 feet across the bar, we don't recommend this shortcut for keel auxiliaries or, indeed, for anything except shoal-draft craft in perfect weather conditions. You may think you're saving a few miles, but you won't save any time if you fetch up on one of the 3- or 4-foot spots on the bar.

The approved entrance to both Rock Hall and Gratitude starts at the south end of Swan Point Bar, marked by Bell 1. From there the channel is wide and clearly marked, with depths of 9 to 18 feet past the lighted R-4 off Huntingfield Point. While most cruising auxiliaries prefer Swan Creek for an overnight anchorage, the historic colonial port of Rock Hall has much to offer as a shopping center and marine supply base. The Rock Hall channel is straightforward, leading between lighted jetties into a small dredged basin, rimmed by docks and almost always crowded with a colorful assortment of workboats, cruisers, and outboards. The harbor is too small and shallow to provide a comfortable anchorage, but the ancient town and its old and new marine facilities are well worth a visit.

For marina services, starting inside the jetty to port, you'll see Pelorus Sailing Limited, Northside Marina, Kendall's Marina, Windmill Point Marina and Motel, Rock Hall Marine Railway, Rock Hall Seafood, and the Sailing Emporium (you'll be able to see the red buildings of the Sailing Emporium from some distance out). A county launch ramp is next to the Sailing Emporium. For seafood, try Cain's Wharf (steamed crabs to order), the Waterman's Crabhouse, or Fin, Fur and Feather, all on the waterfront. Don't look for the Rock Hall Yacht Club in the harbor; its headquarters are on Langford Creek, a long way up Chester River by water, but only a short distance by land.

Perhaps Rock Hall's greatest fame was in colonial times, when it was the terminus of a sailing ferry that carried passengers, horses, and carriages from Annapolis to the Eastern Shore. George Washington made many trips across the Bay, some of which he recorded in his diary; on one such trip he must have had a sou'westerly gale behind him, for he's said to have made the passage in time that would make a modern yachtsman envious!

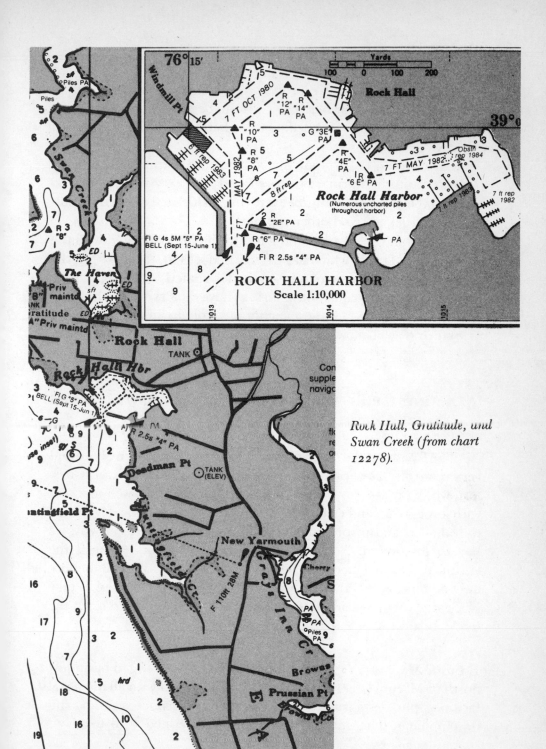

Rock Hall, Gratitude, and Swan Creek (from chart 12278).

2. *Gratitude and Swan Creek* (*12278*). If you are looking for an overnight anchorage or berth you will do better to continue up the main channel north of Rock Hall, where you will have several choices.

Many cruising boats enjoy the convenience and improved facilities of Gratitude Marina, now operated by Larry Reni, with 100 slips, on the point at Gratitude. Overnight dockage is usually available, with fuel, ice, and other supplies.

Inside Swan Creek you'll find a mooring area associated with the Swan Creek Marina, which has extensive docks to starboard. In the second bight to starboard, the area designated as the Haven, is Haven Harbour Marina. Both marinas have repairs and fuel, as well as the usual services. The best anchorage is on up Swan Creek as far as your draft will allow.

X. CHESTER RIVER, INCLUDING KENT ISLAND NARROWS (*12272*).

The Chester is the second longest river on the Eastern Shore and very rewarding for upriver exploration, particularly as far as Chestertown, 24 miles above Love Point, up to which it is well marked, with lovely vistas and estuaries. At Hail Point, in colonial days, ships were hailed and inspected before going farther upriver; why, we haven't discovered. Normal tidal ranges are about 1 foot at the entrance, 1½ at Queenstown, 2 at Chestertown. With Baltimore only 20 miles across the Bay, weddings on the Chester used to take place at 7 A.M., it is said, so that honeymoon couples could catch the 8 A.M. boat.

1. *Castle Marina* (*12272*). On Kent Island, on a dredged basin just north of Macum Creek, is a large modern marina with all the usual facilities, plus restaurant, snack bar, swimming pool, and housing development. The entrance channel was dredged to 6 feet, but watch for shoaling just outside the entrance beacons. Castle Marina usually has facilities for transients, and is a popular rendezvous point for local power squadrons and yacht clubs.

2. *Kent Island Narrows (12272).* About 4 miles up Chester River from Love Point Light on the southern shore is the northern entrance of Kent Island Narrows, which connects the Chester with Eastern Bay. If you are headed from the Chester for St. Michaels on Miles River, or for the Wye, the Narrows may save you a long trip around Kent Island and up Eastern Bay. We say "may" save you, because the saving depends upon the draft of your boat, the tide, and how recently the channel has been dredged. The channel keeps filling in near its northern end in Chester River. In recent years the controlling depths have ranged between 5 and 7 feet, but regardless of what the latest chart may show, it is well to proceed cautiously, taking soundings if your vessel draws over 4 feet. The shoalest parts of the channel are from Chester River entrance to Long Point, and between markers 23 and 31. After that, as you head from Chester River toward the Narrows, depths increase and the channel becomes wider.

In earlier editions of this guide we suggested that you telephone one of the nearby marinas to check on depths before heading for the Narrows, and that still may be good advice if you are planning to take a keel sailboat through. The latest project depth was supposed to be 7 feet, but we've seldom found over 5 feet even after the channel has been redredged. In any case, keelboats should proceed with caution. The bottom is hard sand and you can't slither through a few inches of soft mud, as you can in so many parts of the Chesapeake. In any case, proceed very slowly, preferably under power if you have it, and use your depth sounder constantly in the shoal section. Don't attempt the passage in a strong following wind. The channel is very narrow and if you have an absent-minded professor in your crew, take the helm yourself. The buoys throughout the channel, and on both sides of the bridge, are treated from the point of view of entering Chester River. In other words, the

Kent Narrows. (Photo courtesy of BaySailor.)

system of marking is continuous from Eastern Bay to Chester River. So, when you approach the Narrows from the Chester, you are leaving the river, and hence leave red nun buoys (even numbers) to port, cans (odd numbers) to starboard.

On Saturday, Sunday, and holidays the draw opens only on fixed hours that are changed frequently in the hope of finding a schedule that will accommodate travel both by road and by water until the high level bridge (construction due to begin in 1989) is completed. Notices to mariners or a telephone call to the bridge tender, (301)

643-5963, are your best sources of information. Of course, the opening times are also posted on the draw. If for any reason the bridge cannot open, your one prolonged blast followed by one short blast should be answered by five short blasts from the bridge tender.

Two large marinas are located on the north side of the bridge: Mears Point Marina, with over 500 slips, is on your port hand as you approach from Chester River, and Piney Narrows Marina is to starboard, with both covered and open slips in a dredged basin. Both have ramps for outboards and trail cruisers, and most facilities,

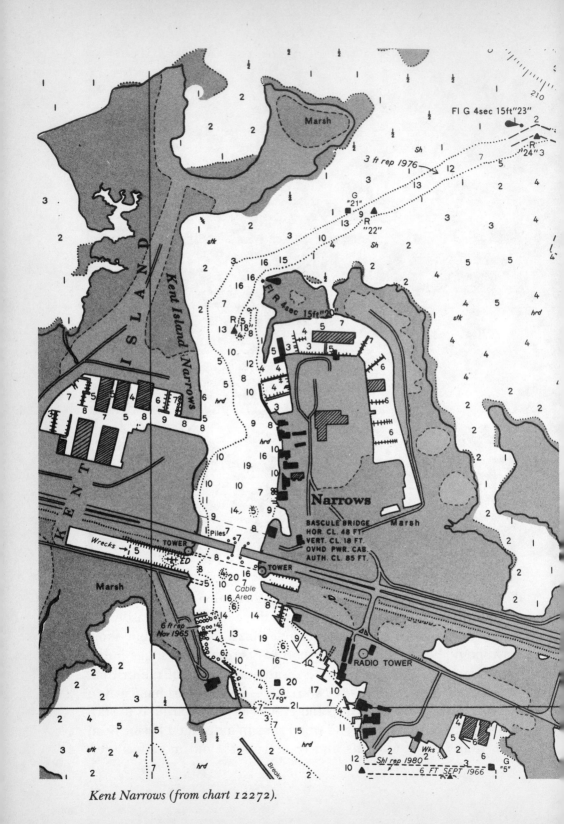

Kent Narrows (from chart 12272).

including gas and diesel. Transient slips are available, and the Poseidon Restaurant is nearby.

Just south of the bridge is a basin, used mainly by workboats. South of that on the point at the western side of the channel, near can 6, is the attractively located Kent Island Yacht Club, with slips, water, rest rooms, bar, kitchen, deep water at the dock, etc. Members of other yacht clubs are welcome.

The current through the Narrows, over a knot at full strength, floods in a northerly direction, following Eastern Bay tides, which are ahead of those on Chester River.

Just south of the bridge, you will find several facilities in addition to the Kent Island Yacht Club. There are several good restaurants, including the Dockside, with slips for use while dining, and the W. A. Thomas yard, with its fuel dock and shoreside restaurant. Nearby is the Fisherman's Inn, where seafood dinners are a specialty. Most of the docks have about 7 feet alongside.

Yachts can usually tie up for the night at one of the docks along the east shore below the bridge, or anchor off these docks in the narrow basin. Don't cut corners too near the bridges in entering the basin from the regular channel.

The land surrounding the Narrows is low and marshy, and many cruising skippers prefer to go 4 miles farther to Queenstown, where they can find good overnight anchorage in that protected harbor.

Three years before Lord Baltimore's expedition founded St. Marys on the Western Shore, William Claiborne in 1631 established a trading post on the southern tip of Kent Island. Claiborne operated under a trading license from the Governor of Virginia and had several fights with Lord Baltimore's forces before finally losing out.

3. *Queenstown (12272).* Between 7 and 8 miles up Chester River from Love Point is one of the best harbors on this part of the Bay. We first visited Queenstown at the end of a cold and wet trip after going up Eastern Bay and through Kent Island Narrows. It was near sundown and the weather cleared just as we dropped our anchor, treating us at the same time to a triple rainbow and one of the most

beautiful sunsets we had ever witnessed, even on the Chesapeake. With such a stage setting above the wooded shores, which became darker green as the sun sank, no wonder we remember Queenstown and like it.

The harbor is easy to enter after dark, as the channel is straight, with two flashing markers to be left to port. A shoal spot midway between the markers was removed by dredging in 1985, making the channel clear for keelboats drawing up to 7 feet.

The outer anchorage is directly opposite the entrance channel, off the remains of an old steamboat wharf, no longer visible, but designated on the chart as "subm. piles." Snug anchorage is found by following the channel (charted at 7 feet) southward into little Queenstown Creek. There is a perfectly protected and attractive anchorage basin off the town dock. The dock is useful for dinghy landing but a bit small and public for overnight tie-up. We spent a delightful night anchored in this basin more than 20 years ago and had it all to ourselves. Today you are likely to find it crowded with workboats and cruising yachts. The channel is well marked by charted beacons.

No gas or facilities are available on the Queenstown waterfront, adding variety and charm, if not convenience, to the harbor. However, stores, post office, gas stations, etc., are all within easy walking distance of the Queenstown landing.

Another alternative for anchoring, though less accessible to supplies, is northward up Queenstown Creek, opposite Salthouse Creek in 7 feet of water. Watch carefully for submerged piles off the ruined wharf, and keep outside of them. These are sometimes privately marked by stakes in summer, but don't count on finding the stakes. The channel to this most private anchorage is unmarked and is narrow in one place.

Even without a sunset or a rainbow, Queenstown is a pretty, unspoiled town, with attractive shores and several famous old estates. One of these, with lovely grounds shaded by tall trees, just back of the steamboat wharf, is known as Bolingly.

The present owners are hospitable to visiting yachtsmen interested in old houses. They also help out wandering mariners in case of need. They inherited the tradition from earlier occupants. Some years ago, so the story goes, a young couple with a baby turned up in their newly purchased boat, thinking they were in Cambridge rather than Queenstown. It was their very first cruise and they apparently misread their road map. After the owner of Bolingly showed them a chart, they were rowed out to a place in the outer harbor where the tall radio masts of Annapolis were visible in the distance, and were advised to steer a course in that direction.

On Blakeford Point is a famous old house of that name. My Lord's Gift, another historic estate, is across the creek to the south, on Coursey Point. In 1814, British landing forces were repulsed in the Battle of Slippery Hill.

Lord Baltimore granted some of the land on Queenstown Creek to Henry Coursey, secretary of the province, by the famous "Thumb Grant": as much land on a certain map as Coursey was able to cover with his thumb. This included My Lord's Gift and part of Blakeford.

4. Reed Creek and Grove Creek (12272). These creeks are not as well known to yachtsmen as Corsica River, but they are most attractive backwaters which have not yet been spoiled by overdevelopment. The common entrance is now buoyed, and it's not difficult to find your way into Reed Creek, which is a "favorite anchorage" of more than one knowledgeable Chesapeake cruising man. The narrow entrance to Grove Creek is tricky, but if you don't draw more than 4 feet you can work your way in slowly to an anchorage in 7 feet just inside the south point in peaceful surroundings. The two creeks still offer almost 5 miles of unspoiled shoreline.

5. Grays Inn Creek (12272). This creek, on the west shore of Chester River, is pretty and has a number of good anchorages, though it is not easy to enter. The best way to avoid the long shoals on each side of the entrance is to leave black can 1 close to port and head for the end of the ancient wharf at Spring Point on the west, or left, side of the creek. Then keep 50 yards off the wharf and stay in the middle of the creek as you go up farther. The Hills Marine Railway (gas, repairs, etc.) is on the north shore of Herringtown Creek, with Steamboat Landing and Skinners Neck Public Ramp nearby.

There are good anchorages farther up Grays Inn Creek in 9 feet above Brown's Point.

Eugene Du Pont had a waterfront farm and dock on the creek, which was sometimes used by the Chesapeake station of the Cruising Club of America for its fall rendezvous.

Church Creek is shallow and sounds hot; it has a Fryingpan Cove.

6. Langford Creek (12272). There seems to be no logic to the mental processes of those who decided whether a creek (or a river) was a river or a creek. For instance, Langford Creek is considerably larger than Corsica River across the way. This large creek is well marked by government buoys from the entrance to the first fork about 2 miles up.

The Rock Hall Yacht Club is located on the south side of Drum Point, on Lawyer's Cove. The approach is too shoal for most cruising auxiliaries, who can find good docking facilities, fuel, ice, and other supplies at the Lankford Bay Marina on the south side of Davis Creek. Re-exploring Langford Creek on a summer cruise in the mid-1980's we found many choice anchorages in both forks of the creek above Cacaway Island. Some of the best are in the middle and upper reaches of the west fork, like Bungay Cove, Shipyard Creek, and the bight on the east side of Millstone Point, where the branch redivides. The east fork of Langford Creek has its share of good anchorages too, but is likely to have more boat traffic on summer weekends.

Many cruising boats anchor and raft off the east side of Cacaway Island or opposite the entrance to Philip Creek.

The only village on Langford Creek is near the entrance, on Long Cove, where there is also a small marine railway. Just below is Deep Cove, with 1 foot at the entrance and 2 or 3 feet inside. When the cove was named in colonial times, it undoubtedly had a deep entrance and anchorage basin. Like so many other "deep" creeks around the Bay, it has shoaled continuously from the erosion that has accompanied advancing civilization.

7. *Corsica River* (*12272*). The most conspicuous landmark for the entrance of Corsica River, which flows into the Chester, is the former estate of John J. Raskob between Holton and Town points on the south shore. Two large brick houses, and various other houses, barns, and fields, occupy a considerable portion of Corsica Neck. The property now belongs to the Soviet government and is an R and R site for Russian Embassy personnel.

The land is fairly low on both shores near the entrance but farther up the banks are higher and the attractiveness of the river increases.

The principal anchorages are as follows:

(1) In the large bight off the former Raskob place, beyond Town Point and outside of Middle Quarter Cove. Be sure to round red nun 2 before going in.

(2) North of red nun 4 at the mouth of Emory Creek. This is a popular anchorage and offers better protection than the one off the Raskob place, particularly from northwest squalls. This is known locally as Red Wharf Cove because of a former steamboat landing of that description.

(3) At the Centreville Landing dock nearly 4 miles upriver. This is the county wharf. There was at least 6 feet at the wharf when we were there. Leave the private channel stakes to port leading up to the dock. There is a small country store at Centreville Landing a short distance up the street; gas may be obtained near the store. This used to be an important grain shipping place.

Unless you are in need of supplies, we recommend anchorage number 2. The upriver dredged channel is not always easy to follow and the surroundings are not inviting.

8. *Upper Chester River to Chestertown* (*12272*). Chester River from the mouth of the Corsica to Chestertown, about 12 miles, is deep, well marked, and easy to navigate. Near the entrance of Island Creek, on a historic plantation (1705), is the Kennersley Pointe Marina, with a channel to a snug, lovely location with slips, electricity, gas, ice, Artesian water, lounges, rest rooms, swimming pool, etc.

Above, in attractive surroundings on the east shore, is the Rolphs Wharf Inn and Marina, with docks (9 feet), gas, diesel fuel, ice, snack bar, lounge, travel lift, rest rooms, showers—all most inviting.

Just above Devils Reach, north of flasher 39, is the white porticoed clubhouse of the Chester River Yacht and Country Club. You can anchor off the dock. There is a strong tidal current.

The anchorage is exposed for a considerable distance to the northeast and a northeaster once raised havoc with a visiting fleet. Fortunately, northeasters are uncommon in the yachting season and if one comes, take shelter below Primrose Point.

Gas and water are obtainable from Kibler's Marina at Chestertown, where all kinds of supplies can be found.

If you have a liking for old houses and history, walk around Chestertown, visit the Old Custom House or Ringold House, and walk through the grounds of Washington College. When this college was founded, George Washington became chairman of the board.

Good dockside facilities are available at Kibler's Marina, which has 64 slips, haulout and repair facilities, and is located conveniently on the waterfront just a block or so from the old Custom House. The Old Wharf Inn serves fine meals. If you wish to explore above the bridge at Chestertown, you will find a narrow channel to Crumpton. (The bridge is manned and opens on demand from April through September. From October through March, give 6 hours' notice of your need to have the bridge opened by calling 301-778-1451.)

Few yachtsmen venture above the bridge, but the trip is rewarding if you have the time. Try anchoring off Buckingham Wharf, or near the windmill at Travilla Wharf, or Deep Landing in 10 to 20 feet of water.

XI. BAY SIDE OF KENT ISLAND (*12271*).

If you are heading south from Chester River and don't take Kent Island Narrows, your course takes you back around Love Point and down the main Bay past the twin Chesapeake bridges and Annapolis on the Western Shore. As Annapolis is a hard place to find transient slips, cruising boats are often looking for a harbor or place to tie up on the Eastern Shore along the 9-mile stretch of Kent Island from the Bay Bridge to Bloody Point. In the past there has been little to recommend along this shore, but now there are four possible man-made harbors which can accommodate shoal or medium-draft powerboats and sailboats under 4-foot draft.

1. Pier 1 Marina (12270). This was developed in the early 1970's, providing a sheltered harbor and complete marina services at the Eastern Shore end of the Bay Bridge. The entrance channel is a dredged cut 150 feet with a controlling depth of about 5 feet (1986), well marked with ranges, leading into a sheltered mooring area and fully protected inner basin capable of handling vessels up to 65 feet. The 225-foot fuel dock carries 8 feet alongside at MLW. Gas and diesel fuel, ice, water, marine supplies, showers, 30-ton lift, and Laundromat are all available. A restaurant is on the premises, with an airstrip and charter services nearby. A shopping center is not far away at Stevensville. The marina fills a real need.

2. Matapeake Harbor of Refuge (12270). Located about 2 miles south of the Bay Bridge, this snug harbor of refuge makes good use of the old ferry landing, breakwaters, and bulkheads at Matapeake. The lighted entrance leads into a fully protected basin maintained by the Maryland Department of Natural Resources and is used by the Maryland Marine Police. It is available only in emergency as a genuine harbor of refuge, and is not intended to be used as a public marina. A few slips may be available next to the marine police dock. Visiting yachts are not encouraged to remain overnight except in emergency conditions, but several small craft have found shelter there in severe Chesapeake storms. Depths in the entrance have reportedly shoaled in spots since the harbor was opened in 1962, but the channel and basin are said to be safe for vessels up to 6-feet draft. A State Marine Police Academy is located on the grounds, which are close to the site of the hydraulic model of Chesapeake

Bay, built in the early 1970's by the federal government. (The model is now closed.) There is a public launching ramp in the harbor.

3. Kentmorr Marina (12270). This man-made harbor is located about 4 1/2 miles south of the Bay Bridge, just beyond the white and orange nun buoy "S" marking the south end of the measured mile shown on chart 12270. The entrance, approached on a course of 122° from the nun, has been dredged to 5 feet and offers no problem to most power cruisers and other shoal-draft craft. But we don't recommend this harbor for keel sailboats and auxiliaries which draw over 4 feet, since the entrance is constantly shoaling after winter storms. The marina has a 95-slip capacity, and can handle yachts up to 40 feet. Complete marine services, boat and engine repair facilities, and modern marine hoists up to 35-ton capacity are available.

4. Queen Anne Marina (12270). The entrance to this relatively new marina is just over a mile south of the Kentmorr entrance, with a 2 1/2 foot dredged channel leading into a shallow salt pond which has been dredged to 4 feet at dockside. All of these dredged channels have a tendency to shoal, and we caution vessels against entering without local knowledge or recent information about controlling depths. Gas, diesel, and all shoreside facilities are available at the marina, but transient slips are scarce.

XII. EASTERN BAY TO THE MILES AND WYE RIVERS (*12270*).

Whether you enter Eastern Bay from the west or from the north through Kent Island Narrows, your first good harbor is Tilghman Creek, around Tilghman Point and to the east of Rich Neck. If you are coming in from the west, you will find—as is so often the case on the Chesapeake—that you must be careful running directly from the red and slightly tilted lighthouse on Bloody Point Bar to the next marker, black bell and flasher, due to the shoal. Extensive shoaling has been reported northeast of Bell 1, and we have actually seen several cruising division sailboats go aground trying to hold a course from the bell to Tilghman Point. We recommend giving the bell a safe berth and then setting a course of 075 degrees for Bell R-2A off Claiborne, until clear of the shoal.

1. Claiborne Landing (12270). For many years Claiborne had a public landing used by Bay steamers and ferries running from Romancoke on Kent Island to the mainland. When the ferry service came to an end with the building of the Chesapeake Bay Bridge in the early 1950's, the Eastern Shore terminal became a public landing and launching ramp used chiefly by local small craft. Cruising boats seldom visited the landing, although the old ferry channel carried 7 feet to the docks. Today there are limited facilities for a few pleasure craft, used mostly by local boats.

2. Tilghman Creek (12270). This is one of the best anchorages and most attractive creeks on the Eastern Shore, and a convenient stopping place for anyone bound for Miles or Wye River, or prior to a trip across the Chesapeake. On entering, approach the conspicuous lighted beacon on a line from red nun 8 in Miles River. Swing wide to the starboard around the beacon, giving it a good berth to your port and then head carefully between can 3 and red nun 4, leaving the latter, of course, to starboard. From there, head past Seth Point, not too close to the point, into any one of the following several fine anchorages in the creek.

(1) Behind Seth Point, to port. This is fairly good and secluded though somewhat open to the northwest.
(2) In the first cove to the starboard, in 11 feet. Anchor in the middle. Some private docks are farther in.
(3) In the second cove to port, in 10 feet. This is the most appealing of all and very snug.
(4) Farther up the creek, just north of a small boatyard.

John Cockey, Jr., now runs the Locust Hill Boat Works at the head of the creek, with 6 feet at the end of the pier. Like many Chesapeake boatyards, he can't haul keelboats, but will take care of craft up to $3\frac{1}{2}$ feet draft. The Boat Works has gas and fresh water at the dock, with showers and overnight accommodations available close by ashore. Supplies can be bought from a store about a half mile away, perhaps telephoned for. The Cockey family, who have been operating this yard for many years, are always most hospitable.

3. *Shipping and Cox Creeks, on Kent Island (12270).* If you like unusual anchorages and don't mind mild cases of running aground, try poking your way with the depth finder up Shipping Creek between the unmarked shoals. You will find several interesting places to lie, out of the beaten track.

One of them is west of the more northerly of the Philpotts Islands, in 11 feet shoaling rapidly to 5 feet, according to how far south you go. Another is in 6 feet below a wharf shown on chart 12270, in the long western branch of Shipping Creek.

Cox Creek is not recommended because there are extensive marshes farther up, where the best anchorages are, and it takes a

Workboats in Crab Alley Creek, off Eastern Bay. (Photo courtesy of BaySailor.)

run of a couple of miles between many unmarked shoals before you can get there.

4. Crab Alley Creek (12270). This creek is interesting and well worth a visit. After picking up cans 1 and 3, head for the west shore of Johnson Island to your starboard. Then anchor in 10 or 11 feet west of the island. If you want to go farther, keep in the middle, leave R-6 to starboard, and go as far as the fork east of Dominion. There are two small marinas in Crab Alley Creek, and two boatyards in Little Creek, both run by Thompsons. Don't try to enter Little Creek without local knowledge.

XIII. WYE RIVER (*12270*).

In our opinion this is one of the most appealing rivers on the Eastern Shore. There are three main branches, Wye East River, or "Front Wye"; Wye River, so called on the chart, or "Back Wye"; and Wye Narrows, which connects the other two branches, 4 or 5 miles up. Unfortunately for boats carrying masts more than 10 feet above

the water, the bridge across the Narrows is now a permanent one. We had heard various stories about having to wake up and help an ancient bridge tender to get the draw open, so we had to investigate for ourselves. There is no longer a draw, unfortunately, and the clearance is approximately 10 feet.

If you have time to go only up one branch, we recommend Front Wye and a trip up Wye Narrows to the bridge. Snug anchorages and attractive vistas will be found around nearly every bend, with some famous old colonial houses to add special interest to your exploration. Wye Island, surrounded by the three branches of the Wye, has been called "one of the beauty spots of the Eastern Shore." We strongly recommend that you explore both branches.

In entering the Wye from the north, it is possible to cut across the shoal below Bennett Point by going between red nun 2 and can 3. After that, watch the chart carefully, gauge the distance to which the shoals extend off the various points to be passed, don't get careless on the way back as we did, and, in general, keep in the middle. You will then have some of the finest river cruising on the Chesapeake. It may be blowing hard outside in the Bay, but you will hardly notice it on the Wye. Mark your points, as you pass; otherwise it is easy to get mixed up in this lovely maze. Take note of the exceptional depths—58 feet off Bruffs Island in the entrance, and 48 feet past Bordley Point. Yet some northern yachtsmen call the Chesapeake a shoal water bay!

The nearest port for gas, supplies, boatyards, and such facilities is at St. Michaels on Miles River.

1. *Wye East River (Front Wye) (12270).* There are so many good anchorages, almost anywhere in the river, that we shall be able to mention only a few of them here.

a. Shaw Bay. Here is the first good anchorage on the way upriver. Anchor behind Bruffs Point and its tall trees. This place is delightful under good weather conditions and is sometimes used for a rendezvous of the Cruising Club of America, the Sailing Club of the

Chesapeake, and other clubs around the Bay. It can be crowded on summer weekends, but is particularly appealing in the fall when the geese are in full flight. The first wheat in America is said to have been raised on Wye Island, north of Shaw Bay.

b. Lloyd Creek. It is not as snug or as easy to navigate as several of the creeks farther up the Wye but it has on its southern shore the famous Wye House, a white colonial mansion built in Revolutionary times by the Lloyd family to replace a house destroyed by the British.

c. Dividing Creek. This is narrow and deep, between high banks of overhanging trees, and is a fascinating place to anchor. But don't land; there are signs which say "No Trespassing." Watch the chart carefully and avoid the 2-foot spot at the entrance. The depths run from 7 to 10 feet for some distance inside, and, at the entrance, if you keep in the channel. In springtime we have watched a family of ospreys teaching their young to fish the creek.

d. Granary Creek. Very similar to Dividing Creek, it is equally intriguing, secluded, and private. It would be impossible to find a snugger anchorage, though in summer it may be cooler outside the entrance.

e. Pickering Creek. Long, narrow, and easy to go aground in, it is still deep enough in the right spots. Sound your way carefully past the bar near the mouth. We prefer Dividing and Granary. Just above Pickering is a bight with 8 to 10 feet in it and soft bottom, where boats often anchor. We have discovered several places on the Wye where the bottom is so soft that it is difficult to get your anchor to hold in a fresh breeze.

f. Skipton Creek—Wye Heights. There is a good anchorage near the entrance of Skipton Creek beyond the point of land at the mouth occupied by another famous estate of colonial times—Wye Heights.

The imposing house with its 4 white pillars and long rose arbor overlooks the junction of the upper and lower parts of Front Wye, Wye Narrows, and Skipton Creek, one of the finest locations on the Eastern Shore.

g. Wye Landing. Just below the landing is one of the many river anchorages, cooler than in some of the narrow creeks but not quite so snug. The landing is used for launching trailer outboards and there are likely to be a good many boats moving about on weekends.

h. Wye Mills. Not far from the head of Wye East River, it is a small village where the famous Wye Oak is located. The largest white oak in Maryland and one of the largest in the United States, it is said to be over 400 years old. It is 95 feet high and its branches spread horizontally for 165 feet.

2. Wye Narrows (12270). Two anchorages here which are out of the narrow channel are in the two wide spots just southeast of the bridge. In going toward the bridge from Wye Heights, be sure to keep well over to the starboard, or east, shore to avoid the half-foot shoal, which projects about to the middle of the channel. As already pointed out, the bridge over the Narrows is now a fixed bridge with about 10 feet vertical clearance.

3. Wye River (Back Wye) (12270). Besides anchorages in various coves or behind bends of this river, some of the best places for the night are in the large bight east of Drum Point, often used for a club rendezvous, and the western part of Wye Narrows up to Covington Creek. Other good anchorages are found in:

a. Grapevine Cove, or in one of the horns of the unnamed cove across the river to the west of Grapevine Point. The latter is easier to get into, as the deep-water entrance is wider.

b. Quarter Creek, which offers good anchorages if you keep in the middle and avoid the shoals on both sides of the entrance.

c. The Upper Wye is well worth exploring, with a dozen delightful spots to spend the night. On your way up you will see the docks and attractive buildings of the Wye Institute to starboard about a mile above Quarter Creek. At the head of navigation you are only a couple of miles south of Queenstown, on Chester River, but almost 30 miles away by water.

XIV. MILES RIVER (*12270*).

This is one of the best-known rivers on the Eastern Shore. Unlike the narrow, zigzag course of the Wye, this river, about a mile wide for 2 miles or so beyond Deep Water Point at the entrance, runs for 4 miles in a southeasterly direction and then for nearly 5 more miles of navigable waters toward the northeast. With few marshes, pleasant shores, and many fine harbors, this is one of the best cruising rivers on the Eastern Shore.

Here, as in so many other rivers, you may not have time to explore, nor is there space to describe all of the many good anchorages. We'll tell of a few of the best ones.

1. Long Haul Creek (*12270*). Just to the starboard, as you enter Miles River, is Long Haul Creek, the headquarters of the active and hospitable Miles River Yacht Club, whose dock and clubhouse is on the port, or south, shore as you come into the creek. Local buoys put out for the yachting season aid in following the channel, which is not difficult. There are range lights on the club dock. Keep close to the Yacht Club side of the south fork of the creek, beyond the dock. The chart shows shoal water projecting almost halfway across this branch from the northern bank. We know from experience that the chart is right. You may possibly be able to obtain a slip from the club, but not on active summer weekends; if slips are not available at the club, you can anchor near the south shore of the lower fork or in the middle of the northern fork. The club has rest rooms, showers, bar, etc.

The club dock, with about 10 feet of water, has water and electricity, but gas and supplies cannot be bought there; they are available conveniently at St. Michaels about a mile away.

Although it can get uncomfortable at the club dock in heavy easterlies, good shelter from all winds can be had around the corner of the southern fork in 9 feet.

If you like peace and quiet, don't plan to cruise into Long Haul Creek during either of the two major regattas—one for sail and the other power—since these are big events on the Eastern Shore and bring hundreds of spectator boats to the area. But if you do blow in at that time, as we have done more than once, don't miss the famous log canoe races on Miles River. These, and the hospitality of the officers and members of the Yacht Club, are always high spots of our frequent visits to this area.

2. *St. Michaels* (*12270*). This is *the* supply base of all Eastern Bay. All kinds of provisions are available. The entrance is easy and well marked. In the center, as you approach, is the St. Michaels Town Dock Marina, with gas, diesel, water, and ice at its dock, and a store and restaurant close at hand. Across the south fork is the Harbour Inn and Marina, an impressive structure with transient slips on the harbor, a pool, restaurant, etc. Despite these facilities, finding a slip or anchorage room in the tight little harbor has become a problem for visiting boats. A few slips may be available at the Higgins Yacht Yard, and the Maritime Museum has opened up a dredged channel to berths in the back harbor.

The Crab Claw restaurant, with its balcony overlooking the harbor, offers limited dockage to boat customers and has good seafood dinners at reasonable prices.

A major attraction of this historic harbor is the Chesapeake Bay Maritime Museum, located on the north side of the basin in the row of old town houses with white balconies and porches. The museum welcomes visiting yachtsmen, and may have room for you to tie up temporarily at one of its dockside slips on weekdays. Supported and operated by an enthusiastic group of Chesapeake boatmen and maritime preservationists, the museum is increasing its fine collection of Bay craft and arti-crafts each year. The restored lighthouse which you leave to starboard as you enter the harbor was saved by the museum, and brought to the present site from Hooper Strait in 1966. You can spend an interesting morning or afternoon browsing through the museum and its grounds. Longfellows is another good seafood restaurant on the waterfront, and the Inn at Perry Cabin provides transportation by boat to its dock in the cove behind the museum. The Cruising Club of America sometimes holds a rendezvous at St. Michaels or Long Haul Creek in the fall, and some of the finest yachts on the Chesapeake are attracted there. Many stores and specialty shops are along the nearby main street.

If you prefer a quiet night, try either Long Haul Creek or Leeds Creek just across Miles River.

3. Leeds Creek (12270). This is a long, narrow creek, well marked at the entrance, and easy to navigate beyond. A good anchorage is in the 8-foot spot below Tunis Mills, or just below the bridge if you draw under 5 feet. Tunis Mills is a small country town, with one or two wharves in varied states of repair. A few supplies and gas (in cans) are obtainable at or near a country store. The creek is very typical and its shores are of medium height, some of them bordered with large vine-covered trees. Tunis Mills was the name given to a large sawmill erected more than a century ago when they were first timbering the Eastern Shore. Two- and three-masted schooners used to load timber and sail to Baltimore or Philadelphia. Now the river is crowded with pleasure craft on summer weekends.

4. Hunting Creek (12270). This creek is well marked with beacons and private markers to aid navigation. The easiest anchorage to reach is behind Long Point in the bight opposite the first red beacon. Or you can go nearly two miles up and find a very snug anchorage in 6 feet, near the head. Follow the beacons, keep in the middle, and avoid points. This creek is one of the best. It ranks high on our list of "favorite anchorages."

5. *Miles River above Hunting Creek* (*12270*). It is possible to carry 5 feet for almost 5 miles above Hunting Creek. One good anchorage is in 9 feet to the north of red spar 18 just below the bridge. One of the most experienced yachtsmen on the Chesapeake, the late C. Lowndes Johnson, had his home here, which we were fortunate to visit. Mr. Johnson was a great help to us in preparing earlier editions of this guide. Fellow members of the Sailing Club of the Chesapeake have established a perpetual trophy in his memory.

Another of many good anchorages is near the entrance of Goldsborough Creek in 7 feet. This is protected closely from the northwest and southeast, but is in a place where a southwest breeze will come over the water, often a real asset on a hot night. On the point which separates this creek from the upper part of Miles River is Myrtle Grove, one of the old places in Talbot County. The drawbridge operates from sunrise to sunset, but the channel above the bridge is not buoyed.

XV. POPLAR ISLAND NARROWS AND POPLAR HARBOR (*12271*).

1. *Poplar Island Narrows* (*12270, 12266*). Seven miles south of the flashing red buoy off Tilghman Point is red nun 8 at the northern entrance of Poplar Island Narrows. This is a first reminder that the buoys southward through the Narrows are to be considered from the point of view of leaving Eastern Bay, rather than entering the Narrows. In other words, red buoys are to be left to *port,* green buoys to *starboard.*

The passage inside of Poplar Island is not difficult, if you follow the buoys carefully, and saves about 2 miles in a run from Eastern

Bay to the mouth of Choptank River. According to the chart the minimum depth is 7 feet, though there is one 6-foot spot. An experienced yachtsman recommends that 6 feet be considered "the practical working draft." Another cruising man reports that the shoal south of Coaches Island is moving eastward, so don't hug green C-3 too close. We touched bottom on the channel side of C-3 and found less than 4 feet at low tide on a fall day in the 1980's, and reported our soundings to the National Ocean Service. The new charts show this shoaling, which was still moving eastward in the late 1980's.

2. *Poplar Harbor* (*12270, 12266*). We have found good anchorages southwest of Jefferson Island, with a controlling depth of 5 feet in the approach channel.

Follow a course of 298° M from C-5 in the Narrows until you have reached the 6-foot area south of Jefferson Island. Then swing north and anchor to the west, or left, of the lower end of Jefferson Island. Follow the bush stakes which are on the northerly side of the entrance channel. There is about 4 feet at the end of Jefferson Island dock. Before World War II many famous Democrats landed for meetings of their Jefferson Island Democratic Club, until the house burned down. FDR used to go there.

In addition to Democrats, crows come to Poplar Island from at least three counties, for it is a famous crow roost.

Poplar and Jefferson islands have had several owners since World War II, and a new dock and shore facilities were built for use as a club and hunting lodge. Later the owners gave the islands to the Smithsonian Institution, in the hope that this government group would be better able to check the constant erosion which threatens them with extinction. Unfortunately, very little seems to have been done and erosion is taking away many acres of island beachfront every year. But for this generation, at least, the islands are a fine place for fishing, and for duck hunting in the fall. It is fun to poke into the harbor with lead line or pole, and to spend the night if the weather is good and you don't draw more than 5 feet.

Knapps Narrows, looking west toward the Bay.

XVI. Knapps Narrows—Tilghman (*12266*).

These narrows save about 5 miles in the passage to Oxford or up the Choptank. At the time of our last trip through the Narrows in 1985 there was at least 7 feet in the channel, but a tendency to shoaling always exists after winter gales. According to local boatmen, the channel does not run straight between the first two light beacons at the Bay entrance, but curves slightly southward. Unlike Kent Island Narrows, the markers on each side of the Narrows, at each entrance, are with reference to entering from that particular side. In other words, when you enter, whether from the west or east, leave green markers to *port*. After passing through the bridge and heading across the wide mouth of the Choptank, leave green markers to *starboard*.

As in other dredged channels on the Chesapeake, don't count too much on the maintenance of the charted depth. However, the situation in Knapps Narrows is generally more favorable than at Kent Island Narrows, and depths of 6 feet in the channel can usually be counted on.

There are two marinas in a small dredged basin just west of the bascule bridge, with gas, dockside slips, ramps, snack bars, and a restaurant. Four other boatyards in the Narrows provide facilities, chiefly for local fishing craft based in the town of Tilghman. This is a busy waterway at almost any time; it's convenient for gas or supplies, or as a stopover for a meal, but not the best place to spend a quiet night. The bridge has a good reputation for opening promptly for boat traffic.

XVII. Choptank River (*12266, 12268*).

Choptank River is the largest river on the Eastern Shore. While the *Coast Pilot* calls it navigable for 53 miles to Greensboro, minimum depths above Denton, about 45 miles up, are only 3¹/₂ feet.

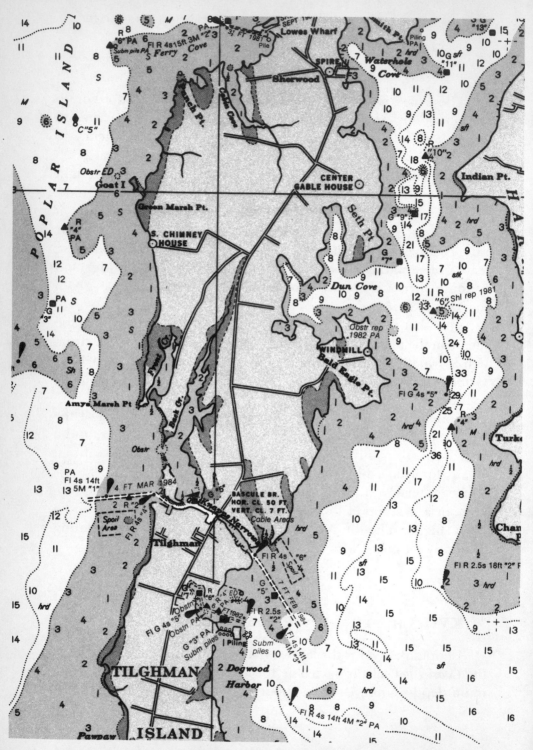

Knapps Narrows and Dun Cove at Tilghman Island (from chart 12266).

Except for confirmed upriver explorers, we do not recommend the Choptank much above Cambridge. The river winds among extensive marshes and much more attractive cruising can be found elsewhere, though the channel to Denton is deep, well marked, and there are many possible anchorages along the edge. "Scenic beauty sort of peters out at the town of Choptank," as one widely traveled yachtsman put it.

As we shall soon see, the Choptank and its tributaries below the fixed bridge, 50-foot vertical clearance, at Cambridge provide some of the best cruising on the Chesapeake. Compared to these waters, the upper Choptank has little to offer.

The mean range of tide is about 1 1/2 feet at Cambridge, 2 feet at Denton, and 2 1/2 feet at Greensboro. Above Choptank, 22 1/2 miles up, the water is fresh.

The principal port on the Choptank, where all kinds of supplies and repair work are available, is at Cambridge, the third largest city on the Eastern Shore. But many yachtsmen call Oxford their favorite port, with its many active boatyards, inns, and shops.

As you enter the wide mouth of Choptank River from the Bay, Sharps Island Light marks the northern edge of an extensive shoal that once was a large island. The island has eroded until today nothing remains but a beacon and submerged piles at its southern end. Robert Burgess notes that in the middle of the last century the island measured some 600 acres and supported several prosperous farms. The first edition of this guide described the island as still having 70 acres when it served as a bombing target in World War II. If approaching from the south, the main channel runs between Qk. Fl. 5 and red nun 6 below the southern end of the shoal.

1. Blackwalnut Cove (12266). A 50-foot-wide, 6-foot channel leads into this cove, but controlling depths may be lower into the dredged basin of 400 square feet. The entrance channel is clearly marked by two lighted beacons. Leave beacons and bush stakes to port. The place is open to the south and is used mainly as a harbor of refuge for small power craft. There is a small yard. Cruising keelboats should stay out.

No dockage facilities or supplies are available. However, the town of Tilghman is about 2 miles away and gas, ice, water, etc., are obtainable at the Narrows, as indicated above.

2. Dogwood Harbor (12266). In earlier editions we indicated that this open harbor could be used by larger vessels; but the roadstead is exposed from northeast to southwest, and the dock at Avalon formerly operated by the Tilghman Packing Company no longer offers convenient access to supplies. Vessels requiring provisions will do better to proceed eastward to Oxford, while those looking for a protected anchorage can head northward into Harris Creek. A new waterfront development was under way in Dogwood Harbor in 1988, with boating facilities on the small island in the harbor.

3. Harris Creek (12266). Navigable with drafts of 6 or 8 feet to Dun Cove and—if you are careful, lucky, and have chart 12267—for some miles beyond, this creek above Knapps Narrows has several first-class anchorages. Once over the bar off Indian Point, where the chart indicates several 4-foot spots and a 6-foot spot (not all easy to locate), about 5 feet can be carried to the county wharf at Wittman up Cummings Creek. There are two small railways in the prongs just east of Cummings Creek. However, on account of extensive, unmarked shoals, we don't recommend going into Cummings Creek or its eastern prongs without local guidance.

The entrance to Harris Creek can be made without difficulty if you are careful to follow these instructions:

Favor the east side of the channel after leaving the Narrows, heading for red nun 4 off Turkey Neck Point and keeping east of lighted beacon 5 where the shoal off Bald Eagle Point extends beyond the marker. Then continue toward red nun 6, leaving it to starboard, and on toward can 7. If you are entering Dun Cove swing to port when you are about halfway between 6 and 7, heading west until you have cleared the shoal to starboard and both arms of Dun Cove have opened up. There are good anchorages in both. If you are continuing up Harris Creek just keep in midchannel, leaving all markers on the proper side.

a. Dun Cove (12266). This lovely cove is on almost everyone's list of "favorite anchorages." It is no longer as secluded as we first found it 40 years ago, but it remains unspoiled and the shoreline and surrounding fields and woodland are virtually unchanged.

Dun Cove is the most convenient anchorage for vessels entering the Choptank through Knapps Narrows. Many cruising boats anchor in 8 or 9 feet west of Bald Eagle Point.

A more protected anchorage is $1/4$ to $1/2$ mile up the northern branch just inside Seaths Point. This is fine if you can keep clear of a 2-foot shoal to port and a 1-foot spot to starboard. If you keep in the middle, you're fine and will have a very secure place to drop your hook in 8 feet. Another still more appealing anchorage for shoal-draft craft is behind the low spit of marsh grass opposite a plane ramp. There is 6 feet of water for about a third of the distance into this cove, and the wreck is farther in than would appear from the chart. This is a "neat" place to go, as our children would remark, and has charm. Though the bottom is hard, it offers good protection from all winds. Favor the starboard shore going in.

Dun Cove is a favorite rendezvous for the Chesapeake Station of the Cruising Club of America and also for the Sailing Club of the Chesapeake. These well-known groups of experienced sailors sometimes join forces in their cruises. Though there are no facilities in Dun Cove, that is considered an asset when the cruising fleets want to raft up and enjoy their own company without the harassing wakes and interruptions which sometimes come when places offer too many enticements to the slip-seeking fraternity.

The swimming in Dun Creek is fine except when there are sea nettles.

b. Waterhole Cove (12266). This is a fair anchorage, but open to the east and south, and with extensive unmarked shoals. You can get a few supplies at Sherwood, an attractive little town with a good general store. There is a county wharf, to which you can get very close.

c. Harris Creek above Waterhole Cove. This creek is navigable for about 3 miles above Waterhole Cove and you can find places to anchor all the way up to the Northeast Branch, but don't stray far from the channel. There are, however, more interesting creeks elsewhere on the Choptank. Other fields are greener—or perhaps more appropriately, other waters are bluer.

4. Broad Creek (12266). "Poke into some of the coves when you are in no hurry," said one cruising man who likes to go into out-of-the-way places. However, if you go into Broad Creek, you are very likely to run aground, as it is full of outlying and unmarked 1- and 2-foot spots. Furthermore, the sand is very hard on some of them. However, both the main branch of Broad Creek and the wide entrance to Edge Creek are better marked than they were a few years ago, and a number of very delightful anchorages can be found in both creeks. Keep your chart handy and use the depth finder or lead line, and you should not have too much trouble with the shoals. The best part of Broad Creek is San Domingo Creek. However, for coolness on a hot night, an anchorage at the mouth of Broad between Nelson Island and N-2 is recommended by an experienced yachtsman. This is better than it looks, because a long 2-foot bar and Nelson Island partly break the sea and the holding ground is good.

a. Balls Creek and Leadenham Creek (12266). These are both attractive and unspoiled waterways, worth exploring if you have time. But, like most of the other tributaries of Broad Creek, you'll want to keep a sharp lookout for those unmarked shoals. We like the little bight just east of Caulk Cove in Leadenham Creek.

b. San Domingo Creek (12266). This is the back door to St. Michaels. With 4-feet draft or less you can go nearly to the end of the creek and do your shopping at St. Michaels, less than half a mile away. If

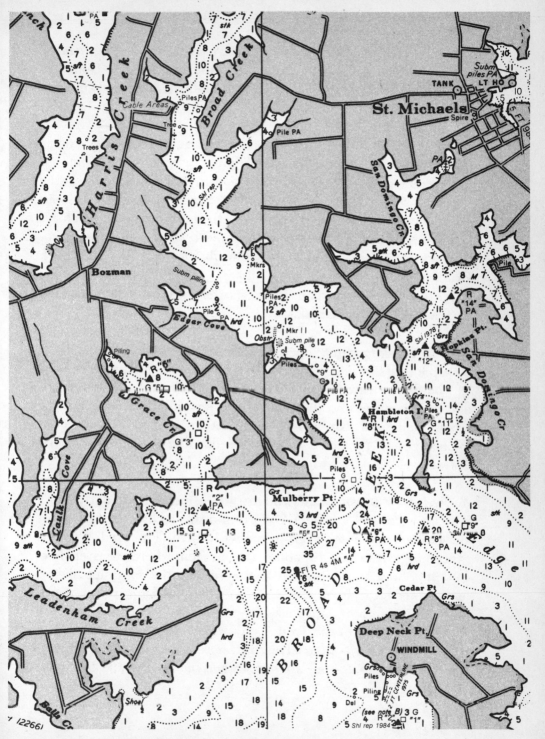

Broad Creek and its tributaries (from chart 12270).

you draw under 7 feet, you have to walk only 3/4 mile to St. Michaels and will have a good anchorage. One authority calls San Domingo Creek "one of the most attractive places on the Bay" and the spot between Hopkins Point and the upper end of Hambleton Island a "dream anchorage."

Watch the long shoals at the mouth of Edge Creek, particularly the one around Hambleton Island, on your way to San Domingo and again look out for the 2-foot spots off Hopkins Point and at the entrance of the east fork just above. Crooked Intention (about 1680), beautifully situated on the north shore of the St. Michaels branch, is one of the Bay's charming old houses—small, well proportioned, and constructed of whitewashed brick.

c. Solitude Creek, as its name implies, offers a quiet anchorage at the eastern end of Edge Creek.

5. Irish Creek (12266). The entrance to this creek will challenge your piloting skill and you must watch for shoaling between "3" and "4," but if you leave C-1 well to port, hug close to N-2 to starboard, and then steer true north up the creek, favoring the opposite shore from Lucy Point, you will be rewarded by a choice of attractive anchorages in protected waters. We like the 9-foot spot in the entrance to Haskins Cove.

6. Tred Avon River (12266). Many yachtsmen, particularly those who cruise by sail, consider Oxford and the Tred Avon the tops of the Eastern Shore. We won't argue with them. The Tred Avon has everything, from Oxford, about 2 miles from where the river flows into the Choptank, to its many lovely creeks with their quiet anchorages protected from all winds. Along some of these creeks, if you know where to look, are tucked away famous old houses of early times. The shores of the Tred Avon are not so high or imposing as those of the Severn or Sassafras, but there is something about them which appeals to us; they are not rugged but restful, and they have charm.

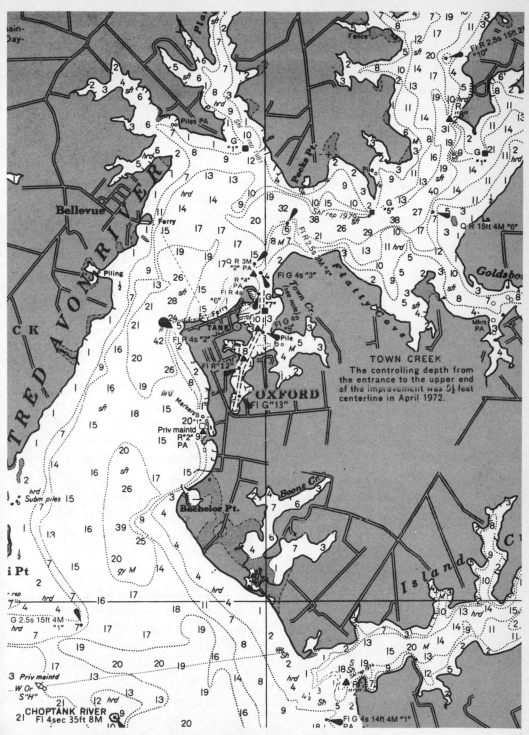

Approach to Tred Avon River and Oxford (from chart 12266).

In entering the Tred Avon, whether from the direction of Knapps Narrows or from the bell off Cook Point at the entrance of the Choptank, head for Choptank River Light, a rather low steel structure which has replaced the old red-roofed lighthouse. As you approach the light, swing to port around the lighted marker off Benoni Point and head for the light at Oxford toward the north, giving Bachelor Point a sufficient berth to avoid the 4-foot shoal. A prominent white water tank on Town Creek is on the eastern side of Oxford. There is considerable soft mud in the Tred Avon and the holding is poor in some places.

a. Oxford (12266). If we were asked to pick out our favorite port on the Eastern Shore, our choice would be easy. The answer would be Oxford. Other harbors are more beautiful, snugger, and have facilities at least as convenient, but in no other place that we know of will you find a better combination of these things, plus the atmosphere of friendliness which does so much to make a yachtsman feel at home.

When we once visited Oxford many years ago, it was late in the evening and our ice was nearly gone. The ice company had closed for the night, so we dropped in at the grocery store on Morris Street, which fortunately hadn't closed, to see if they could help us out. They didn't have the ice but found the telephone number of an official of A. B. Harris & Co., Wholesale Seafood Packers. This official not only was undisturbed at our late call, but insisted on leaving the ice for us at Ralph Wiley's dock during the evening. That was back in the 1950's, but it's still typical of Oxford, which was a famous colonial seaport before the American Revolution, and is a friendly haven for yachtsmen today.

In approaching Oxford, you will first see Bachelor Point Harbor and the Pier Street Marina and Restaurant to starboard, and then as you round the point with the light on it, the white club house and the pier of the Tred Avon Yacht Club, where members of recognized yacht clubs are welcomed. This club is especially interested in sailing and sailing yachts. There is plenty of water at the pier, even for deep-draft boats, and visitors may dock there briefly.

Many yachts anchor in the bight east of the Yacht Club and north of the town, but this is often crowded and quite exposed when the wind pipes up. We prefer Town Creek beyond, where yachts are well protected and can either anchor in the creek or tie up at a slip at one of several dock areas just beyond the entrance channel to starboard, including Mears Yacht Haven, the Oxford Boatyard, and the Town Creek Marina and Restaurant. Farther up the creek there are other boatyards and marinas. Ralph Wiley's old yard is now operated by Cutts and Case. The creek has been dredged and you can carry 10 feet into the Oxford Boatyard, and 8 feet to the head of the creek.

In entering Town Creek keep well outside of a direct line from the red beacon on the point where the Yacht Club is located, and the lighted beacon at the entrance of the creek.

The bottom of Town Creek used to be soft, oozy mud, where boats sometimes dragged in severe thunder squalls, but it is reported on reliable authority that dredging operations have removed most of this and exposed a hard, clay bottom with excellent holding ground.

While many large boats tie up at the Oxford Boatyard, where gas, diesel fuel, hauling, repairs, and other facilities and services are provided, boats drawing less than 6 feet can usually find a slip at one of the smaller yards. Cutts and Case have maintained Ralph Wiley's fine reputation for superior boat building and repair work. Ralph retired in 1966 after more than 30 years as one of the Bay's most creative yacht designers and builders.

Just beyond is Crockett Bros., with an excellent layout, including a moving lift, repairs, etc. Shannahan's Marine Yard is at the end of the creek. Bates Marine Basin is on the east shore.

For yacht facilities, as well as a snug harbor, Oxford is unsurpassed on the Eastern Shore. But it has more than these; it has charm and "atmosphere." You can tie up at the Town Creek Marina and Restaurant, at the foot of Tilghman Street on Town Creek, and have a fine meal piped aboard.

The principal street in Oxford is named after Robert Morris, father of the famous financier of the Revolution. The elder Morris was a leading citizen of colonial Oxford, and at one time was a colorful Captain of the Port. On the southwest side of this street is a famous grapevine planted in 1775 and still bearing fruit. The Robert Morris Inn has been renovated, with a colonial atmosphere, a cocktail lounge, and excellent food. Yachtsmen, drop in!

Oxford is relatively easy to reach by land, and you can fly into Easton, 10 miles away, so it is a place where you can meet guests or pick up a charter boat.

b. *The Tred Avon above Oxford* (*12266*). There are too many creeks with good anchorages in them for us to do more than mention a few between Oxford and Easton Point, about 9 miles upriver, to which about 6 feet can be carried.

(*1*) *Plaindealing Creek* (*12266*). On the west shore, this creek is long, narrow, and more private than Oxford. A good anchorage can be found about halfway up, in 6 or 7 feet. Though there is some sweep to the north and south, the creek is well protected from seas.

(*2*) *Goldsborough Creek* (*12266*). On the east shore, this creek has fine anchorages around the bend in 7 or 8 feet. On our first visit many years ago, we saw a yacht aground on the long 3-foot shoal at the entrance and lost our ambition to go in ourselves. The entrance didn't look easy on the old charts. Later we went in without trouble, and enjoyed a pleasant overnight anchorage in 8 feet off the dock on the north shore. Otwell, a famous old house, called "one of the finds of the Eastern Shore," is situated on the point north of Goldsborough Creek.

(*3*) *Trippe Creek* (*12266*). This large creek on the east bank has two locally marked shoals at the entrance, and half a dozen fine anchorages in protected waters beyond. Several well-known Chesapeake yachtsmen have moorings in the creek, which is a favorite rendezvous spot for the Sailing Club and other Bay organizations. Our favorite places to anchor for the night are in the entrance to Snug Harbor on the north shore, and in the bight east of Deepwater Point in a Maxfield Parrish setting. This is a "favorite anchorage" for many Eastern Shore cruising yachtsmen.

(4) *Martins Cove* (*12266*). Here is a tiny gem of a creek (which you can miss if you don't look sharply) off a large yellow house, formerly The Oak Haven Inn. A lawn goes down to the water in front of the house and a large oak tree overhangs a tiny creek at the end of the cove to the south. This intriguing harbor, unnamed on the chart, is known locally as Martins Cove.

You can find it to the port as you go up the river, just above Fl. R-10 and below N-12. The chart shows 7 feet about halfway up the cove and our sounding confirmed this. A Norman-style house is on the northern shore. The two forks, each with 5 feet of water, give the creek the shape of a Y.

(5) *Double Mills and Long Point* (*12266*). We found a number of large yachts, from the Corinthian Yacht Club of Philadelphia, at anchor just north of Double Mills Point and in the bight between that point and Long Point one night, but this is usually a quiet anchorage and a first-class place for the night except in northeasters or easterlies. It is usually cool in summer.

(6) *Maxmore Creek* (*12266*). This creek offers a good anchorage just north of Long Point; but keep close to Long Point and don't try leaving C-15 to port as you go in, as the can applies to the river, not the creek, and marks a long shoal extending two-thirds of the way across the river.

(7) *Peachblossom Creek* (*12266*). The name of this creek is hard to resist, and its attractions live up to its name. Some of the finest houses in the region are found along its shores. Best anchorages are in, or off, Le Gates Cove on the north bank, and in the bight to the southeast.

(8) *Dixon Creek* (*12266*). There is a private dock at the port side of the entrance of this creek. The land is relatively low and the point separating this fork from the main river to Easton is marshy. Keep well over to the west bank of the river as you go up and avoid the long shoal off Watermelon Point. Shipshead Creek, opposite Dixon, also has good anchorages.

On the point which separates Dixon Creek from the main river to Easton is the famous Manour of Ratcliffe, built in 1749 by Henry Hollyday (ancestor of the photographer H. Robins Hollyday) on land patented to Captain Robert Morris in 1659. The house is Georgian colonial and can be glimpsed from the main river behind a magnificent box garden.

(9) Easton Point (12266). Drafts up to 8 feet can be carried to the docks at Easton Point, where gasoline, oil, and water are obtainable. You can tie up in 6 feet of water at the Easton Point Marina. The large town of Easton, where all kinds of supplies and shopping are available, is about a mile from Easton Point. At Easton is the Tidewater Inn, one of the best hotels on the coast.

7. Choptank River from the Tred Avon to Cambridge (12266). Two of the outstanding creeks on the Eastern Shore—Island and La Trappe—are on the Choptank between Oxford and Cambridge. If your yacht draws over 4 feet or if you want privacy, either of these creeks is to be preferred to Cambridge for overnight.

a. Island Creek (12266). The entrance to Island Creek is only about a mile above C-1 at the entrance to the Tred Avon. Chart 12266 shows 5 feet in the dredged and well-lighted entrance channel. Once you are through the channel, Island Creek is easy to navigate and in most parts deep water goes close to the shore. The only places where you have to watch your depths carefully are at the last two points to the north, or northern bank, near the head of the creek. The second of these shoals, to the north, where the creek forks, projects farther southward than the chart indicates.

The best anchorages on the creek are as follows:

(1) In what looks like a tiny cove just around the point to starboard of the entrance. Actually there is room for several boats. This, however, is exposed to a sweep to the northeast. An intriguing spot!

(2) Well up the first long branch of the creek at its northern side in 8 or 10 feet; but this isn't as snug as farther up.

(3) In the bight across the creek and about opposite the "K" of Island Creek as shown on the chart.

(4) If you don't draw over 3 feet you can go to the end of the northern fork, where Kenneth Millett, well-loved yachtsman who died in Hurricane Carol at Padanaram, Mass., used to have a boatyard.

There are several interesting estates along the shores of the creek. It is a pretty place, but you will have to go to Oxford or Cambridge for supplies.

b. La Trappe Creek (12266). This is one of the finest creeks on the Bay, with a miniature Sandy Hook to port of the entrance, behind which you can anchor in 7 feet of water. Give the end of the spit a good berth. The sandy beach is no longer available for swimming, unless you obtain special permission in advance from the owner. Too many thoughtless boatmen have littered the area with beer cans and refuse from beach parties in the past. If supplies are needed, Cambridge is only 4 miles away, or they can be obtained at Oxford on the way.

The entrance to this creek is marked by a large, conspicuous, green lighted beacon, looking like a small lighthouse, followed by a red day beacon. There is plenty of water in the entrance, 10 feet according to the chart.

Across from the sand spit, the shores are high and wooded, and above the white sand the glistening waters of the Choptank can be seen stretching southward for several miles.

At the end of a long road on a point above "Sandy Hook," on the west shore is Beauvoir, built in 1670, and owned in the 1950's by Thomas T. Firth, well known for his photographs of the Chesa-

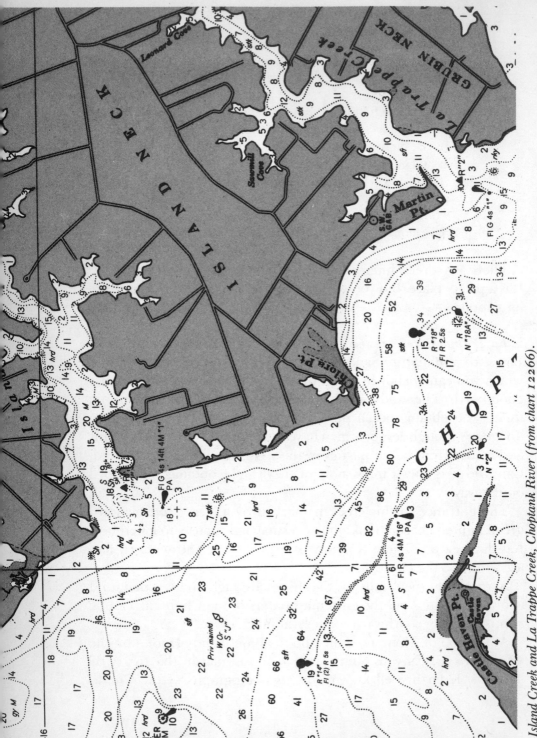

Island Creek and La Trappe Creek, Choptank River (from chart 12266).

peake. Mr. Firth was also the owner of Hampden, just beyond Saw Mill Cove on the same side of the creek. This is the oldest house in Talbot County, and was built along the substantial lines of English farmhouses of that day. Across the creek is Compton, built in 1770.

A delightful anchorage, with 6 feet, is to be found in Saw Mill Cove, about halfway up the creek. "A peaceful spot, an old hideout," said one cruising man of Saw Mill Cove.

It is possible to go up La Trappe Creek to La Trappe Landing, with at least 5 feet at MLW all the way.

Near the head of the creek you will find the Dickerson Boat Builders yard, moved here from Church Creek in the Little Choptank and now building fine fiberglass auxiliaries.

c. Castle Haven (12266). On the south shore of the Choptank, it offers good shelter behind the point from all directions except east to south. The wharf is privately owned and not open to the public.

8. Cambridge (12266). This historic waterfront city has much to offer cruising sailors. In earlier editions we noted that Cambridge seemed to attract more power cruisers than sail. That was because the shallow entrance channels to Cambridge Creek and to the Yacht Club and Municipal Marina favored shoal draft vessels. But conditions have been improving dramatically ever since Cambridge embarked on its waterfront transformation in the late sixties and seventies. Now you will find enough water for most sailing craft and power cruisers, with attractive marine facilities at both locations.

The prominent white clubhouse of the Cambridge Yacht Club has occupied the northwest corner of the channel into the Municipal Basin since 1938, when the basin and surrounding park were completed. The clubhouse was a gift of Eugene Du Pont, and was designed to represent the superstructure of a ship. The club is hospitable to visiting yachtsmen from other clubs, but most of its slips, like those in the basin, are occupied by local boats. But it is worth checking with the dock masters, who may have a guest slip available.

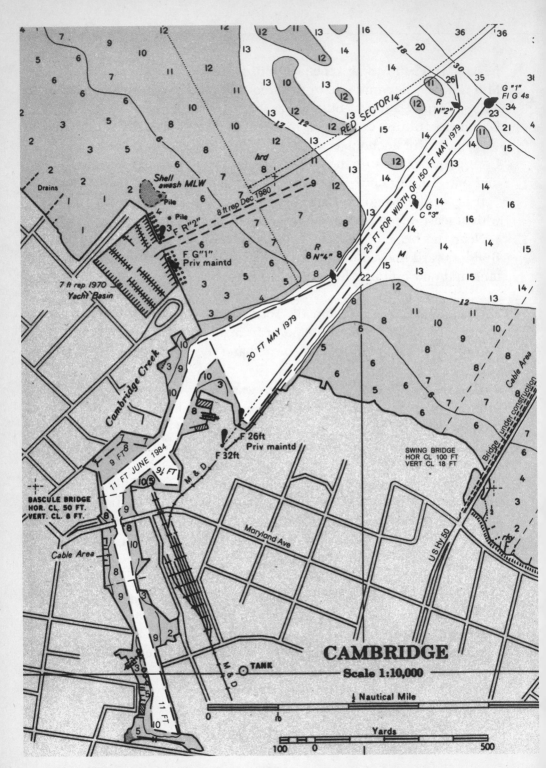

Cambridge Harbor (from chart 12266).

In approaching the yacht basin, head directly into the opening at right angles to the wall. Don't try to cut corners. The basin has red and green lights at the entrance. It is an attractive place.

The entrance to Cambridge Creek was originally dredged to 25 feet to accommodate tankers and small commercial vessels, but had shoaled to less than 20 feet by the 1980's. (See chart 14.) The triangle-shaped turning basin carries deep water to the entrance to the creek, but if you are coming around from the yacht basin be careful to keep well outside the shoal north of the bulkhead, preferably leaving N-4 to starboard to enter the dredged turning basin. The creek inside has been dredged to 13 feet as far as the bascule bridge. The former Cambridge Shipyard is now operated by Yacht Maintenance of Cambridge, with slips for transients and full service facilities, and the Phillips Oil Company Marina has a 600-foot service dock. Overnight berths may be hard to find on summer weekends. The Johnson's Marine Center has dockage service, and Clayton's on the Creek has transient dockage for diners at its restaurant.

In the early fall you will find many old working skipjacks tied up in the harbor, waiting for the opening of the oyster dredging season on November 1.

A new highway bridge over Choptank River at Cambridge has a vertical clearance of 50 feet in the fixed mid-channel span. The bridge replaces the former swing span.

9. The Choptank above Cambridge (12268).

a. Warwick River—Secretary (12268). This has a well-marked, dredged channel with 5-foot depths (1985) to the storage and distributing depot of the Dorchester Oil Co., who will usually give permission to tie up at their dock in 10 feet just below the bridge. The Snug Harbor Marina offers such facilities as gas, water, ice, and a snack bar, and there is a small store nearby.

b. Cabin Creek (12268). If you have come this far upriver keep your eye open for this little creek to starboard, with its Poor Boys Yacht

Cambridge, on Choptank River. (Photo courtesy of BaySailor.)

Club at Suicide Bridge, and Uncle Joe's Place close by. You can carry 5 feet almost a mile to the privately maintained marker on the south bank.

c. *Choptank* (*12268*). Anchor in the channel. There is only a foot or two at low tide in the basin. An old-timer recalled steamboat days on the river: "I have seen seven steamboats on the Choptank at the same time, right from here. Them days have gone; they are just a memory. Three different lines had steamers on the river."

d. *Tuckahoe Creek* (*12268*). If you like poking around narrow streams among out-of-the-way marshes, you may enjoy this creek, 41 miles above the mouth of the Choptank. Chart 12268 makes it much easier to navigate than it used to be, when boatmen had to depend on the old small-scale charts which gave depths only to Tuckahoe Bridge.

This fixed bridge has a vertical clearance of 17 feet. Small craft which can get under this and draw no more than 5 feet may poke their way another 8 miles up this snakelike marshy creek, provided they can "smell out" the channel, which is unmarked.

If you try Tuckahoe Creek, you are a real enthusiast for gunk-holes. We know a veteran yachtsman who told us that he spent a quiet and interesting night between the triangular-shaped island on the second bend below Stony Point and a marshy point. It takes a good deal to discourage such yachtsmen.

CHAPTER SIX

HARBORS OF THE UPPER WESTERN SHORE—ABOVE POTOMAC RIVER

I. NORTHEAST RIVER (*12275*).

This river, like so many others on the Chesapeake, was first explored by Captain John Smith, who found that the narrow channel led only to the head of the Bay at what is now the town of North East. The river is out of the way for most boats cruising between the Chesapeake and Delaware Canal and Annapolis, but a dozen well-equipped marinas and two yacht clubs provide berthing facilities for many out-of-state boat owners who use this area as their gateway to the Chesapeake. Sailboat skippers complain about the narrow channel, but to those who cruise by power it offers no difficulty, and the high and lively shores compensate for the time required to make this side trip. To reach Charlestown, the principal port, it is necessary to follow a channel for 7 or 8 miles from Turkey Point along the edge of the Havre de Grace flats, more appealing to duck hunters than to yachtsmen. Some of the highest land on the Chesapeake is on Elk Neck.

One place to go is the well-equipped McDaniel Yacht Basin on Ford Run, Northeast Heights. An 8-foot channel leads into the basin. They have gas, diesel fuel, water, many slips, electricity, showers, toilets, an attractive marine supply store, telephone, repairs, hauling ramp, etc. Just to the south is the Northeast River Yacht Club with a fine restaurant and other facilities. Depth at the dock is 4½ feet. The Sailing Club of the Chesapeake visited the club in the late 1980's with more than 30 "guest boats," which were miraculously rafted in the tiny basin. The North East Yacht Sales Marina and Shelter Cove Yacht Basin are nearby, and the Bay Boat Works with slips is at Hance Point. At Charlestown are the Wellwood Yacht Club, Avalon Yacht Basin, and Charlestown Marina, all with good facilities. Since the holding ground is not good, a tie-up at one of these places is recommended.

II. SUSQUEHANNA RIVER—HAVRE DE GRACE (*12274*).

Like Northeast River, the Susquehanna can be reached only by a long run, about 6 miles, through a narrow channel bordering the Havre de Grace flats. The river is one of the prettiest on the Bay, and it is possible to continue up it as far as Port Deposit. The ConRail bridge has 52 feet of vertical clearance and opens with 24 hours of notice, should your boat require more. The overhead power cable, with a clearance of 127 feet, should pose no problem. The three fixed bridges you will encounter have a minimum clearance of 86 feet.

Havre de Grace itself is a convenient rendezvous for those coming by road or rail from the points between New York and Washington.

One of the most distinctive things about the Susquehanna among Chesapeake rivers is that it has some rocks. If New Englanders get homesick on the Chesapeake for a good rock, they can find one by running off the edge of the channel to the east just before coming

Concord Point Lighthouse, Havre de Grace. (Photo courtesy of Ed Smith.)

to the dredged yacht basin south of City Park. The rocks were carried to this point in the glacial age.

The granite lighthouse on Concord Point was an aid to navigation from the time it was built, in 1827, until 1975. Now it is a registered historic landmark, open for visitors on Sundays, 1–5 P.M., April through October, or by appointment, (301) 939-2165.

On this shore are the Penn's Beach Marina, the Havre de Grace Marina, and the Tidewater Marina, which, with 8 feet of depth at the dock, can accommodate deeper draft boats than the others.

A few moorings are available to visiting yachtsmen for overnight on the assumption that purchases are made of gas, etc. Groceries are obtainable about 2 blocks away; the stores are even open at certain times on Sunday.

The moorings at this spot are open for some distance to the north and south, though the extensive shoals break up any heavy seas. Some yachts anchor nearer the bridge, particularly if those on board want to do some shopping.

Motor cruisers drawing under 3 1/2 feet can anchor in the city of Havre de Grace Yacht Basin, south of City Park. A low island gives shelter from southerly seas if not winds. There is a dock at the park, apt to be swarming with people of all ages on holidays and week-ends. As may be gathered, the place is anything but private.

Most of the waterfront facilities have ramps for launching out-boards or trailer-cruisers. Half a dozen other boatyards and marinas are located across the river at Perryville, but Havre de Grace is more convenient for most cruising boats.

The Havre de Grace Track, where Man o' War once ran in a lovely setting, has gone. In September, 1781, Rochambeau's army camped here on their way to Yorktown.

III. SPESUTIE ISLAND TO SENECA CREEK (*12275, 12274*).

This area, which includes the Aberdeen Proving Grounds, is restricted to the public, though parts of Bush River and Gun-powder River are accessible on weekends and at certain other specified times. Current regulations are published in the *Coast Pilot*, and should be checked before entering the area. Patrol boats will direct you out of the danger area during periods of target practice, when shells send up geysers of water. Because of the restrictions, we are omitting from this guide any detailed description of 15 miles of the Western Shore, which have little to offer cruising boats and are much less attractive than the nearby harbors previously described on the Eastern Shore. Outboards and trailer-cruisers coming to the Chesapeake from the west will find launching ramps and small-craft facilities at Bauer's Trojan Harbor, or the Bush River Boat Works above the town of that name, beyond the bridge on Bush River, and at the Gunpowder Cove Marina at the head of Gunpowder River; but more accessible launching places are available at Havre de Grace or Middle River.

IV. MIDDLE RIVER (*12278 OR 12279*).

Middle River is headquarters for one of the most attractively located older yacht clubs on the Bay, the Baltimore Yacht Club. There isn't much to attract most visiting cruising boats farther up this "too-civilized" river, though there are marinas and boatyards at the head of the river, and in Norman, Dark Head, and other creeks. But there is a great deal to interest yachtsmen behind Sue Island, where the club has its piers, and on Sue Island, where the good-looking white clubhouse is perched on the highest part.

Entrance is made from the Bay channel southeast of Pooles Island between the flashing marker at Pooles Island Bar and the black and white nun 40-B a mile to the southwest. Proceeding northwesterly you will have no difficulty picking up the flashing red and green markers with radar reflectors between Spry Island (now totally submerged) and Hart-Miller Island (the two islands are joined now by a small beach, constructed when the 1,000-acre spoil impoundment was created on the eastern side of the islands), and the quick-flashing R-4 south of Bowley Bar at the mouth of Middle River. If you are approaching from the south, give the shoal off Booby Point a wide berth. From the channel entrance at R-4 you should be able to run almost due west to the lighted entrance marker in Sue Creek, but keep a sharp eye on the shoal off Turkey Point, which reaches farther out than shown on the chart. Once you are inside the creek you'll find at least 6 feet off the end of the 5 Yacht Club piers, and 5 feet in the creek. The best anchorage, according to the club dock master, is in the bight west of the piers and north of the point marked "CR" on chart 12279.

The club has no transient slips available, unless you know a member who has made arrangements in advance for you to visit the club. Fuel and ice are usually available, however, and the dock master can direct you to marinas in the area where other supplies may be available. One of the newest and best facilities is located in Galloway Creek, back of Bowley Point, about a mile north of Sue Island. Hawk Cove is exposed to the north, but provides good anchorages in 8 to 10 feet of water between Hart-Miller Island and Rocky Point at the entrance to Back River. From the anchorage, you can wade—if you have a shallow draft boat—or dinghy ashore (no public docks) to walk or picnic (tables and fire ring grills provided) or camp in the wooded area on Hart Island. The area is crowded. A 6-mph speed limit within 250 yards of the island is enforced by the marine police, and park rangers oversee things shoreside.

V. BACK RIVER (*12278* OR *12279*).

The entrance to Back River passes through Hawk Cove and not far from the Baltimore Yacht Club headquarters at Sue Island, which is a preferable anchorage. Strangers find the numerous unmarked shoals difficult, and the river has few attractions for visiting cruising boats. A number of boatyards and marinas up the river provide services and facilities for local craft.

VI. PATAPSCO RIVER AND BALTIMORE (*12278 OR 12279, 12281*).

This is the river that leads to Baltimore, one of the nation's largest seaports. It's a busy river, full of ocean carriers and commercial traffic. In earlier editions we noted that most cruising yachts bypassed Baltimore in favor of better small-craft harbors on both sides of the Bay. But no longer is Baltimore neglected by yachtsmen. With the development of Baltimore's historic Inner Harbor, yachts are coming from far and near to sample one of the most exciting urban anchorages in North America.

Here on the shores of this same harbor the city of Baltimore was founded in 1729, and much of Maryland's maritime history took place. It was an important shipbuilding center in colonial times, and a thriving port during successive eras of sail and steam.

Today a spectacular transformation of the old inner harbor has emerged from more than a decade of waterfront reconstruction and mid-city redevelopment. Cruising sailors who visit the port of Baltimore now find an overflowing cornucopia of historic landmarks and modern waterfront facilities. On the way up the river you will pass Fort McHenry, where you may be able to tie alongside the wharf for a visit to the historic site where the "Star Spangled Banner" had its inspiration in the bombardment of September 13–14, 1814.

Continuing a few miles to the Inner Harbor, you will find many reminders of the area's seafaring past. Less than a mile beyond Fort McHenry you will pass Fells Point to starboard. Fells Point is a maritime landmark now being redeveloped as a downtown yachting center. Scarcely 1½ miles beyond Fells Point you enter the Inner Harbor, with its multiple attractions: the famous old frigate *Constellation*, the National Aquarium, and harborside shops and restaurants of all kinds.

There are seven or eight bays, creeks, and branches leading off Patapsco River, all navigable and all offering marine facilities of

Baltimore Inner Harbor. (Photo courtesy of BaySailor.)

some sort. The most interesting to cruising boats are Bodkin Creek, Rock Creek, and Stony Creek, all on the south side, and the Northwest Branch leading to Fells Point and the Inner Harbor. The other main branches—Old Road Bay and Bear Creek, on the north shore, and Curtis Creek on the south side of the Patapsco, are essentially commercial, although they provide many service and repair facilities and are used by local small craft.

Entering the Patapsco from the north or south, you can follow the well-marked ship channels to their junction between Sparrows Point and Bodkin Creek.

1. Bodkin Creek (12278 or 12279). This creek provides the most convenient anchorage on the Patapsco and, with Sue Island and

Rock Creek, one of the three best anchorages above Gibson Island on the Western Shore of the Chesapeake. It is easy to enter if you don't try to cut corners at Bodkin Point and are careful to follow the line of buoys. Keep close to Cedar Point at the entrance to avoid the 1-foot spot to starboard.

The best and most attractive anchorages are south of what is called Spit Neck on the chart and Split Neck locally. The former Kastner and Humm boatyard on Graveyard Point is now run by Ventnor Marine Service, which has installed new piers with many slips, used almost entirely by powerboats. The Hammock Island Marina nearby has slips for sailboats, and offers wet storage. When we were there we couldn't find anybody who had heard of Graveyard Point, except a boat owner who had read it on the chart. Since

Fells Point, on Patapsco River. (Photo courtesy of BaySailor.)

Main Creek is called Deep Creek, we felt like members of *The New Yorker*'s old Department of Utter Confusion before we had been there long.

Other good anchorages are in the bight beyond the point or in Jubb Cove farther up. The latter is very pretty, with steep shores and tall trees.

Back Creek, the northern tributary of Bodkin, is deep but more difficult for strangers to enter; however, if you avoid the unmarked shoals at the mouth, you will find an attractive anchorage in 9 feet just east of Hickory Point. Close by is one of the oldest farmhouses in Maryland. Hancock's Resolution, built in the mid-1600's and now owned by Historic Annapolis. A security guard watches over the house. Steps have been taken by Historic Annapolis to halt its decline, but the house has not yet been restored. Woods have been allowed to grow up around it, somewhat hiding it from view now.

2. *Rock Creek* (*12278 or 12279*). The entrance is easily identified by the "White Rocks," said to look like the back of a partially submerged elephant. Rock Creek is the principal center of yachting activities on the Patapsco. There, on Fairview Point, is the former summer station and now *the* headquarters of the Maryland Yacht Club. There are several piers here with many slips that have electricity. Gas, water, ice, and soft drinks are obtainable and a spare mooring may be available. The club has a dining room and visiting yachtsmen may have their meals there, with permission from the club, which is hospitable to members of other recognized yacht clubs.

The former Rogers Marina, now called Fairview Marine Corp., is located just inside the narrow point extending southward about halfway up Wall Cove. There is deep water at their pier, where gas, diesel fuel, water, electricity, marine supplies, etc., are available as well as a number of slips, usually occupied. Many large auxiliaries and motor cruisers come to this well-equipped place. Rogers invented a spar turning lathe, capable of turning spars up to 80 feet; it was worth seeing. There is a very good anchorage off the

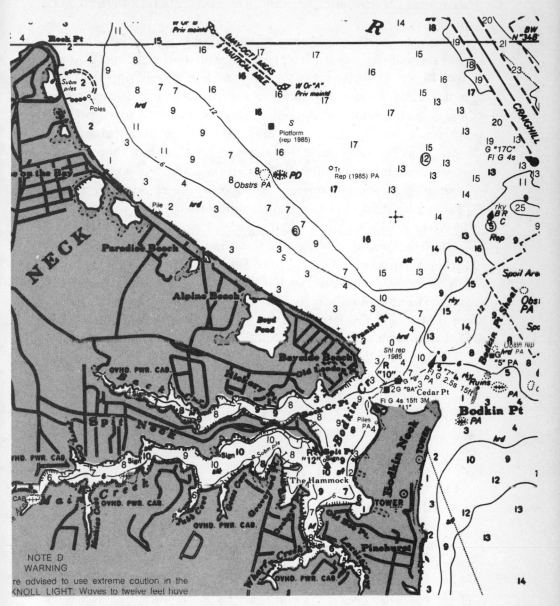

Bodkin Creek, Patapsco River (from chart 12278).

marina in 11 feet, where the point offers protection from northwest squalls.

Across the creek is an array of motorboats along the shores of active summer resorts at Riviera Beach, Sunset Beach, and Cottage Grove Beach. If you are very sociable and like to be in the midst of a great deal of activity, and if you want ideal facilities in very good shelter, Rock Creek will appeal to you. If you want more privacy, with fewer houses and more trees, you have a better chance of finding it at Bodkin Creek. These two creeks, both of them attractive with much to offer, are the best on the Patapsco. They are also the most easily accessible from Chesapeake Bay's open waters.

Farther up Rock Creek are several other yacht clubs and marinas: the White Rocks Yachting Center, with a long fuel dock and many slips on the point southeast of Maryland Yacht Club; the Oak Harbor Marina on the east side of Rock Creek on a sheltered cove with 12 feet (they have a travel lift capable of handling powerboats up to 50 feet and a railway that can haul sailboats up to 50 feet and 6 feet draft); and the Pasadena Yacht Yard on the west side of the creek, also with slips, gas, and hauling facilities.

The nearest store is about a mile away from the yacht club, but provisions can be ordered by telephone and delivered.

3. Stony Creek (12279). This creek is marked by the prominent rocks at the entrance, which should be left to port. The *Coast Pilot* advises favoring the west side of the channel due to shoaling from Stony Point.

The creek is fairly attractive but too close to summer resorts crowded with houses to suit those who like privacy. A good anchorage is in the large bight to the right just after entering. There are a number of private piers along the shores and a nice sandy beach. Several stores are in the settlement nearby. Stony Creek Boat Works, with slips, gas, and other facilities, is just inside of the drawbridge. There are other boatyards and marinas in Nabbs Creek and Back Cove, where there are well-protected anchorages. Boats can be hauled drawing up to 6 feet and gasoline and other supplies are available. This is a deep creek with many snug bights but, like other ports near a large city, it is too popular with the outboard fraternity to encourage overnight cruisers.

4. *Jones Creek on Old Road Bay* (*12278 or 12279*). This creek is almost never used by cruising people because of its industrial surroundings. There is a narrow, not very well marked entrance between the shoals. Water is available at a pier and supplies are a short distance away. There is a large iron and steel works, the Bethlehem Shipbuilding Co. plant, and a railroad terminus on Sparrows Point at the entrance of the creek, which gives a cue to the scenery.

5. *Bear Creek* (*12278 or 12279*). Although there are a number of boatyards and marinas on Bear Creek and its tributaries, we find the area too commercial to attract many cruising boats. Lynch Cove is the largest and deepest of the tributaries, but the water is discolored by pollution from the nearby Bethlehem plant, and you must pass through three bridges to reach the cove.

Several large boatyards and marinas are operating in Lynch Cove. If you need emergency repairs in the Patapsco, this is a good place to look for help. You'll find leading firms listed in the *Boating Almanac*.

6. *Curtis Creek* (*12281, 12278, or 12279*). There is little to attract cruising boats to Curtis Creek, which is very commercial, dirty, and inhospitable to small craft. The Coast Guard has one of its largest East Coast bases near the entrance to the creek, with a shipbuilding facility capable of turning out the latest types of steel and fiberglass CG vessels.

7. *Middle Branch* (*12281, 12278, or 12279*). This used to be important to yachtsmen because it was headquarters of the Maryland Yacht Club, whose large, good-looking clubhouse on attractive Broening Park was a welcome sight to the yachting fraternity as they

traveled along Highway 40. However, as we have pointed out, the clubhouse has long since been sold, and the site is now used for the South Baltimore General Hospital, which occupies most of the former park and clubhouse grounds.

Several marinas are located just around the point, close to the highway bridge, but most of the slips are used by Baltimore boat owners.

8. *The Inner Harbor and Fells Point* (*12278, 12279, 12282*). A nautical Rip Van Winkle would rub his eyes in amazement if he could come back to see the transformation of the old inner harbor and Fells Point. What was once the center of colonial shipping and

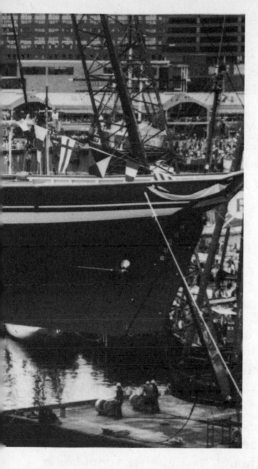

The new Pride of Baltimore II *being launched April 30, 1988, in Baltimore Inner Harbor. (Photo courtesy of Greg Pease.)*

shipbuilding, and later the busy dock area of steamboat days, has become a maritime civic center, a historic memorial, and an active rendezvous point for seagoing visitors and landlocked strollers and tourists alike.

But the Inner Harbor is much more than any of these. Three sides of the rectangular basin are lined with ships of all sizes. The masts of the old frigate *Constellation* dominate the northwest corner of the basin; smaller tall ships occupy the piers where the *Pride of Baltimore II* ties up when in port; and several hundred sailing yachts and power cruisers are berthed at the Inner Harbor Marina at the southeast corner of the basin. Large cruise steamers base in the harbor, while small sightseeing craft move around the river waterfront. Visiting yachts may tie up at the seawall or anchor in the basin with permission of the harbormaster, whose office is just back of the large ship piers on the southwest side of the seawall.

If you don't find a berth or an anchorage in the Inner Harbor, try Fells Point, where the Anchorage Marina has transient slips at its large and expanding facility. The Fells Point area is less than 2 miles from the Inner Harbor by water or land, and has its own shoreside attractions in local pubs, inns, and restaurants. A water taxi operates between the two harbors.

VII. MAGOTHY RIVER AND GIBSON ISLAND (*12278*, *12282*).

For boats heading down the Bay, the entrance to the Magothy is 5 miles south of the Patapsco and about 6 miles north of Severn River and Annapolis. This is close to the center of the Chesapeake cruising grounds, and Magothy River offers some of the best creeks and harbors on the Bay.

While no one should cruise the Chesapeake without a visit to Gibson Island Harbor, the creeks and harbors on both sides of the river should not be overlooked. Although the shorefront population has increased rapidly over the past 30 years, urbanization has not spoiled this lovely river and its estuaries.

1. Gibson Island (*12282, 12279*). Just as Pulpit Harbor is the yachtsman's perfect harbor on the coast of Maine, and as Hadley or Quissett is to the Buzzards Bay area, so is Gibson Island to the Chesapeake.

Here in truth is a sailor's dream come true—one of America's most charming harbors and current headquarters for the Gibson Island Yacht Squadron.

In the first edition of this guide we needed more than a page to describe the entrance to the Magothy and the intricate channel

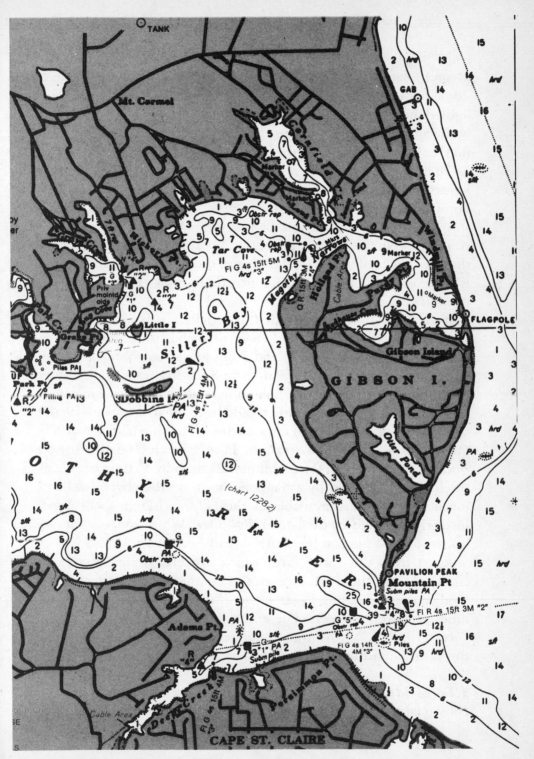

Gibson Island and Magothy River (from chart 12278).

(then largely unmarked) leading from Mountain Point through Magothy Narrows into the two protected harbors of Gibson Island. Today both the river entrance and inner channel are well marked by lighted beacons and buoys. Don't crowd Mountain Point Bar between the flashing beacons, and carry on to the large green marker before heading northwest toward the lighted beacon east of Dobbins Island. From there you can swing northeast to the two lighted beacons in the narrows between Long Point and Holland Point, and then follow the private markers maintained by the Gibson Island Club, around the bight inside Windmill Point, where you'll find yourself in a completely landlocked harbor among one of the finest fleets of yachts on the Chesapeake. Except in a hurricane, when seas could break over the eastern causeway, there is complete protection in all weather.

If the inner harbor is crowded (it usually is during the boating season) you can probably find room to anchor in the first cove to your right as you round Holland Point at the northern tip of the island. While the Gibson Island Yacht Squadron welcomes visitors from other recognized yacht clubs, it has only a few guest moorings, and arrangements for their use should be made in advance with the commodore or a member of the squadron. The club launch will take guests ashore on three blasts of the horn. The club boathouse and dock are located about the center of the causeway on the east side of the harbor, identified by a flagpole shown on the chart. Fuel and marine supplies are available at the Gibson Island Yacht Yard, formerly operated by the late H. R. "Buzz" White and now run by his son John White, on the south side of Redhouse Cove.

Apart from the Yacht Yard, which operates under concession from the club, there are no stores or commercial activities of any kind on the island, but, instead, one of the most attractive communities we have ever seen. The entire island is the property of the Gibson Island Club, the unique and well-run parent organization of the Yacht Squadron, founded in 1921 by W. Stuart Symington, Jr.

2. Cornfield Creek (12282), North Shore of Magothy. This is north of Gibson Island and less attractive than the island anchorages or other creeks on the Magothy. Keep in the middle as you go in the narrow, unmarked channel. There is a wharf with 8 feet, also gas and water, just inside the entrance on Long Point, where some docks are shown on the chart. No supplies are available nearer than half a mile away.

3. *Dobbins Island* (*12282*), *North Shore of Magothy*. This little wooded island lies at the southwest end of Sillery Bay and about a mile west of Gibson Island. The bight between Dobbins and Little Island is a favorite anchorage for cruising boats, and is often the scene of yacht club rendezvous. Don't try to cross the bar at the west end of Sillery Bay; it shoals to less than the 3 feet shown on the chart. There's a sandy beach that extends off the western tip of Dobbins, with a high cliff behind it.

4. *Deep Creek* (*12282*), *South Shore of Magothy*. This is the first creek to port after passing Persimmon Point at the entrance of Magothy River. We wouldn't suggest stopping, since the creeks farther up are better. Fairwinds Marina is on the southeast shore near the lighted beacon at the narrow entrance, and has fuel, slips, travel lift, and launching ramp. The channel above this is narrow and winding, with locally maintained stake markers leading to another marina.

5. *Forked Creek* (*12282*), *South Shore of Magothy*. This is a lovely spot, bordered on the east shore to the fork by the beautiful Lynch estate. Opposite the sharp point which is about halfway along the east shore, and almost in the middle of the entrance to the fork, are two privately maintained markers, which you leave close to starboard on entering the east fork. The chart does not show the depth at the entrance, but our soundings showed at least 5 feet in the channel, and 10 to 14 feet inside the east fork.

Keep in the middle in going up the east, or main, fork. There are several good anchorages with perfect shelter and over 10 feet of water south of the sharp point. The surrounding land is high and wooded, with few houses and no commercial activities. No landing facilities or supplies are available. Stay out of Coolspring Cove; the entrance is too shallow, although it is deep inside.

6. *Broad Creek* (*12282*), *North Shore of Magothy*. The entrance is now marked by red and green buoys and there is deep water to the tiny island at the head. Favor the east shore to avoid a 2-foot spot north of Rock Point. The high wooded shores are very attractive and the creek is seldom overcrowded.

7. *Blackhole Creek* (*12282*), *North Shore of Magothy*. This tight little harbor is the home of the Potapskut Sailing Association, which maintains an attractive clubhouse with slips and moorings for over 30 cruising sailboats and launching ramps for a fine fleet of small class sailboats. Visiting yachtsmen are welcome, even though there is not much room for anchorage off the club docks. The narrow entrance is well marked. The best anchorage is just behind the small island.

8. *Mill Creek* (*12282*), *South Shore of Magothy*. This is another fine anchorage. Though not so private as Forked Creek, it has facilities that are lacking at the other creek. Leave the uncharted red barrel to starboard where the creeks separate; then swing fairly wide to avoid the shoal with piles outside of the boatyard docks to port. Don't head for these docks until you have passed between the second private red barrel and a stake. Then swing slowly to port and head for the dock of the Ferry Point Yacht Basin on the east shore just inside the Mill Creek entrance. There is 10 feet at the dock, which has gas, water, electricity, and a few slips. A good anchorage is in the middle beyond the boatyard. Favor the starboard shore in going up.

9. *Dividing Creek* (*12282*), *South Shore of Magothy*. This creek, like Mill Creek, provides perfect shelter and is also a pretty place, though there are many more houses along its banks than at Mill. After leaving the red barrel to starboard, favor the starboard (west) shore in getting up the creek, as there is a sandbar not shown clearly on the chart off the prominent point about halfway up.

One of the many good anchorages is in 7 feet just inside the entrance to the left (east fork) near the head of the creek. The fairly high land—for the Chesapeake—and the tall trees make this a particularly inviting spot. There is a boatyard and marina part way up the creek.

The store which stood on the Crystal Beach shore of Dividing Creek, near the entrance to Mill and Dividing creeks, has been leveled, and a new house is being built on the site.

10. Cypress Creek (12282), South Shore of Magothy. Two green beacons show the way into this creek, where there are good anchorages in each fork. To the port, before the creek forks, are two boatyards and a third marina across the fork. If you need supplies, Cypress Marine (to port) will help you out with transportation to nearby grocery and convenience stores and restaurants.

The creek has one serious drawback. It is too popular, and the shores are lined with houses and private docks, with the swarms of inevitable outboards—even in April, when we were there.

11. Cattail Creek (12282), South Shore of Magothy. This is, or was, an especially attractive creek. The shores are fairly high and wooded, with most of the houses tucked away unobtrusively among the trees.

The chart shows a "marine railway" just outside the entrance of the creek, on the south shore of the river. This is no longer there, as the owner of the private pier explained, but two private lighted markers are now maintained off the pier. In entering Cattail Creek watch carefully for the very long shoal which projects southeast of Focal (formerly Falcon) Point, and is now marked on the north, or river, side by government marker 15. These changing private and public markers bring to mind the time we explored Cattail Creek for the first edition of this guide.

"A buoy is supposed to mark the end of this point," said our local informant, "but it's been washed away to the wrong place. See it up there where it's doing no good. I suppose they'll put it back some-day." That was before 1950 and "they" meant the Magothy River Association, which looked after private buoys among other things. But strangers could never be quite sure whether the private markers were in the right place or on which side they should be left. Today most of the main rivers and creeks are well marked by the Coast Guard.

After you have skirted the shoal off Focal Point, favor the star-board (north) shore. The point across the creek is high, wooded, and conspicuous.

A very snug anchorage is well up the creek in 7 feet just after the creek turns south beyond the 9-foot spot (chart 12282).

12. The Upper Magothy—Above Cattail Creek (12282). The Upper Magothy beyond Cattail Creek is narrow and above the Focal Point bar offers no especial difficulties until you are well upriver, if you keep in the middle.

On the point on the east shore, just beyond Focal Point, is an Indian totem pole, made and put there, we were told, by the boys of a school founded by Grace Church, formerly located on this point.

A white boathouse, on Boundary Stone Point, marks the spot where the Magothy proper forks to the left and Cockey Creek to the right. The Magothy above here is too cluttered up with houses, much too civilized to be as attractive as it is below. However, two of the creeks—Old Man and Cockey—are of special interest. At River-dale is a launching ramp and a fine restaurant where you can tie up.

a. Old Man Creek (12282). This creek is pretty and much more attractive than the main river at this point. The houses are larger and not as crowded together. There are good anchorages in the first and second bights on the south shore. There is a small boatyard well up the creek.

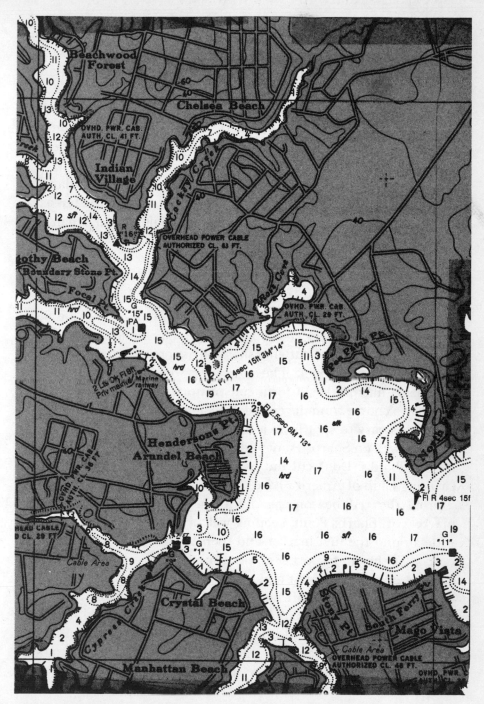

Upper Magothy River (from chart 12282).

b. Cockey Creek (12282, 12279). The banks are high, but while the trees are more prominent than the houses on the east bank, the reverse is true on the west shore. When we were there a building boom seemed to be in progress. The banks are so high and the houses so near the edge we had a feeling that, if anchored below, we couldn't take a spoonful of soup in the cabin without people in the houses knowing whether we spilled it. Opposite Indian Village is a marina with slips, gas, supplies, etc.

If you like being "the sinecure of all eyes," as one Mrs. Malaprop said, you'll enjoy it here. For our taste, the creek is better as a convenient and attractive summer resort for Baltimoreans than it is as a cruising objective.

VIII. WHITEHALL BAY AND CREEK (12282, 12283).

South of the Chesapeake Bay Bridge and before entering Severn River you will pass Hackett Point (which should be allowed a wide berth around the outlying shoal), which marks the entrance to Whitehall Bay and Creek. The entrance is wide, but the deep-water channel is narrow. Head for a conspicuous red beacon off North Shoal on a course from the end of Tolly Point. This marker, which is not always easy to spot from a distance, will appear in line with a concrete wall on Sharps Point and to the right of some conspicuous red sandbanks. Don't cut the North Shoal. Even members of the Cruising Club of America have tried this without success.

From the red beacon, head for the red and green channel markers off Sharps Point, keeping well off the shoal to port. Swing wide around the first marker and then head so as to keep the red beacon farther in to port. Behind a miniature Sandy Hook to the south is one of the tiniest and snuggest deep-water coves we have ever seen. You can dive off the inside of the sand spit into a passage not much more than a boat's length wide, unless a yacht with a deep keel is so close to the sand that she gets in your way. We have seen two large and deep draft yachts almost block the passage when tied up alongside each other at the dock. The deep water continues inside of the little cove.

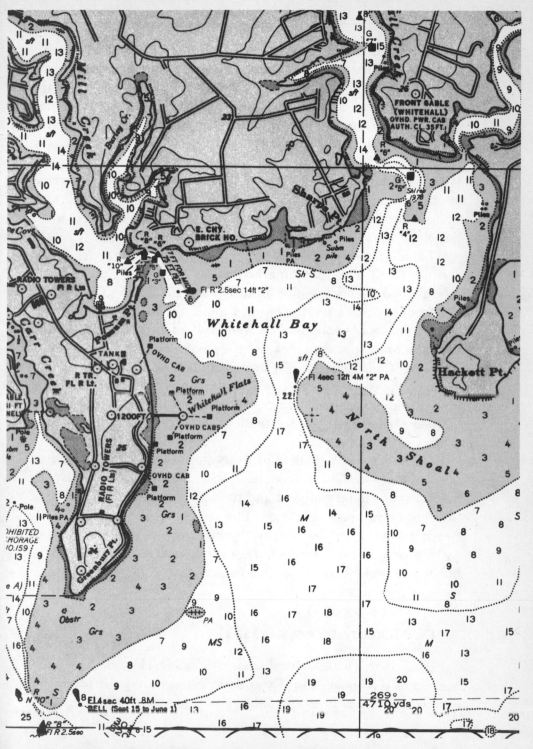

Whitehall Bay, Whitehall Creek, and Mill Creek (from chart 12282).

Carleton Mitchell, former rear commodore of the Cruising Club of America, once owned the beautiful estate which rises above the cove, where he then moored his famous yawl *Finisterre*. Since the cove is very small and private, we suggest that visiting yachtsmen anchor farther up the creek on one of the many snug spots on the upper forks. On the east side of the entrance to the creek, facing Sharps Point, you will get just a glimpse of the famous portico of Whitehall Manor, built by the last colonial governor of Maryland just before the American Revolution. Owned today by Mr. and Mrs. Charles Scarlett, it has been restored to its original condition and is one of the great houses of Maryland.

Whitehall Creek is navigable for about 2 miles above Sharps Point and the shoals are clearly marked as far as Ridout Creek, where several good anchorages are found. When the Sailing Club of the Chesapeake holds a rendezvous in Ridout, the rafted yachts almost reach from shore to shore. The Whitehall Yacht Yard is farther up the main branch of the creek, on the east side, and there are snug anchorages with 7 and 8 feet around the bend beyond. The yard, formerly known as Ritter's, has been expanded in recent years, and now provides slips for over 100 boats, and a railway capable of hauling yachts up to 50 feet with 8-foot draft. Engine and hull repairs are available.

Whitehall Bay itself, behind Hackett Point, is a favorite rendezvous point for Chesapeake Bay yachtsmen, and you will usually find a fleet of handsome sail and power yachts anchored or rafted together on summer weekends. The sandy beach belongs to Holly Beach Farm, owned by "Peggy" Spence, and should not be used without permission. The anchorage is exposed to southerly winds, but is recommended by local boatmen as a cool spot for warm summer evenings.

IX. MEREDITH CREEK (*12282*).

Don't try this without local advice, if not local knowledge. There are unmarked shoals and if you don't get aground outside of the entrance on the 1- or 2-foot spots, you probably will inside. It is a lovely spot, though, if you can make it. "Nothing about Meredith Creek is ever in a hurry . . . there is peace and serenity that comforts a sailor's soul," wrote Carleton Mitchell.

X. MILL CREEK (*12282*).

This large creek on the eastern side of Whitehall Bay, back of the radio towers, has a narrow dredged entrance—now well marked—which opens up into an attractive anchorage just around the last marker, in the entrance to Burley Creek. Once inside, there is 10 to 14 feet of water to Martins Cove and above. Cruising boats will find less developed places to explore up the Severn.

XI. SEVERN RIVER AND ANNAPOLIS (*12282, 12283*).

The Severn is one of the most beautiful rivers on the Bay and also one of the most rewarding for upriver exploration. It is likewise the easiest to identify from a distance, with the high radio towers on its northern entrance point. The shores are high and wooded; the creeks are unexcelled in snugness and charm, though some of them can be hot in summer. Five miles up the river is Round Bay, wide enough for good sailing, small enough for protection against heavy seas. Don't miss a trip up the "Hudson River of Maryland," as someone has called it. The lower Severn bridge opens on call, except during rush hours. The old railroad bridge between the new (Route 50) and old lower Severn River highway bridges has been completely removed.

1. Carr Creek (*12283*). This creek near the Navy radio towers is no longer closed to navigation, but the dredged entrance is narrow and boats are warned to keep out when the red flag is flying.

2. Chesapeake Harbor (*12283*). This newly developed yacht basin is on the south side of the Severn less than a mile before the entrance to Back Creek. A new dredged channel with private markers leads to a large basin with all the facilities. You can identify the place by the condos that cluster around it.

3. *Back Creek* (12283). This creek on the west side offers the first good anchorage upon entering Severn River and is the most accessible port in the area when you are cruising along the Bay in a hurry; it provides easy access to Annapolis as well as many boating facilities. While it does not have the rare charm of Spa Creek, it has much to offer, both of facilities and fine anchorages.

Head for the outer, lighted beacon 1 off Chinks Point. After you have left all three black beacons to port, an active, busy shore opens

Back Creek and Spa Creek, divided by the Eastport Peninsula. (Photo courtesy of BaySailor.)

up to starboard, crowded with boat slips and a continuous line of marinas, with no hint of the peaceful and lovely anchorages farther up.

Immediately to starboard are Horn Point Boat Harbor Marina and Lilly Brothers Yacht Yard (formerly Vosbury's), furnishing slips, water, electricity, toilets, showers, etc., and 9 feet of water, but little privacy. The cove beyond is lined with large and small boatyards and marinas, with several large new apartment houses farther up on the Eastport side. Eastport itself is developing rapidly, and stores, shopping centers, and restaurants are now only a few blocks distant.

Anchoring for the night is possible, but not advisable, in the lower

part of the creek, where traffic may be heavy. Farther up the creek you may find room to anchor in the bight off the eastern side opposite the Watergate apartments, or above the point and shoal in 7 feet of water. But these can no longer be called "snug" or "quiet" anchorages, as they were when the first edition of this guide came out.

Many new marinas and boatyards have appeared on Back Creek in the past 15 years, and older yards have changed hands. In 1987 we counted over 1,200 slips or moorings for sail and power yachts in this one creek alone, or almost half of the total dock facilities in Annapolis as a whole. And yet it was difficult at times for visitors to find overnight dockage anywhere in this busy port. Some of the larger marinas beyond the Yacht Yard at the entrance are to starboard: Aloha Yacht Sales and Service, the Seafarer's Yacht Club, and the Mears Marina and Severn River Yacht Club, with 300 slips, mostly occupied by cruising sailboats. They have tennis courts and a swimming pool available to slip holders. The Watergate Marina is reserved just for the apartment residents. To port, as you enter the creek, are three large well-equipped marinas and boatyards: Annapolis Landing Marina, nearest the entrance; Port Annapolis Marina, opposite the Watergate apartments; and Bert Jabin's Yacht Yard near the head of the creek. Among other boating facilities within reach of Back Creek are chandlers, sail makers, mast and rigging firms, electronic and marine hardware stores. You can arrange for day sailing or weekend charters from Annapolis Sailing School, whose office is on Sixth Street, just behind the Mears Marina.

4. Annapolis (12282, 12283). It is hard to discuss Annapolis without sounding like a tourist guidebook or letting one's eloquence soar into the wild blue yonder. For interest, charm, snug anchorages, friendly people, all sorts of facilities, and historic landmarks, it is hard to beat.

As a base from which to cruise the Chesapeake—north, south, east, or west—it is unexcelled. From a quiet slip beside the willows

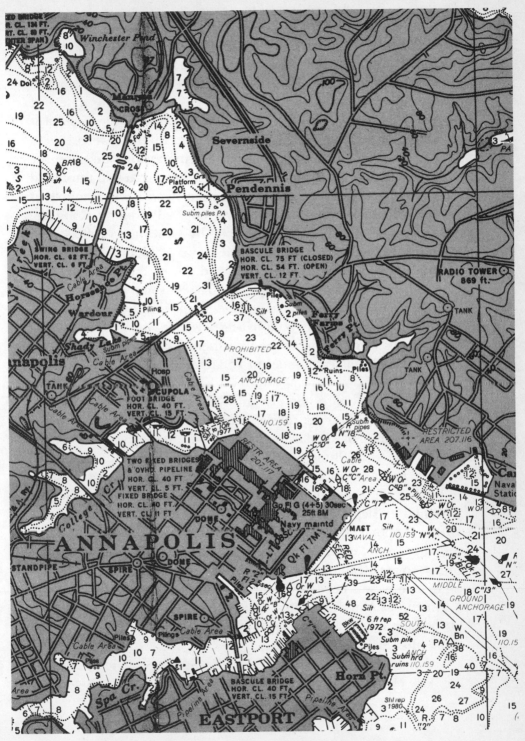

Severn River, Spa Creek, and Back Creek (from chart 12282).

of Spa Creek, it is 10½ miles northward to the mouth of the Magothy, or 14 miles to Gibson Island. In the other direction, to the mouth of the South River, it is only 9 miles, and 2 miles farther to Rhode and West rivers. Across the Bay, the best cruising waters of the Eastern Shore lie within a few hours' run. And if the weather is too rough for comfort on the Bay, take a trip up the Severn.

Once, on a weekend in spring, when storm warnings flew over the Naval Academy seawall and a torn sail during a trial trip reminded us that the red flag should be taken seriously, we spent a couple of days wandering about Annapolis. We enjoyed strolling along the intimate and friendly streets laid out by Governor Nicholson in 1693, and through the grounds of the Naval Academy; it was pleasant to drop by at Weems and Plath, and at Fawcett's (where charts may also be obtained). Perhaps we passed some of the famous colonial houses without knowing it, though we didn't miss Maryland's historic statehouse, built in 1775, where George Washington resigned his commission to the Continental Congress, which then met in the old senate chamber in 1784. We didn't consider it a lost weekend.

The entrance to the Severn and Annapolis has no particular difficulties; but don't get careless and cut corners just because you aren't a big ship, particularly off Horn Point. It took a stiff breeze to heel us over enough to get off—soon after our Chesapeake education had begun. Honor the Fl. 6 sec. white light that marks the shoal there now. The shoal marker should have a sign on it saying "George Washington Slept Here," because he did one stormy night in the 1780's. He notes in his diary that the boat carrying him and some of his party from Rock Hall to Annapolis went aground there and was unable to get off until the next morning. George slept with his boots on in case he was needed on deck during the stormy night.

Annapolis Harbor is almost too busy to provide a comfortable anchorage, but a few locations can be suggested for anchoring or tying up:

(1) In the main harbor at the outer entrance of Spa Creek, 20 moorings were placed in the anchorage area by the city of Annapolis in the fall

of 1987, and plans called for adding at least 20 more. Anyone using one of these moorings must pay a fee to the harbormaster, whose office is located on the City Dock. A dinghy landing is available in front of the Market House, at the end of the Market Slip (known locally as Ego Alley), and rest room facilities and showers are available in the building where the harbormaster is located. The area is well sheltered, except for about 3/4 mile to the northeast. Should you find room to anchor in this area, be advised that the holding ground is poor; the bottom is soft ooze.

The City Dock has slips, which are convenient for shopping and eating out, but it's hard to find one that's not in use.

(2) At the large Gulf dock operated by the Yacht Basin Company or their slips adjoining and northeast of the Annapolis Yacht Club, or at the prominently located Annapolis Hilton Inn, east of the Spa Creek Bridge, or at the Arnold C. Gay Yacht Yard, west of the bridge.

(3) Transient slips may be available at some of the yacht yards and marinas on the Eastport side of Spa Creek, including White Rocks Yachting Center, Annapolis City Marina, Pier 4 Marina, O'Leary's Seafood Restaurant, and the Annapolis Harbor Boat Yard, all east of the Spa Creek Bridge, and the Spa Creek Yacht Club Marina, Petrini Yacht Yard and Marina, and Sarles Boat and Engine Shop, all west of the bridge.

Water taxi service is available to all Annapolis anchorage areas.

Remember that depths in all of these anchorages may be reduced considerably below charted depths by any prolonged northwest blow, most frequent in spring or fall.

The Annapolis Yacht Club sometimes has dock or mooring space for members of recognized yacht clubs and, in any case, is most hospitable to visiting yachtsmen. This club was organized in 1886 as the Severn Boat Club and took its present name in 1937; it is one of the best-known yacht clubs on the Chesapeake and among the leaders in the promotion of yachting not only on the Bay but also outside. In 1939, it sponsored an ocean race from New London to Annapolis which was continued on alternate years after World War II, first from Newport to Annapolis, and then since the mid-1950's from the Maryland capital to Newport, under joint sponsorship of the Annapolis Yacht Club, Naval Academy Sailing Squadron, and the New York Yacht Club. The present clubhouse, built in 1962 on the site of the old club on the "town side" of Spa Creek by the bridge, has a fine restaurant and is a popular gathering place for Bay yachtsmen.

Several other active yacht clubs center their activities here. The Sailing Club of the Chesapeake, without a clubhouse but with many members from the Baltimore-Washington-Annapolis area, had almost 300 members and nearly 250 cruising sailboats in 1985 and has become an effective promoter of cruising on the Bay. The Severn Sailing Association, with its headquarters on Horn Point, has done an outstanding job in developing one-design sailing on the Chesapeake and in training new generations of small-boat sailors. They have been hosts of many regional, national, and international regattas on the Severn. The Maryland Capital Yacht Club, with dock and clubhouse facilities on Horn Point, welcomes visiting yachtsmen from other accredited clubs. The Eastport Yacht Club in Eastport and the Severn River Yacht Club on Back Creek are among the newer clubs that are active promoters of cruising and racing on the Bay.

The long and narrow City Dock Basin, properly known as the Market Slip but mostly referred to as Ego Alley, has been a center of maritime activity since colonial times, and is crowded today with fishing craft, crabbers, oyster tongers, and skipjacks in season. The channel is dredged to 6 feet at the bulkheads, and if you are lucky you may find a space to tie up long enough to purchase supplies nearby.

Marine supplies and provisions are available all around the Market Square, Dock Street, and Compromise Street. Fawcett's Boat Supplies, on Compromise Street next to the Hilton, has just about everything a boatman may need. Among eating places within walking distance are the Harbour House right on the waterfront, Maryland Inn on Church Circle, the Barrister Inn on State Circle, Middleton Tavern, which was established in 1750 and faces the restored City Market, and the Hilton on Compromise close by the Annapolis Yacht Club. Other popular eating places, like McGarvey's Saloon and Griffin's, facing the market, are found all around Market Square and Dock Street.

Annapolis is said to have the largest concentration of boatyards of any harbor of its size in the United States. The Yacht Haven has taken over the old John Trumpy Yacht Yard on Spa Creek and is operating a new marine complex that offers a variety of yacht services. Many other fine marinas and boatyards line the shores of the creek. If you are slightly bewildered by this formidable array of maritime facilities, just ask for a free copy of the new *Port Book,* a most useful directory listing all of the boating services available in Annapolis. You'll find no fewer than 150 marine service firms operating in Annapolis.

Recently there has been a revival of interest in restoring the historic waterfront of Annapolis. This began with the preservation of the old eighteenth-century Custom House, facing the City Dock on Market Square at the foot of Main Street. As a local authority put it: "The growth of yachting is reviving a great maritime past. More than half the buildings facing Market Square today are eighteenth- or early nineteenth-century structures." Historic Annapolis, Inc., a nonprofit organization, has played a leading role in a restoration program which may make Annapolis "as significant to Americans as Williamsburg and Mystic Seaport."

5. Spa Creek (12283). This busy in-town creek has retained its own distinctive character through successive periods of maritime history in Annapolis. A boatyard was operating on the present site of the Arnold C. Gay Marina, at the foot of Shipwright Street, as early as 1696, and the creek has offered friendly protection to all manner of vessels in eras of sail and steam and power since that time. It has changed in many ways since the first edition of this guide was written, when Arnie Gay was just taking over the old Thomas Langan yard with its friendly clublike atmosphere that so impressed Fessenden Blanchard and other cruising yachtsmen in the late 1940's. At that period you might have found a score of cruising boats in the creek, occupying slips or moored in the stream above the old swing bridge. Today, you'll find hundreds of fine pleasure craft lining both sides of the creek, with tall masts predominating at Petrini's yard, on the Eastport side, and Gay's slips on the "Town" shore, while powerboats are clustered at Sarles and many private piers and bulkheads around the creek. Men and boats have changed, but the friendly atmosphere and salty character of the creek remain; you can still find a place to drop your hook for overnight anchorage above the bridge.

The bridge across Spa Creek just beyond the Annapolis Yacht Club has a vertical clearance of 15 feet; if you need more than that, blow your horn. Car traffic is heavy at rush hours, and the bridge is closed to boats from 7:30 to 9:00 A.M. and 4:30 to 6:00 P.M. on week-days, except state and federal holidays. After going through the bridge, favor the starboard or north shore, leaving the new slips of the Annapolis Yacht Club "Annex" to port and keeping clear of the shoal marked by a green day marker off the next point on the Eastport shore. You can get to the boatyards on the Eastport shore just below the point by keeping well below this buoy as you head in. On this shore, just above the bridge, is Petrini's Boat Yard, with plenty of water at the dock, many fine yachts, and a variety of repair and maintenance work available. Sarles Boat and Engine Works farther up concentrates largely on powerboats; it has both covered and uncovered slips.

Until the creek turns southwest as you go up, favor the starboard shore; after that keep in the middle. There are several fine anchorages in Spa Creek. One is in the bight on the north shore just above the yard; a better, especially pretty place, known as "Hurricane Hole," is in 5 feet just below where the creek starts to fork. (Near the "S" of Spa Creek on chart 12283.) Bugeyes and pungies used to come there to ride out hurricanes.

6. *Weems Creek (12282), Southwest Shore of Severn.* This is the first creek above the bridges. Favor the port shore on entering in order to avoid the long, unmarked bar on the upriver side. The most convenient anchorage is just inside the entrance, where the creek opens out wider. A more protected spot is in the middle near the bridge. This creek has some good-looking houses on its port bank and is readily accessible to West Annapolis, where supplies can be bought.

However, it is less snug and secluded than some of the creeks far-ther up.

7. *Luce Creek (12282), Southwest Shore of Severn.* This creek is very snug but use care in entering. As the chart shows, there are shoals on both sides but plenty of water in the middle if you stay there. The entrance may be spotted by a row of several brick houses on the shore to port. This is a beautiful creek with deep water inside and up the branches. When we were there, a large sailing yacht was moored in the narrow cove with 12 feet behind the spit on the south side of the entrance. If this cove is occupied, there are several good anchorages farther in. Residents of a new community have built a private marina on the southeast shore, but no transient facilities are available.

8. *Saltworks Creek (12282), Southwest Shore of Severn.* This creek, sometimes called Salt Bay, is just above Luce Creek and the only one on the Severn in which we have so far touched bottom. This is the place where we once misread a private marker (at that time a red-white-black striped spar) in the middle of the entrance, referred to in Chapter Two when we were discussing reasons for going aground on the Chesapeake.

We guessed wrong on the color and left it to port when we should have left it to starboard, for it is on the end of a 3-foot shoal projecting from the upriver point at the creek's entrance, almost halfway across.

Once inside, we found the creek pretty, with several fine places to anchor. One of these is in 14 feet near where the old chart said "stk." Several others are farther up the middle.

9. *Chase Creek (12282), Northeast Shore of Severn.* This is across the river from Saltworks Creek and has a wide entrance with two forks. It also has the characteristic shoal extending from the upriver side of the entrance, now marked by a lighted red buoy, N-2. A green frame structure seems to mark the end of this shoal, but play safe;

give it a good berth and keep closer to the south shore to starboard. Keep in the center between the two hooks at the fork.

The upper, or left, fork looks snugger and more attractive. One good-sized sailing yacht was moored just behind the northern hook in 15 feet when we were there, and another farther in just where the left fork branches again.

A number of small houses face the entrance and the place, though pretty, isn't as appealing to the cruising man who likes seclusion as the two across the river, to be described next.

10. Clements Creek (12282), Southwest Shore of Severn. This creek has been easy to identify by the golf course just above it. It is one of the most attractive areas on the Severn, and presents no difficulties in entering. When we first explored the area not a house was in sight along the shores, and the high land above the golf course was heavily wooded. But the area has been developed over the past decade, and the golf course is now the site of an attractive residential community that has not changed the character of the riverfront as much as we feared it might. It still provides a snug anchorage, about halfway up the creek. As in most of the other creeks on the Severn, no supplies or facilities are available.

11. Brewer Creek (12282), Southwest Shore of Severn. This is just above Clements Creek and has been one of our favorite anchorages on the Severn. But it is also changing character, as new waterfront homes are being built along its high banks and once thickly wooded shores. In entering favor the north shore to the narrow part, and then stay in the middle, where you can carry deep water almost to the end. Anchor anywhere from half to three-quarters of the way up. It's hard not to overdo the word "snug" on the Chesapeake, but it belongs here, if anywhere.

12. Round Bay (12282), Sunken Island Creek, Little Round Bay Creek. This is a perfect body of water for small-boat sailing. About 5 miles up the Severn and 2 miles wide at its widest in either direction, Round Bay gives the upriver explorer who has sails a good chance to

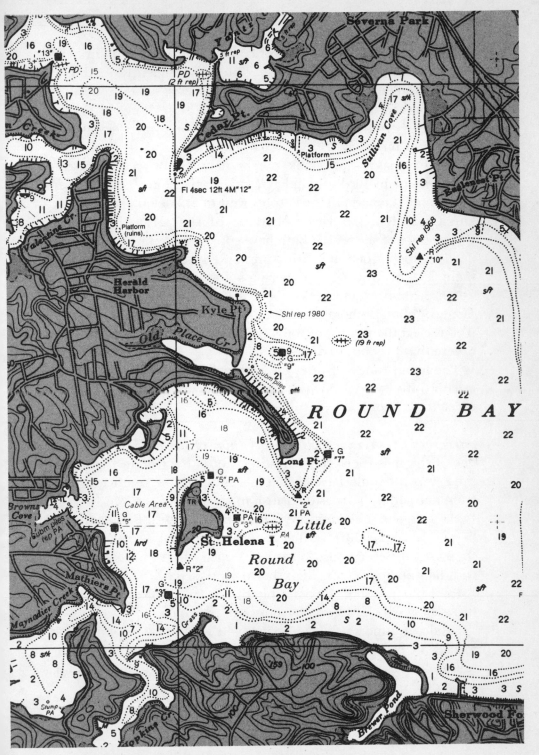

Round Bay on Severn River (from chart 12282).

use them. He may have plenty of company on weekends from the racing fleets of small yachts whose white sails frequently dot the Bay.

One of the most beautiful vistas we have ever seen was our view up the Severn on a late October day, with high shores of flaming color, clearly framing the blue strip of sparkling water beyond that was Round Bay.

The bay has no navigable creeks between Brewer and Cedar Point except in Little Round Bay, where there are two: Hopkins Creek and Maynadier Creek, southwest of St. Helena Island. Hopkins Creek is a "favorite anchorage" of Dick Hutchings, a past commodore of the S.C.C. Both have considerable marshland at the heads, which, combined with unmarked outlying shoals, makes them less inviting (except perhaps for the latter creek in hot weather) than other creeks above and below the bay. There are plenty of good anchorages in deep water all around St. Helena, and if you select the right spot you'll have a good chance to pick up any breeze that may be stirring.

The mean range of tides on Round Bay is about 1 foot and is greatly influenced by winds. The tidal current velocity seldom exceeds $1/2$ knot.

13. Forked Creek (12282), Northeast Shore of Severn. This used to be one of the most perfect, interesting, and attractive anchorages on the Severn. It could have been a fine hideout for American vessels from marauding parties of British in the days of the War of 1812. Perhaps it was. The entrance is hard to find but it finally appears beyond a sandy bluff with several private wharves on the north shore of the Severn, just to the right, or north, of a wooded point with hills 40 and 60 feet high shown on the chart.

Favor the port shore on entering; the sharp point to the starboard has a shoal which projects farther than the chart indicates.

Inside, around to the starboard, you will find a splendid land-locked anchorage in 14 feet. Farther up, in 10 feet, good-sized sailing craft can moor among the trees. But the place has built up a good deal recently, and is threatened by suburban sprawl.

On the left fork is the well-regarded Sappington's Yacht Yard, Inc., where gas and water may be obtained and motor and hull repairing is done. A few moorings are available at times and there are a number of slips, usually filled up, however, in the busy season. At this yard there are 2 railways and a lift capable of hauling boats up to 60 feet in length and 8 or 9 feet draft. There is 12 feet at the dock. The yard has complete engine and repair facilities and allows do-it-yourself repairs.

Supplies can be had by telephoning from the yard to Severna Park about 2½ miles away, where there are stores which will deliver if not called too late. Taxis may be obtained instead and you can visit the park.

At Severna Park are buses, drugstores, grocery stores, etc. The Governor Ritchie Highway, between Baltimore and Annapolis, passes by only a little over a mile from Forked Creek.

14. Rock Cove (12282). This cove, just above Forked Creek, gives good shelter under ordinary conditions and would perhaps be cooler in summer, though not nearly so attractive or interesting.

15. Indian Landing and Upper Severn (12282). Above Rock Cove the river is deep as far as Indian Landing, with a number of anchorages in the bight south of Point Lookout and the larger bight east of Indian Landing. The Sailing Club of the Chesapeake held a Fourth of July rendezvous with more than 30 cruising boats anchored off the sandy islet shown on chart 12282.

XII. SOUTH RIVER (*12270, 12271*).

The beauty of South River is in its creeks, which rival those on the Severn. The principal shoals are buoyed for about 5 miles up and the river is well worth exploration, at least as far as the first bridge—now a high fixed bridge with 50-foot clearance. For most of this distance, the channel runs in a northwesterly direction, so it is a good reach either way under sail in one of the southwesterly breezes so frequent during the summer months. But don't just run or reach up and back and miss the best part. Poke into some of those creeks; several of them are among the best on the Chesapeake. Watch for the crab pot buoys in entering the river. To avoid the increased traffic, go there on weekdays.

The bridge at Edgewater has a vertical clearance of 53 feet at mean high water. Above this bridge are three good creeks: Gingerville, Beards, and Broad. If you have time and are in an exploratory mood, you will enjoy going up farther. The fixed bridge, at Riva, has a vertical clearance of 25 feet. Speed limit above the bridge and in the various tributaries is 8 mph.

New marinas and boatyards have appeared in all parts of South River in the past decade, making this one of the busiest rivers in the Upper Bay area. Mooring facilities and slips are available in Selby Bay, the Glebe, and Warehouse Creek, on the south side of the river, and on both sides of the first bridge. The Liberty Yacht Club at the north end of the bridge, and Pier 7 and the South River Yacht Club at the south end, provide slips and ramps for launching. Above the bridge the Oak Grove Marina occupies the point to starboard at the entrance to Gingerville Creek. Paul's Restaurant and Mike's Crab House, both at the south end of Riva Bridge, another mile upriver, have docking facilities for boating customers.

On the high land between the head of Glebe Creek and Rhode River is the South River Club, which has been in existence since 1722, and whose records have been preserved in the minute book since 1742. This is probably the oldest active social club in America—perhaps because the discussion of religion or politics was not permitted.

1. *Selby Bay* (*12270, 12271*). This is too large for comfort in a stiff breeze but offers fair anchorage under ordinary conditions, and an opportunity on hot nights to get the wind over a considerable stretch of water. Even in high winds there is little sea and the holding ground is good. There is a 1-foot spot nearly in the middle.

A good sandy beach is located on the inside of Turkey Point, but

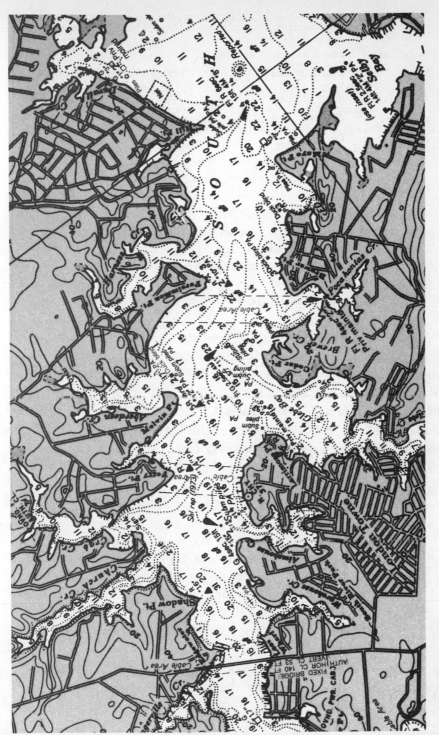

South River (from chart 12270).

it is privately owned and not available to cruising boats. One of the Chesapeake's most insatiable explorers reports an interesting tidal effect:

> There is a nice tidal phenomenon here—something like a bore—between the first change of tide and the final change of current, both in Chesapeake Bay and the river. The result is a succession of waves appearing out of nowhere and running around the point every ten minutes or so, noticeable on an ultrastill and windless day or night. Any unbelievers in the crowd? Then sit yourself down in the water on the Point when conditions are as described above and get your eyes about six inches above the surface; no moving boats, no wind, everything like glass. Wait a few minutes. About the time you wonder what the joke is, you'll see the water suddenly rise about six inches and a dozen waves form up off the Point and roll around inside Selby Bay.

Farther up Selby Bay you will find several larger marinas which have replaced older boatyards with modern slips and storage facilities. Holiday Point Marina, Selby Bay Yacht Basin, and Anchor Yacht Basin usually have transient slips, and offer ramps or travel lifts for trailer boats. Gas and diesel fuel are available. The summer quarters of the Selby Bay Yacht Club are located nearby. Lake Ramsey is busier than you'd suspect from just scanning the chart; many cruising yachts and boats of like size moor inside the lake, as do a host of smaller craft.

Another yachtsman writes,

> The place known as Ramsey Lake was formerly called Ramsey's Gut and all the water in the lake passed out through the stone walls that are now the abutments of the bridge on the west side of the lake. It was the last tide mill on the Upper Bay and went out of use many years ago. This is a famous spot for dipping crabs with a hand net as they come out of the lake.

2. *Duvall Creek (12270, 12271), Northeast Shore of South River.* Despite the 2-foot bar which the chart shows at the entrance, a growing fleet of local cruising boats use this creek and a yachtsman who lives there claims that the chart underestimates the depths under normal conditions. So if you want to try it when the tide is well up, leave a duck blind close to starboard and head for the privately maintained markers through the narrow channel. There is plenty of water in the second branch to port, with a pretty and quiet anchorage.

3. Harness Creek (12270, 12271), Northeast Shore of South River. This is the nearest good harbor to the entrance of South River. After passing the 4-foot spot on the lower point, keep fairly close to the starboard shore to avoid the characteristic shoal on the upriver side of the entrance. While there are many good anchorages in Harness Creek, there is one gunkhole which is "out of this world," partway up the east shore in 8 feet near the "Cr" of Harness Creek on the chart.

"You mooch in close," as Colonel Birnn well expresses it, "until what you think is a solid marsh line shows a gap, barely wide enough for your boat. Then you go in with a lot of water under but not much around you. High banks in back; no sign of life . . . even the D.A. himself will never find you there." Others may have the idea too, so get there first.

There are a number of small houses along the west shore after you round Thunder and Lightning Point, the local name for the first point to the left of Persimmon Point. A house there was once struck by lightning. No supplies are available. The creek is a favorite with Chesapeake yachtsmen, and you may find a rendezvous rafting up on almost any summer weekend.

4. Brewer Creek (12270, 12271), Southwest Shore of South River. The surroundings are fairly high, wooded, and pretty, but there are two bad unmarked shoals at the entrance. The creek is open to the north for some distance and a recently dredged channel allows entrance for most cruising boats into the attractive inner cove.

5. *Glebe Creek (12270, 12271), Southwest Shore of South River.* If you like to have plenty of company and a lot going on, you will like this place; but don't go there for quiet waters on a Saturday night in summer. The creek is also too large to be snug until you go well up beyond the long hookline point on the south shore, where you will find many small cottages and small motorboats. Waves will reach you, but not from the wind.

Pick up Fl green 11, and head a fair distance off wooded Cedar Point, avoiding the 2-foot spot to port and the usual upriver shoal to starboard, which is marked by oyster stakes and projects over half-way across the entrance. After you pass this shoal, a well-equipped yacht yard may be seen to starboard. This is now operated by the Holiday Point Marinas, whose former owner told us that the chart is very deceptive, as it is easier to reach his dock than the chart indicates. Just head straight into the first little cove beyond the creek's upper entrance, favoring the starboard shore. There is 14 or 15 feet reported at the dock, where gas, water, and ice are obtainable. Groceries can be found at a store in Woodland Beach, a short distance away.

There is an unbuoyed sunken island with 2 feet over it in the middle of the wide part of Glebe Creek. So follow around the shore to port. You will have less shelter but also less company if you anchor off Cedar Point instead of going farther up creek.

6. *Aberdeen Creek (12270, 12271), Northeast Shore of South River.* Keep fairly close to the starboard shore and avoid the long upriver shoal off Melvin Point. Continue near the starboard shore up creek. This is a pretty place, though fairly wide and open to the south. A number of Chesapeake Bay yachtsmen keep their boats in the creek, which is a favorite rendezvous point for several yacht clubs.

7. *Almshouse Creek (12270, 12271), Southwest Shore of South River.* This is the most attractive creek which we visited on the southwest shore of South River. The houses are larger and less evident than on some of the other creeks. In entering keep well south of lighted beacon 15 until you are in the middle of the entrance, watching the upriver shoal off Larramore Point and not getting too close to the Woodland Beach shore. When inside, head just off the end of the long narrow point with the road, on the port shore. Then keep in the center. Supplies are at Woodland Beach.

A good anchorage is in the first bight to the starboard. The old Almshouse for which the creek was named has been restored to resemble as far as possible its original look when built to serve as an inn sometime between 1744 and 1750. London Town Publik House, as it is known now, is the only remaining structure from the once-thriving seaport of London Town. Its dock is no longer a ferry landing, serving such distinguished travelers as George Washington, Thomas Jefferson, and Francis Scott Key. Instead it welcomes cruisers who wish to visit the brick Georgian-style structure and grounds. Visiting hours are 10 A.M. to 4 P.M., Tuesday–Saturday, noon to 4 P.M. Sunday, closed Monday and all during January and February. The surrounding 8 acres of ground, planted with native trees, shrubs, and flowers, is of interest as well. No gas or facilities are available on the creek.

8. Crab Creek (12270, 12271), North Shore of South River. Like most of the creeks on the north shore, this quiet backwater has retained its charm despite an increasing number of houses around its wooded shores. There are no difficulties in entering if you leave South River when the twin chimneys on the London Town Publik House are in line with the flagpole; turn north, favoring the starboard shore until you see a short black pile off the point dividing Church and Crab creeks; then leave the pile well to port before turning into the little cove to port or heading on up the creek through the narrow entrance channel. There is barely room to anchor in the cove, which has several private piers extending out to deep water, but several good anchorages may be found farther up, past the sandy hook on the east side of the entrance. The chart may leave you in doubt about the depth of this narrow channel, but you will find nothing less than 12 feet if you hug the sandy spit; keep about 75 feet off the beach, and make an S turn to avoid the shoals to port at the entrance. The shores inside are high and wooded, with most of the houses screened by trees and shrubbery. The best anchorages can be found in 8 to 10 feet of water above the second point to starboard, but if your vessel draws less than 5 feet you can explore almost to the headwaters. No supplies or facilities are available.

9. *Church Creek (12270, 12271), North Shore of South River.* This creek is just above Crab Creek and shares the wide approach from South River. It is also one of the most beautiful creeks on the Chesapeake, with some of the best anchorages on the river, but is lacking in supplies and facilities, which are obtainable across the river. Head for the point to the east of the entrance and then follow the starboard shore to avoid the 2-foot shoal off the upriver point. A yachtsman who lives on the creek advises going in on a line from Ferry Point and a clearing on the point which projects southward nearly halfway up the west shore.

A perfect anchorage is in the cove to port just inside the entrance in 10 feet, especially in the northern fork. There are other snug anchorages farther up, with one of the loveliest located in 11 feet beyond the first sharp point on the starboard, or east, shore. The land is steep and wooded, and the houses few and tucked away in the woods.

10. *Warehouse Creek (12270, 12271), South Shore of South River.* This is a fairly attractive creek, though not comparable in privacy or charm to Church and Crab creeks across the river. In entering, keep well to the right after passing the prominent white house with the red roof on the left side of the entrance. A good anchorage is in 8 feet inside.

Around the point to starboard in the tiny cove beyond the 10-foot marking on the chart is a small boatyard, Dayton Trubee and Company, which continues to give cruisers a friendly reception in the tradition of the yachtsman who previously owned the property. There is 10 feet at the end of the dock and if room is available boats may tie up overnight. Water may be obtained from the dock and some stores are not far away on the highway, which goes across the bridge.

11. Lees Wharf (12271), South Shore of South River. The old wharf area has become a leading charterboat center, with Pier 7 providing dock space and related facilities for small-boat charters, both sail and power. The old South River Yacht Club building houses a variety of yacht sales and services. Two restaurants, Mike's Crab House and Paul's, are open year-round, serving lunch and dinner. The fuel dock carries 10 to 12 feet alongside.

XIII. RHODE RIVER (*12271*).

Our first night of cruising on the Chesapeake was spent in the moonlight on Rhode River. We couldn't have had a better introduction to the Bay, and can well understand the popularity of the river as a weekend rendezvous for yachtsmen from Baltimore and Annapolis.

A large white building with a cupola, on Dutchman Point, is a good landmark for the entrance. A square marker of red framework on the end of the shoal should of course be left to starboard. On rounding the black beacon just beyond the cable area, one of the most attractive and unspoiled anchorages on the Bay opens into view. We anchored on that first night close to the east shore of Big Island, south of a point which projected far enough eastward to aid in offering good shelter from northwest squalls. If the wind is strong from the east, it would be best to run around the northern end of the island and anchor in 7 feet to the west of it—another good anchorage with fine holding ground. The Smithsonian Institution of Washington owns most of the land back of Contees Wharf, which is now used for ecological research.

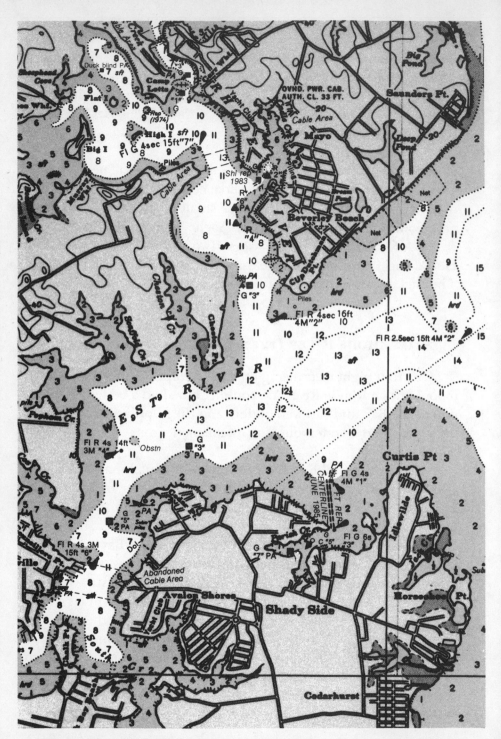

Rhode and West rivers (from chart 12270).

1. Cadle Creek. Located on the eastern side of Rhode River, this creek is too heavily populated to suit lovers of quiet and privacy, and too crowded with powerboats. There is also only 4 feet at the entrance, a deterrent to keelboats. Boats drawing less than this may want to tie up in the private yacht shelter around the hook. The West River Yacht Club is near the head of the north arm of this creek, to port. Gas and supplies are available and there are two small railways.

2. Bear Creek. Beyond Cadle Creek on the east shore of Rhode River, Bear Creek is used considerably by sailing craft. It now has two boatyard-marinas. Orme's Blue Water Marina, directly inside of Carr's Wharf, has slips for deep-draft sailboats and launching facilities. Rhode River Marina, farther up, is used chiefly by powerboats, but has a marine railway and a good repair shop. Favor the starboard shore going in. Holiday Hill Marina is beyond.

Other possibilities in Rhode River are past the YMCA Camp Letts and up Sellman Creek, or between High and Big islands. Here is another favorite anchorage, where you generally see larger yachts than in the cove down the river.

If you want gas, supplies, facilities, and shore meals, you will find them in abundance on West River, if not on Cadle Creek or Bear Creek.

XIV. WEST RIVER (*12270, 12271*).

West River is one of the most popular—and populated—boating centers on the Western Shore. It is a beehive of activity during the yachting season, swarming with boats of many sizes and descriptions; its shores are lined with docks, seafood restaurants, an outstanding boatyard, and two progressive yacht clubs.

In entering, keep well north of the shoal off Curtis Point. A course from red flasher 2 to lighted beacon 4 at the mouth of the river will clear everything. Farther in, watch your chart and buoys carefully for 1-foot spots on either side. Mean tidal range is 1 foot.

1. Parish Creek (12270, 12271), at Entrance of West River. This is just inside Curtis Point, east of the entrance to West River. In order to avoid the shoal off Curtis Point, wait until the lighted beacons are in line or nearly so before heading for the outer one. The narrow dredged channel is well marked by beacons but had shoaled to less than 5 feet. Dredging was discussed in 1987 and may have taken place when you read this, so depths may have increased. Proceed cautiously.

While Parish Creek has facilities such as gas, a boatyard, etc., it has become very commercial and too crowded for our taste—certainly so for an overnight stop. While many motorboats are berthed there, visiting yachtsmen usually prefer to go to other parts of West River, particularly Galesville or Avalon Shores.

2. Avalon Shores and South Creek (12271), East Side of West River. The Chesapeake Yacht Club is located on the point southwest of the spot where "Avalon Shores" is written on the chart, and may have a slip available.

If you prefer to anchor out, a fair anchorage off the yacht club docks in 8 feet of water is available, although this is open to the north.

3. Galesville and Lerch Creek (12270), West Shore of West River. "Everybody" goes to Galesville, according to one authority, and it is here that several fine seafood restaurants will be found, as well as one of the oldest boatyards on the Chesapeake, founded in 1865 by Emile Hartge. It is an increasingly active sailing port.

The Hartge Yacht Yard today is just around the point south of Galesville, on the starboard side of the entrance to Lerch Creek. There is 6 feet of water at the dock at low tide and moorings are furnished if slips are unavailable. The dock has gas, fresh water, ice, electricity, and rest rooms. Small grocery stores are about 1/4 mile away.

We first visited Hartge's in 1948 and called on Captain Oscar

Hartge, finding him full of Chesapeake lore and a great authority on the Bay. A member of the family said, "We are newcomers; we have only been here 75 years." Captain Oscar won a yacht race when he was over 70, competing with Naval Academy skippers, on one of the academy boats. Since our early visit, the captain has passed away and the yard has been run by other members of the Hartge clan.

To this day Hartge's Yard has maintained its fine reputation and has expanded its facilities by the addition of many new, covered slips, additional piers, and an enclosed working slip where good-sized cruising boats can be worked on for deck and inside repairs without hauling. The yard has several railways and can haul yachts up to 65 feet in length and 6-foot draft. Marine hardware is carried among other things.

Galesville Yacht Yard, at the entrance to Galesville on the starboard hand, has built a new bulkhead and pier with slips for up to 150 sail- and powerboats in 6 feet or more of water. The Pirates Cove Restaurant serves good seafood meals and sometimes has transient slips at its own pier. Many powerboats use Shady Oaks Marina above Hartge's. The West River Sailing Club has an attractive clubhouse just north of Councillors Point, and is an active force in promoting sailing in this part of the Bay.

On a hill north of the town is famous Tulip Hill, built by Samuel Galloway in 1745, a fine example of colonial architecture.

According to Swepson Earle there is a "well-authenticated story which has some foundation that there was a secret underground passage leading from the lower terraces near West River to the cellar of the mansion through which slaves were supposed to have been smuggled." In support of this, Mr. Earle calls attention to an advertisement which appeared on March 22, 1753.

> Just imported from London in the Brigantine *Grove,* Captain Robert Wilson, to be sold by the subscriber on board the said brigantine in West River, for sterling or current money, a parcel of healthy indentured servants among whom are tradesmen and husbandmen.
>
> Samuel Galloway

Galesville, West River.

Rockhold Creek and Deale.
(Photo courtesy of BaySailor.)

George Washington's diary records visits with Sam Galloway at Tulip Hill, on trips from Mount Vernon to Annapolis.

West River has a history.

XV. HERRING BAY, ROCKHOLD CREEK, AND DEALE (*12266, 12267, 12270, 12271*).

This is the last shelter for small craft proceeding southward until Solomons Island is reached 32 miles away. That is, except possibly for some of the newly dredged basins—of uncertain depths—along this otherwise inhospitable shore.

Herring Bay is a broad bight indenting the western shore between Curtis Point and Holland Point. It is fringed by a 2-mile-long bar with depths of 3 to 5 feet, affording limited protection in the approaches to three distinctive boating communities: (1) Herrington Harbor, inside Holland Point at the southeast end of Herring Bay; (2) Rockhold Creek, at the northwest, entered through a dredged channel that also leads to (3) the active boating center of Deale.

All three of these locations provide a wide choice of open and covered slips, repair facilities, and boat supplies, but not all of them have enough deep water for overnight anchorage.

257

*1. **Herrington Harbor.*** This harbor has a privately maintained dredged channel about ¹/₂ mile southeast of the Fl 4 sec. light at the end of Long Bar, leading to a basin and marina with 7-foot depths and some 600 slips. Most of the slips are occupied by sail or power cruisers owned locally or by people from the Washington and Baltimore metropolitan areas. A limited number of transient slips are usually available. There is anchorage room in deep water outside the Herrington Harbor entrance, but this area is exposed to north-to-northeast winds.

*2. **Rockhold Creek.*** The dredged channel has a project depth of 7 feet, and has been kept close to that figure during the eighties. But if there's any doubt, check with the Coast Guard or one of the local marinas. New boatyards and other facilities have proliferated during the past decade along both branches of the creek, making this area one of the busiest boating centers south of Annapolis. Herrington Harbor North has a large facility at the mouth of Rockhold Creek, with many sailboat slips.

*3. **Deale.*** This is an old and popular boating town best known for its large fleet of fishing boats—native Chesapeake deadrise hulls used for fishing, crabbing, and clamming in the summer and oyster tonging in the winter. In recent years, Deale has become an active center for cruising boats, both power and sail, with many new yards, like Shipwright Harbor, expanding the number of slips and marine services.

XVI. HERRING BAY TO THE PATUXENT RIVER (*12266, 12267, 12264*).

This long stretch of fossil-laden cliffs is interesting and impressive, high in most part, rugged, and broken only by several dredged basins. The sweep of wind and tide is constantly filling in the channels of these artificial harbors, so chart depths are completely unreliable, as would be any depths which we might give here. It all depends on how recently dredging has taken place.

As an example, the following is what an outstanding Chesapeake yachtsman, whose chief delight is to poke into small places, wrote us about one of the dredged harbors. The promoter of the marina said that he would have an 8-foot channel.

> . . . Willing to bet anyone lots of money it won't be 8 feet for long, and if it ever is dredged to 8 feet, that it soon after degenerates to a 2¹/₂- to 3-foot-deep channel, although the pond harbor is deep enough. Reason: who, outside of some of the inhabitants of the new development, is going to take an interest? John J. Government isn't going to keep it dredged—so who's going to stand the expense?

Despite the pessimistic prospects, motor cruisers drawing 4 feet or less may find it very profitable to go into one of these marinas, provided the wind isn't blowing too hard onshore, and that they proceed cautiously. Once inside, there is usually a snug anchorage with good facilities, gas, water, etc. Whether you find a harbor or not, this is one of the most interesting sections of shoreline on the Bay.

Bob Burgess of the Mariner's Museum, Newport News, writes interestingly of "Chesapeake's Oldest Inhabitants," who lie buried in the cliffs or strewn along the beaches below Herring Bay.

> The best of these [Miocene] deposits are in the Calvert Cliffs, which form the eastern portion of Calvert County, Maryland, bordering Chesapeake Bay. Here, for a distance of 35 miles, from Chesapeake Beach to Drum Point, there is an almost unbroken exposure of fossil-laden strata. In some places the cliffs rise to a height of more than 100 feet.
>
> Scientists have proof that during the middle Miocene times— 3,000,000 to 10,000,000 years ago—a considerable portion of the present tidewater country was submerged. The area was then tropical and coral; porpoises, sharks, whales, crocodiles, giant barnacles and a multitude of shell fish inhabited the waters. As the creatures died, they settled to the bottom of the sea and their remains were gradually

covered up with silt. Ages passed and through upheavals, the floor of the sea was thrust above the surface, forming new land. Through the millenniums many of the buried creatures and shells became fossilized. Even a greater number disintegrated.

The best beds along this stretch are located at Chesapeake Beach and south of that point, Plum Point, and Governors Run. But almost anywhere along the shore where the high bluffs are prominent, they may be found.

Boatmen look upon the yellow Calvert Cliffs as an uninviting shoreline offering few harbors of refuge. But these bluffs may take on another meaning if one walks along the beach at their base and discovers some of the specimens described . . . one can't help but stand in awe as he gazes at the steep rugged banks and the fossilized remains of marine life which was once part of a world too far in the past for us to envisage.

1. Chesapeake Beach—Fishing Creek (12267). Although our chart showed 5 feet when we were there in the summer of 1985, reliable authorities among the fishermen agreed that the entrance channel had shoaled to less than that at low water. A large fleet of sport fishing boats uses the harbor, and there are good facilities for powerboats in the basin inside the Rod 'n' Reel Club. Launching ramp is at Kellam's Marina. Our advice is to stay out if you have a keel sailboat, but to try it cautiously if you have a motor cruiser drawing under 4 feet.

A well-known yachtsman advises favoring the area north of the entrance marker 1 and avoiding some piles which are the ruins of the old pier. Come in on a line with the jetties.

Inside you will find 8 or 9 feet of water and you can tie up (perhaps double) along the dock to port, and have a good meal at the Rod 'n' Reel Club in the large white building. See the fellow at the gas dock; he is dockmaster and authority for all the goings-on. He'll tell you where to lie or how to get up a fishing party—for which the place is noted.

Gas, diesel oil, water, ice, etc., are available at the dock, and groceries are nearby. It is an interesting place, if you can get in, and offers good shelter, though it is not pretty and there is a large marsh. It is also apt to be crowded and too active with fishing parties coming and going to be considered a restful place, to put it mildly. Great for fish and fossils, though! And, if it has been dredged recently, it offers shelter from a storm, if you get there before the seas begin pounding on the entrance channel.

Chesapeake Beach is not an old town compared to many others around the Bay. It was laid out by the promoters of the Chesapeake Beach Railway, and chartered, with a post office opened, in 1894. The first passenger train reached the town in June, 1900, and the amusement park, which included a mile-long boardwalk, a roller coaster, and a merry-go-round among its attractions, was opened that same season. The railway, which ran from a station at the District Line at Seat Pleasant, Md., and had connecting service to Baltimore, had peak passenger traffic in 1920, but interest dwindled and passenger service was discontinued on April 15, 1935. The amusement park did not close until 1972. The original frame station building, used as a storage room by the operators of the amusement park, has been restored to its former appearance and operates as a railroad museum. The grounds of the amusement park are now the site of an expensive condominium development, and boutique-style shops are opening up in town.

2. Breezy Point Harbor (12266, 12267). This private project is used by Bay fishing boats and small powerboats, but is not suitable for cruising yachts or keel sailboats drawing over 3 1/2 feet. In an emergency you could get gas at the fuel dock if you could clear the entrance channel.

3. Flag Harbor (12264, 12265, 12263). This is another dredged private project, which was more ambitious and well planned than many other similar undertakings. Although jetties were built at the entrance and a channel dredged to the Flag Harbor Yacht Basin inside, it has been difficult to keep the approach open for boats drawing more than 4 feet.

The entrance is narrow and the L-shaped basin inside is completely lined with fishing boats, outboards, and a few small cruisers. There is still 5 feet at some slips but our soundings at the gas dock showed only 4½ feet at MLW. We counted over 150 boats in the harbor but only a few sailboats. A keelboat drawing over 4 feet should not attempt to enter except at high tide or with local pilotage.

Just north of Flag Harbor a prominent landmark intrudes on the unbroken shoreline of Calvert Cliffs: the first nuclear power generating plant built on the Chesapeake, completed after several years of controversy over its possible environmental effects on the Bay. Another man-made change in this part of the Bay became evident in the mid-1970's when an offshore terminal was built at Cove Point for discharge of liquefied natural gas from giant tankers. The huge terminal had become inactive by the 1980's, because the liquefied natural gas, which came from Iran, was unavailable. But the terminal is maintained and lighted.

XVII. PATUXENT RIVER (*12264*).

There is an ancient story about how the Greeks chose their leader for the Battle of Marathon. Each general was asked to nominate his first and second choice for the top place. When the votes were counted it was found that each warrior had picked himself for the number-one job; all but one, however, had picked Miltiades next. Thus Miltiades was chosen.

If Chesapeake yachtsmen were asked to choose their favorite harbors, they might act very much like the generals of ancient Greece. Unless they already lived near the mouth of the Patuxent, they'd probably choose Gibson Island or Annapolis, Georgetown or Oxford, or one of the many creeks which Chesapeake yachtsmen love to haunt. But mentioned on every list, near the top, would be Solomons Island, at the mouth of the Patuxent River—or one of the lovely creeks which fan out like the horns of an elk north of Solomons on the chart.

For recent editions of the Guide we have been asking our cruising friends to list their favorite anchorages, and Solomons is named on virtually everyone's list as one of the outstanding harbors on the Chesapeake, and the Patuxent mentioned as one of the not-to-be missed rivers. Fortunately for yachtsmen whose time is limited, the best harbors and most of the interesting places on the Patuxent are near the mouth, or 7 to 8 miles up, where St. Leonard Creek enters the river, and the famous Sotterley Estate looks down from the heights of Sotterley Point on the waters below.

Though navigable with 7 feet as far as Bristol Landing, 40 miles above Drum Point at the entrance, the upper reaches of the Patuxent become relatively low and marshy, and few yachtsmen will want to go above Benedict, 18½ miles from the mouth. The mean range of tide is about 1 foot at the entrance, 1½ feet at Benedict, and 2½ feet at Nottingham.

As you enter the Patuxent from the north, the high bluffs at Little Cove Point are conspicuous. Drum Point Light is at the end of a low point with a hump, and higher land emerges a short distance in. The land is low at Hog and Cedar points to the south of the entrance.

In former times it was not an uncommon sight to see 15 or 20 sailing vessels anchored near the shore between Drum Point and Solomons Island, north of the shoal. The sea is usually negligible for large boats, as the bar to the southward breaks it. This sometimes proves to be a cool and satisfactory anchorage on a hot summer night, but be sure to stay out of the channel.

The south shore of the lower Patuxent and the waters on that side are restricted by the sprawling Patuxent Naval Air Base, with its low-flying planes and other activities unhealthful for visiting yachts. The basins along this shore are for Navy use only. See the *Coast Pilot* for detailed regulations.

1. Solomons Island (12284). There are two entrances to Solomons, one along the Drum Point shore north of the green cans on the triangular-shaped shoal; the other (for night use especially) around the south of this shoal. If you take the latter route, give the shoal a good berth to starboard after rounding the red flasher and bell 4. The best plan is to keep over toward the Chesapeake Biological Laboratory Wharf on the east shore of the island and leave this and the light inside fairly close to port.

Solomons Island is low and flat with many houses, docks, fishing boats—interesting, if not pretty. A causeway connects it with the mainland. The harbor north of the island offers good shelter from all winds and all sorts of facilities. After leaving close to port the conspicuous oil tanks and dock at the entrance, you will find an array of docks beyond, beginning with a long gas dock and the centrally located Harbor Island Marina with slips to which 10 feet can be carried. Fuel, water, and ice are available there, or at several large and well-equipped marinas around the harbor.

On the southwest shore of the harbor are other docks, including the one connected with Bowens Inn, the end of which, with 8 feet, is reserved for visiting yachts. Gas, water, showers, etc., are available. The Solomons Island Yacht Club is close by Bowens and may have a few slips available for visitors from recognized clubs.

Boats can either tie up at one of the docks or anchor in the harbor, where there is usually enough room to swing. In a northeaster, it is well to move up the northwest arm and anchor behind the point in 15 feet.

The harbor is not always quiet; Navy boats, fishermen, and yachts are apt to keep the waters moving. Mill Creek is better if you want privacy.

Take a walk around the island before supper. The little fishing port we knew 30 years ago has changed over the years. Today it is a bustling yachting center, with all kinds of maritime activity. New marinas line the waterfront, and new restaurants, like Solomons Pier facing the Patuxent River, are vying for the tourist trade. Visit the Calvert Marine Museum, on Back Creek, and the Chesapeake Marine Biological Laboratory on the point overlooking the entrance.

Zahniser's has an impressive fleet of cruising sailboats at its docks on Back Creek, and operates a marine railway, lift, and engine

The old Drum Point Lighthouse has been moved to the grounds of the Calvert Marine Museum, where it is open to visitors. (Photo courtesy of Paula Johnson/ Calvert Marine Museum.)

repair shop. Solomons Beacon Marina, Shepherd's Yacht Yard, and Spring Cove Marina also have many modern facilities. Calvert Marina, on the site of the World War II Amphibious Navy Training Base, offers facilities and services for both power and sail.

The shortage of hotel rooms in Solomons is gone. Accommodations are available at a Comfort Inn, with 60 rooms, on the site of Shepherd's Marina, which it took over, and at a Holiday Inn, with 170 rooms, restaurant, and conference center and 90-slip marina. Both are on Back Creek.

2. *Mill Creek (12264, 12265, 12284), North Shore of Patuxent River.* There are at least 10 Mill Creeks on the Chesapeake. Three of them are on the Patuxent, two near the mouth on opposite shores, and one just below Benedict. There may have been mills on all of them, but since we found two "Deep Creeks" with only a foot or two of water in them, the mills are probably missing too.

The Mill Creek that runs into Solomons Island Harbor is one of the very best, and ranks high on our list of favorite anchorages. In fact, it's one of the best and most convenient on the entire Bay. We'd strongly recommend going up this creek for a quiet night after stopping for a while at Solomons to look around and get stocked up.

In the bight a short way up the east shore are the docks of the old M. M. Davis Boat Yard, which built many famous Chesapeake vessels before World War II, minesweepers during the war, and later was operated by the Century Boat Company's Cruisalong Division. The yard is no longer operating as a yacht facility, but is an El Paso terminal.

Farther up, above Pancake Point, Mill Creek is full of beautiful, snug anchorages, each one seeming more perfect than the one before. Favor the Olivet shore in turning eastward into the upper part of the creek, since the shoal on the point above the "Mill" in the name projects farther north than is clear from the chart. After that keep in the middle.

In the first edition of this guide we reported almost no houses in sight above Olivet; today you will see many new homes and waterfront piers which, fortunately, have not spoiled this attractive creek. One fine anchorage is inside Pancake Point, to starboard in 8 feet; another, less attractive one but more convenient for supplies is on the north shore just beyond Olivet. Watch the dangerous high tension cable over Brooks Cove (42-foot clearance). If you can get under this, you can find quiet anchorage in a lovely spot.

3. St. John Creek (12265), North Shore of Patuxent. In entering, keep in the middle because there is a shoal southwest of Olivet Point. A good anchorage is in a bight with 9 feet just above Olivet, but a better one is near the head of the creek. Houses on the west bank and Olivet on the east make this creek less picturesque than Mill, though it is pretty near the head.

4. Back Creek (12265), North Shore of Patuxent. This creek is pretty in some of its coves but suffers from the presence of large buildings lining the banks. Though we prefer Mill Creek, Back has many good anchorages, with lots of marinas and shore facilities.

5. Town Creek (12265), South Shore of Patuxent. This is the first navigable creek on the south shore. It offers good shelter, but the creeks immediately above or across the river are prettier. The new high-rise bridge towers overhead in the best parts of the anchorage. Town Creek Marina and Homeport Marina offer facilities for transients. Town Creek Marine Railway can take care of repairs you might need.

6. Mill Creek (12264, 12265), South Shore of Patuxent. Like Mill Creek at Solomons, this creek is also pretty and wooded. There are several good anchorages beyond Carr's Wharf, to the left as you enter:

(1) In 12 feet around the entrance point to the left.
(2) Up the short, fork-shaped arm south of the first anchorage in 9 feet.

(3) Up the long southwest arm, off the point at the fork, where there is a very good-looking brick house with white pillars. Or you can go farther up either fork.

7. Cuckhold Creek (*12264, 12265*), *South Shore of Patuxent*. Give the shoal off the southwest corner of Half Pone Point a wide berth; it projects a long way out. Cuckhold is a typical Chesapeake creek with many good anchorages. On some other bodies of water it would be "something to write home about." On the Chesapeake it is not unusual. It can, however, be hot in summer. Weeks Marina can make hull and engine repairs.

8. Hellen Creek (*12264, 12265*), *North Shore of Patuxent*. This creek has a very shoal entrance and local authorities advise staying out.

9. St. Leonard Creek (*12264, 12265*), *North Shore of Patuxent*. This creek is big enough to be called a river, and beautiful enough to rival anything on the Chesapeake. In the upper part there are numerous marshes, but near the entrance are several anchorages which "can't be beat." One of them, which is almost surrounded by hills, some rising to 130 feet, is behind Petersons Point at the entrance. Here is perfect security in 8 to 12 feet of water. The White Sands Yacht Club, a commercial marina with gas dock (8 or 9 feet), marine supplies, slips, and a good restaurant, has been built at the entrance of Johns Creek; and there is another marina across St. Leonard Creek a half mile below. Thus, while still lovely, St. Leonard Creek is getting "civilized." Sometimes strong northerlies sweep down the creek making shelter desirable in one of the snug coves.

The mouth of St. Leonard was the scene of a famous naval engagement on June 26, 1814, when a blockading British fleet consisting of two frigates, a brig, two schooners, and a number of smaller craft was driven off by a surprise dawn attack led by Commodore Barney with a small flotilla of open barges. Barney was unable to follow up his surprise victory, however, and the British force later contributed troops to the attack on Washington that resulted in the burning of the Capitol.

10. Patuxent River above St. Leonard Creek (12264, 12265).

a. Sotterley. On the south side of the Patuxent almost directly across from St. Leonard Creek you will find an ancient wharf on Sotterley Point. For yachtsmen, this is a courtesy wharf, where you may tie up without charge for a visit to the historic Sotterley plantation, one of the best-preserved colonial mansions. The old mansion and its tenant houses date back to 1717 and occupy a ridge with fields and lawns sweeping down to the river. The estate is open to visitors by appointment in spring and fall, and without appointment from June through September. There's a telephone on the wharf to phone the house, and transportation may be available to take you up the hill. The Cruising Club of America and the Sailing Club of the Chesapeake have arranged rendezvous at Sotterley in recent years.

b. Battle Creek. This has some bad 2-foot spots on either side of the entrance and depths are not adequately charted. In this battle, we'd recommend discretion instead of valor. The names Prison Point and Kill Point are reminders that the creek is well named. Calvert Town used to be on this peninsula until the British fleet sailed up the Patuxent in 1814 and destroyed it.

c. Benedict (12264, 12265) and Indian Creek. Benedict is the principal town on the upper Patuxent and is 18½ miles above the entrance. The former ferry has been replaced by a swing bridge with 15½ feet vertical clearance when closed. Gas and water are available at the dock and stores are nearby in the town. The anchorage is protected from the northwest only; there is better shelter for boats drawing under 4 feet in Indian Creek below. This creek, however, is incompletely charted and one should proceed cautiously.

Patuxent River is navigable for another 10 miles or more above Benedict, but the channel is unmarked most of the way beyond

Chalk Point (site of another electric power plant) and there are no protected anchorages outside the channel.

XVIII. St. Jerome Creek (*12233*).

Don't try this creek in a hard onshore wind, or if you draw 3½ feet or more, but it is a very handy refuge for shoal-draft cruisers between the Patuxent and the Potomac. The depth in the dredged channel—5 feet according to our chart—cannot be depended on.

Between Points No Point and Look-in, leave the two red markers to starboard heading north to the narrow entrance, where you leave the Fl. R beacon on St. Jerome Point to starboard. The best anchorage is just north of the lighted beacon 9.

Here's how an earlier authority told us to enter when there was only one navigational aid:

> On entering the channel, favor the Deep Point side, turn abruptly at the outer red range, and head not for the Airedale dock, but for the far (west) end of the large leaning shed past the dock, between this dock and the red turning buoy.
>
> Gas is obtainable at the dock, but there is little else. However, there's usually an obliging motorist around who's going inland a couple of miles for supplies, and he might as well take you, and welcome. Anchor, if you must, near the dock, but don't block the channel. It's best to continue around that red marker off the shed, passing close to the inner black range to a point (usually locally stake marked) halfway between the range and Fisher's Point. Ease over to Malone Bay for anchorage or, better yet, left rudder at this halfway point and turn up the north arm of the creek, where you'll find 5 to 7 feet of water at low tide. I go in to a cove due east of the point which separates the words "Jerome" and "Creek" on the chart.
>
> How do strangers come to grief in the creek? According to the local boys it is often by flinching away from the deep water close to Deep Point and getting too close to St. Jerome Point. Occasionally by blindly continuing from the outer red range toward the inner black one, ignoring the red turning marker near the dock. Probably most often by heading directly for the dock from the red range, or vice versa. . . . It's best not to charge in too boldly.

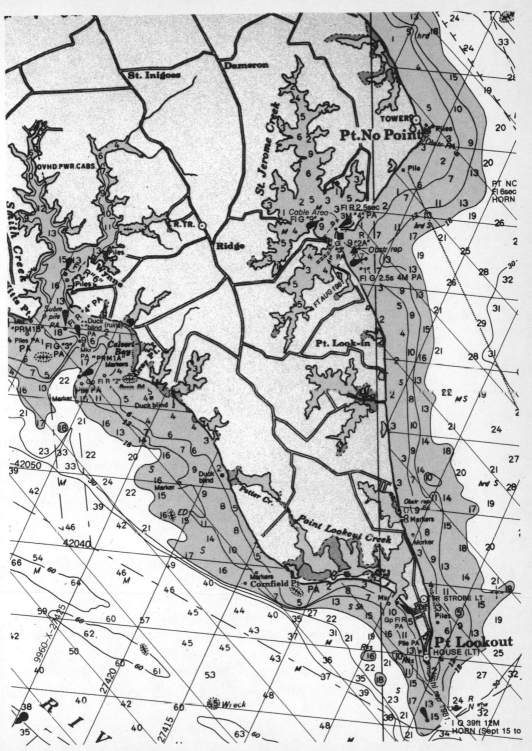

St. Jerome Creek, Potomac River entrance, Smith Creek (from chart 12230).

CHAPTER SEVEN

POTOMAC RIVER
TO WASHINGTON

Here is a spacious cruising area to rival the best in the Chesapeake.

The mouth of the Potomac gives no hint of the hidden charms above. The points on both sides of the 10-mile-wide entrance are low and would be inconspicuous were it not for the high, silver-tinted water tank and hotel on Point Lookout. No majestic cliffs or pine-clad, rocky islands are there to lure the yachtsman as he heads southward along the Western Shore. Instead, he is apt to find a vast expanse of placid waters almost as wide as those of the Chesapeake itself. There will be no suggestion of the lovely landlocked harbors concealed in the bays, rivers, and creeks which make the Lower Potomac one of the finest cruising areas on the Chesapeake. "Seek and ye shall find."

Though most of the best cruising is within 30 miles of the entrance, motor cruisers with enough speed can usually carry the flood tide all, or almost all, the way from Point Lookout to Washington, 95 miles upriver. Awaiting them in Washington Channel will be a secure berth and every possible facility. Since the good harbors in the last 65 miles of the run to Washington are not up to those below, it would be wise, if cruisers are in no great hurry, to break up the trip somewhere below the Governor Henry W. Nice Memorial Bridge carrying Route 301 across the Potomac at Dahlgren, Va. It would be still better to spend at least a week on the Lower Potomac. On both the Maryland and Virginia shores there is much to see.

The mean range of tide is about 1 1/2 feet in the lower part of the river, 2 feet at Blakiston Island, and 3 feet at Washington. However, winds or freshets may considerably influence the height of the tides, as they do the velocity of the current. (See the Atlantic Coast Current and Tide Tables.)

Skippers or crews who want to go to church on Sunday should look on the Maryland shore if they are Catholics, on the Virginia shore if they are Protestants. It will be easier in that way to find the church of the faith for which they are looking. That's the way it was in the seventeenth century, and it's not too different today.

As already indicated, there are various restricted and prohibited areas on the Potomac; these are shown on the charts and explained in detail in the *Coast Pilot*. Fortunately, the restricted areas are not where the best cruising is to be found. Even in these areas the restrictions are by no means always in effect. Keep your eyes open for Navy Range boats—large white craft which are apt to be found anywhere from St. Clements Island to Dahlgren or farther up. Whenever you see one of these boats be sure to report for instructions as to where you can go. The Navy seldom does any artillery firing on weekends or holidays.

Cornfield Harbor just inside Point Lookout is a large, open bight, too exposed to be comfortable as an overnight anchorage except in calm summer weather.

Maryland has developed 495 acres of Point Lookout as a state park. There is a dredged cut there between stone jetties connecting Cornfield Harbor and Lake Conoy, within the park. The 100-foot-wide channel was dredged to a mid-channel depth of 6 feet, 4 feet at the sides. This is primarily a small-boat harbor but it is also designated as a harbor of refuge. You may go in and anchor during the day, but you may not stay overnight, except in an extreme emergency. Facilities ashore include camp sites, beaches, nature and history trails, launch ramps, boat rentals, fishing head boats, surf fishing, and a visitor center. The park is on the site of a Union Forces hospital and Camp Hoffman, where more than 20,000 Confederate prisoners endured miserable months and years with inadequate shelter and food between 1863 and 1865. Little remains from the Civil War period. For more information about the park, call (301) 872-5688. For specific information concerning boating, call (301) 872-4342.

Before starting our voyage up the river, we should like to warn yachtsmen that the mouth of the Potomac has a bad reputation for squalls—so get into port early. There are some splendid harbors awaiting. Smith Creek, on the Maryland shore, is only 6 or 7 miles from Point Lookout. Coan River on the Virginia shore is only 7 or 8 miles away.

Despite the names "Hurry" and "Lively" for two tidewater villages on the Potomac, cruising on this famous river is usually as easy and restful as these sleepy hamlets themselves.

I. Smith Creek and Wynne (*12285, 12233*), Maryland Shore of Potomac.

This is the most accessible and one of the best anchorages on the Potomac. It is often used as a harbor of refuge for boats passing up or down the Bay in inclement weather when the mouth of the Potomac can be rough and uncomfortable for small craft of any type. The entrance, once considered difficult for strangers because of several abandoned range beacons, has been remarked with four lighted beacons that are easy to follow into the creek. If approaching from the west or southwest, vessels should give a wide berth to the shoal that extends almost a mile south of Kitts Point beyond the sunken wreck shown on the charts. The entrance channel is now well marked, but you should proceed cautiously, swinging hard to port on passing close to beacon 3 to avoid the 2-foot spot just north of the marker. This shoal extends almost all the way to R-4, and boats drawing more than 6 feet may drag at this point since the channel is narrow; but the bottom is soft and you will be in deep water again before reaching red beacon 4. From there on the channel is deep and straight to the last marker beyond the docks at Wynne. These are not the best places to tie up because the fishing pier is usually crowded with local boats and the fish and oyster dock is commercial.

If you keep on up the creek and then turn northeast toward Jutland Creek you will have a choice of good anchorages or a well-run marina and boatyard on the sharp point of land to starboard. You can probably obtain a slip or a guest mooring from Point Lookout Marina (formerly Clayton Marina), with 12 feet of water at the dock and many facilities.

There are also fine anchorages above Wynne in Jutland Creek, known locally as the East Branch of Wynne Creek. A Chesapeake cruising man writes:

> Jutland Creek is still one of the loveliest, unspoiled, wooded creeks in the lower Potomac area. We anchor well up the creek, around the bend, just out of sight of the boatyard, opposite a large osprey nest on the west bank.

Other good anchorages on Smith Creek are near the head of the main branch or in one of the forks.

II. St. Marys River (*12285, 12233*), Maryland Shore of Potomac.

On a spring day in 1634, Leonard Calvert, brother of Lord Baltimore, sailed the *Ark* and the *Dove* into St. Marys River and founded on its eastern shore the first settlement in Maryland. He

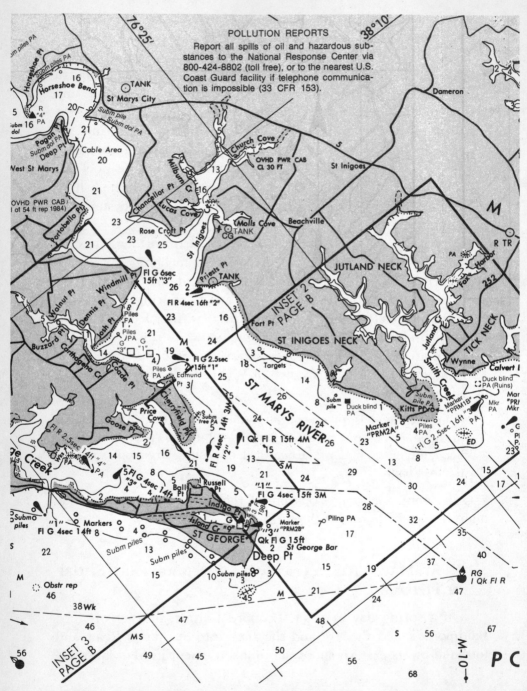

St. Marys River on Potomac River (from chart 12285).

called it St. Marys City and it became the first capital of the province. The town languished after the capital was moved to Annapolis in 1695 and eventually disappeared almost entirely. In 1934 the original statehouse was reconstructed, and this handsome brick building commands a spectacular view over the river from its broad lawn. Extensive archaeological digs have been conducted here in the past few years. Nearby are the colonial-style buildings of St. Mary's College. These all combine to make the site of this old city an interesting and attractive objective for yachtsmen cruising along the Potomac.

Even without its historic significance, St. Marys River is very much worth a side trip. For the river is very pretty, especially in its upper part where wooded hills and fertile, well-kept farmlands come down to the water's edge, and one of the finest creeks on the Chesapeake—St. Inigoes—offers perfect shelter. It is only about 8 miles from the entrance to the island with the intriguing name Tippity Wichity.

1. St. George Creek (12285, 12233). This creek on the west shore of St. Marys River is less attractive than Smith Creek and St. Inigoes on the eastern shore. The entrance is well marked between the outlying shoals, and lighted beacons take you as far as St. George Harbor, home port of the Harry Lundeberg School of Seamanship, operated by the International Seamen's Union as a training school for merchant seamen. The school has taken over docks and shore facilities of the former Coast Guard base at Piney Point, and has dredged the harbor to accommodate deep-draft vessels at its bulkheads.

The yawl *Manitou,* once sailed by President John F. Kennedy, is exhibited at the dock area, and you can see a log canoe, a skipjack, and a bugeye at the nearby boat shed. There are no tie-up facilities for visiting yachts. School officials ask that you not bring your own boat in, but invite you to visit their facilities—by land—between 9 A.M. and 5 P.M. the first Sunday of every month.

2. St. Inigoes Creek (12285, 12233), East Shore of St. Marys River. Here are the best anchorages on St. Marys River. Near the entrance

After the Governor's Cup Race in August, the fleet rafts up at the St. Mary's College docks or anchors in the Horseshoe Bend of St. Marys River. (Photo courtesy of St. Mary's College.)

to starboard the land is low, with some marshes, but to the port on the northern shore the woods are thick and fairly high. Like the river itself, the creek becomes more attractive farther up.

On the point opposite Lucas Cove, and just beyond Molls Cove, on the south shore, is Cross Manor, said to be one of the oldest houses in Maryland and to have been built in 1644, ten years after the founding of St. Marys City. The famous box hedges are now almost large enough to be called trees. (In fact, on our last visit to St. Inigoes in the mid-1980s, we had trouble finding the house, now almost hidden behind the box hedge.)

The anchorage that appealed to us was one just beyond the point where Cross Manor is situated. Here, where the creek widens, you can drop your hook in 13 feet and lie securely, with the old house and its box hedges looking down from the hill above.

Other good anchorages are in Milburn Creek or in Church Cove. Apparently, as in other cases, local names don't agree with the chart. Moll Cove (on the chart) is Church Cove locally—there is a church at the end. Lucas Cove (chart) is Moll's Cove and Church Cove (chart) is a fork of St. Inigoes Creek. We almost lost confidence in our ability to read a chart while we tried to figure out with the local authorities which place was where.

3. St. Marys City (12233), East Shore of St. Marys River. On a hill overlooking St. Marys River at Church Point is the modern counterpart of old St. Marys City.

As you approach Horseshoe Bend, to starboard you may see the replica of the Dove, one of the two sailing vessels that brought the first settlers to this spot in 1635. You may visit the Dove if she is in her home port. You may not, at this writing, tie up to her dock, but you may be able to after planned improvements have been made.

Continuing past the dock and the statehouse, you'll see a large wooden cross marking Church Point, and then, inside the bend, the docks and buildings of St. Mary's College. You may tie up briefly, and the dock master will give you permission to use the college swimming pool and showers. (Donation requested.) No marina services or supplies are available. Refreshed, you can anchor out and dinghy ashore to visit historic St. Marys City, a living history museum of early life in the colonial town a short walk away up the hill. Buy tickets at the visitors center or Farthing's Ordinary, a restaurant serving lunch during the summer. The museum is open on weekends, from April to mid-December, and, additionally, daily from Memorial Day to Labor Day, 10 A.M. to 5 P.M.

St. Mary's College, a coeducational liberal arts institution that is part of the state university system, is noted for its sail training programs and is now an active participant in intercollegiate racing as well as major events on the Bay. The Governor's Cup Race, held in mid-August each year, is an overnight race from Annapolis to St. Mary's City that grew to be the largest race in terms of participants (over 300) on the Bay. The huge fleet moors and rafts for a day of waterfront activities at the college after the race (see photo pages 278–279). A number of yacht clubs hold rendezvous in this popular anchorage, with the college cooperating in shore events.

III. COAN RIVER AND THE GLEBE (*12285, 12233*), VIRGINIA SHORE OF POTOMAC.

Coan River and its tributary, Glebe Creek, are favorite stopping places for Florida-bound yachtsmen—justifiably so, because they have much to offer besides accessibility from the Bay.

1. Main Branch of Coan River (12285, 12233). The outer channel is not difficult but watch the chart carefully inside to avoid outlying shoals. For instance, don't head directly from red beacon 10 to beacon 12; swing to starboard to avoid the shoal off Walnut Point. The most convenient anchorage is south of the end of Walnut Point. The Coan River Marina there has 7 feet of water at the dock, slips for transients, gas, ice, and repair facilities.

But the snuggest and prettiest anchorage is 2 or 3 miles upriver between Bundick and Hawk Nest points, provided you can get

Coan River on the lower Potomac (from chart 12233).

under the 60-foot-high cable. Gas, water, and a store are available at Bundick and there is 9 feet at the wharf.

2. *Kingscote Creek, Coan River, Virginia (12285, 12233).* There is a popular and convenient anchorage in Kingscote Creek, west of Lewisetta, where gas, ice, and supplies are available. However, this is open to the south and southeast for some distance. A snugger place may be found in one of the long, narrow coves on the west shore, but here you would be away from the conveniences at Lewisetta. The *Coast Pilot* reports a depth of 4 feet at the landing, but we found less than that in 1986. The land on the point is low. Local buoys, not shown on the chart, mark the entrance to the creek between the two outlying shoals. A veteran Potomac yachtsman comments: "Very friendly people ashore."

3. *The Glebe (12285, 12233), Coan River, Virginia.* A glebe is a plot of land granted to a clergyman as part of his benefice during his tenure of office. The granting of such plots must have been a common occurrence, judging by the number of glebes one comes across around the Chesapeake. In the various forks of this Glebe, there are several anchorages. On the first sharp point to the starboard was a very old boatyard, possibly the oldest on the Bay. It was established in 1820 by a Headley and was run by Giles and Sam Headley when we first visited Coan River in 1950, but it was no longer operating by 1980. There are good anchorages in all of the coves and creeks up the Glebe.

IV. YEOCOMICO RIVER (*12285, 12233*), VIRGINIA.

This also is a popular stopping place for cruising boats, with so many good anchorages that we can mention only a few of the best.

"Like the arms of an octopus" well describes the appearance on the chart of the Yeocomico and its tributaries—and *their* tribu-

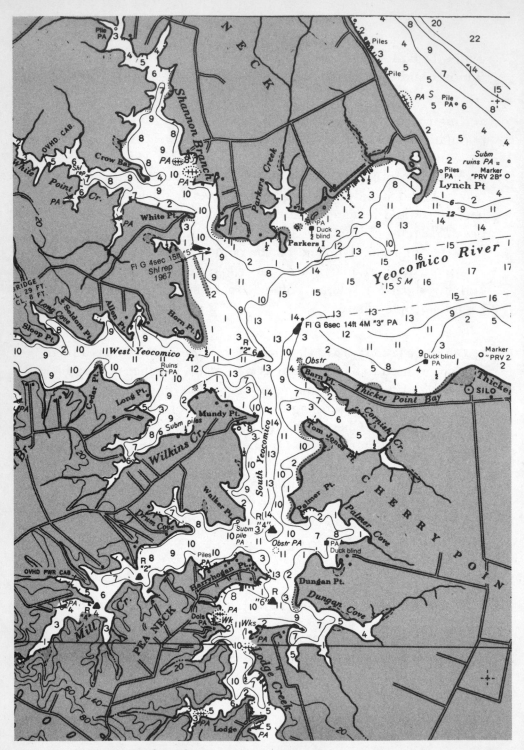

Yeocomico River (from chart 12233).

taries—up to the little coves where the hook is finally dropped. There are three main branches described below, each of which has many good anchorages and coves along its shores.

1. South Yeocomico (12285, 12233). If we had to choose a favorite branch, we would probably favor the South Yeocomico for the variety of its anchorages and shorefront facilities. Here you will find good anchorages in six coves and creeks. Close to the entrance you will find good holding ground south of Barn Point in Cornish Creek. Better protection is offered in most of the creeks farther up, particularly Lodge Creek, where Olverson's Marina has excellent accommodations, and south of Harryhogan Point, in 10 feet near the Krentz Marine Railway, with extensive building and repair facilities. This yard built the last working skipjack (in 1954) for the oyster fleet.

There is (or was) a post office, where we first heard the story of how Harryhogan came by its name. When we asked whom the town was named after, the postmistress replied with a smile, "Oh, it's not named after a person, but was given this name by Captain John Smith, who heard the Indians call the creek 'Arrayogan,' which the Captain transcribed as Harryhogan. That's what it has been called ever since."

2. West Yeocomico River (12285, 12233), Virginia. Kinsale, at the head of this branch, is the leading town on the Yeocomico. Kinsale Marina is very well equipped and has gas, water, ice, etc., and a store on the steep hillside above.

The West Yeocomico almost equals the South Yeocomico in the number of snug anchorages in protected coves. Poke into Long Cove on the north shore between Sloop Point and Sheldon Point, drop your hook in 8 feet; or try any of the horseshoe bends in the Hampton Hall branch. The Moorings Restaurant at the Yeocomico Marina, north of Allen Point, has a fine reputation.

3. Shannon Branch and White Point Creek (12285, 12233). Most northerly of the three branches, the Shannon has its share of attractive anchorages and a well-run boatyard, the White Point Marina, near the mouth of White Point Creek.

V. LOWER MACHODOC CREEK (*12285, 12286*), VIRGINIA.

This isn't as appealing as either the Yeocomico below or Nomini above, though it is easy to enter and supplies are more accessible at the facilities in Branson Cove.

VI. NOMINI BAY (*12285, 12286*), VIRGINIA SHORE OF THE POTOMAC.

Nomini Creek, Virginia. This is one of our favorite spots on the Potomac. Perhaps it was the beauty of the cold January day when an intelligent fisherman took us out from Mount Holly, near the head, through the long channel to the Bay. Anyway, we took a strong liking to the place. So have others.

We met a yachtsman and his wife in the course of our exploration who later wrote us about Nomini Creek and Mount Holly.

> You'll find Mount Holly on the chart. It's a headache getting in, but its beauty is worth the effort, plus the fact that it is only a short taxi ride from there to Stratford and Wakefield, respectively the birthplaces of Robert E. Lee and George Washington, and two of the most beautiful places you can imagine. You enter this through Nomini Bay, but be sure you do it with good visibility for the markers must be followed exactly and they are none too clear.

At the time of our last visit there was about 6 feet in the narrow channel. The channel runs straight from the black framework beacon off the entrance breakwater (partly submerged at high tide) and red nun 4, to the black stake beacon off Icehouse Point. From there it goes straight to the marker off Hickory Point. This nun is sometimes hard to see, so if you can't pick it up, head for a white house among the trees on the point shaped like the claw of a lobster directly ahead of the channel line.

After passing this red nun, pay no attention to the numerous oyster stakes that look like channel markers, but are not. Give the lobster claw point a wide berth, as a shoal makes out. Then swing to starboard and follow the shore until you are past the 1-foot shoal with the pile on the opposite shore. After that, keep in the middle for a very pretty trip to Mount Holly.

The best anchorages are as follows:

(1) On the port shore south of Hickory Point. Anchor between the white and brick houses. This is too large to be cozy.

(2) In the cove to the starboard, south of the lobster claw in 8 feet. This is very pretty and snuggest of all.

(3) Between Mount Holly and Nomini, in 6 to 10 feet just outside of the bridge. At Nomini there is a dock with 10 feet, with gas, water, ice, and a store nearby; or you can get such supplies at McGuire's Wharf on your way, as shown on the chart.

VII. CURRIOMAN BAY (*12285, 12286*), VIRGINIA SHORE OF THE POTOMAC.

This is too large for comfort under some conditions, though fair shelter can be found under the hook at the northwest end, and this cove is near enough to the fossils of Nomini Cliffs for some interesting explorations. Despite the 2 feet shown on the chart, the Sea Scouts who had been there and poked their way in, following a rowboat, told us that the minimum depth at mean low water in the north *channel* was 6 feet. But don't go dashing in as if you knew where the channel was—unless you do know. Follow the Sea Scouts' example; you will get the thrill that comes to mountaineers who avoid the usual trails. But don't try it with a keelboat.

The better entrance, and the one recommended to conservative mariners, is the south one, which is well buoyed, if you pick the correct red nun to head for (the middle one) after picking up N-2 outside. Don't get confused by the nuns nearby marking the entrance to Nomini Creek.

It is fun to explore the creeks (with uncharted depths) along the west shore; but try it in your dinghy first. Some "Poor Jack" evidently came to grief at a creek of that name, for the chart shows a wreck just outside. Perhaps a northwest squall got him as it swept down the Bay. Fresh water is available just above Cold Harbor and Currioman creeks.

Currioman Bay is interesting but if you want security, supplies, and the intimacy of lovely shores close at hand, Nomini Creek is to be preferred.

VIII. BRETON BAY (*12285, 12286*), MARYLAND SHORE OF THE POTOMAC.

Breton Bay offers some of the best cruising waters on the Potomac, with two good creeks for snug anchorages, and a good-sized town with many facilities—Leonardtown—perched on a hill at the head of the Bay, 5 or 6 miles up. If you don't get too close to the shore in some places, as the chart shows, you will find navigation fairly easy; but watch the shoals at Lovers Point and across, and two others near the entrance of the channel to Leonardtown.

1. Combs Creek (12285, 12286), Breton Bay, Maryland. According to chart 12286, this might be a good creek to avoid. Two charted entrance buoys are to be seen marking the narrow channel between two 1-foot spots. Inside, however, the depths are charted at 5 to 8 feet. Along this creek are several boatyards, gas docks, and some first-rate anchorages.

According to a leading local authority who ran one of the boatyards, the right hand marker, to be left to starboard, has an arrow and a reflector. Head for the passage between these markers, leaving the Huggins Point flasher directly over your stern. This will clear the shoals on either side. After passing between the markers the channel swings sharply to port and then to starboard—perhaps a double gybe for sailboats, apt to be a bit hazardous in a strong wind. The entrance is between two sandy spits.

Our local authority reports 5 feet in the entrance channel at low water, with deeper water inside.

The boatyards on the creek include Dock o' the Bay Marina and Restaurant, on the point with the narrow channel just to port of the creek's entrance. This is a large yard and we are told that the channel is not difficult. Other nearby facilities include Combs Creek Marina and the Harbor View Inn, which has a few slips and a snack bar. Gas, water, and other facilities are available.

Yachts with masts reaching up to 50 feet should keep below the overhead cable with that clearance shown on the chart.

A good anchorage is around the second sand spit to starboard. This creek offers fine protection from all winds and is a fairly attractive place. Holding ground is said to be good.

2. *Cherry Cove Creek (12285, 12286), Breton Bay, Maryland.* Cherry Cove is a cozy cove; you won't find much company there but lots of shelter and solitude. Nothing remarkably good or bad insofar as nocturnal insects are concerned either.

Like Combs Creek, if the chart were the only guide you would certainly stay out. Three markers, with reflectors and arrows all to be left to port, show the way in. The banks on either side of the entrance shelve steeply.

From the soundings indicated on the chart the cove looks suitable for not much more than an outboard skiff. However, we've been in and out of there even at moderately low water in 3- and 4-foot drafters and the channel is clear and apparent. It's even easier now, since reflector arrow markers have been locally placed. You approach from the south, keeping outside the grass, pick up the first arrow, and the others will guide you into the cove. In going in, favor the southwest point, the one on the port hand; you'll find at least 7 feet of water in the pass, probably closer to 11 feet.

Inside the cove there's about 5- to 7-feet depth for a quarter mile or so . . . there may be a few bush stakes marking the channel but they are hardly necessary. Just keep halfway between the banks.

There's good anchorage inside the northeast hook of the passage in about 5 or 6 feet of water. The addition of reflector markers indicates night travel by others, thus making an anchor light a worthwhile protection.

3. Leonardtown (12285, 12286), Breton Bay, Maryland. There is not much at Leonardtown to draw cruising yachts all the way to the head of the bay, unless you urgently need provisions not available at the smaller communities. You may find a transient slip at the Leonardtown wharf, with 6 feet alongside the dock, but recent visitors have reported other facilities are limited. Most of the shops and stores are up the hill above the wharf. From atop another hill a famous old mansion—Tudor Hall—looks down on the Bay through a grove of white oaks. There are several good anchorages just below the town, along the north shore. The land here is high and wooded.

On your way up or down the bay you might look in at Abell's Wharf in the bight north of Lovers Point on the south shore, where 6 feet or more can be carried to the dock. In earlier days this was a steamboat landing.

IX. ST. CLEMENTS BAY (12285, 12286), MARYLAND SHORE OF THE POTOMAC.

The entrance is full of shoals and requires some careful navigation, as does the bay inside. St. Clements Bay has some good cruising waters with several fine creeks for anchorages on the west shore; these include Deep Creek, one of the best on the Chesapeake.

Famous St. Clements Island, with its giant cross and abandoned lighthouse tower, is a good landmark for the western entrance up St. Clements Bay. The cross was erected in 1934 in memory of the landing on the island of the first Catholics to reach what is now the

United States: the expedition on the *Ark* and the *Dove*. There they held their first mass.

All that remains of sunken Heron Island is a bar to block the middle of the entrance to St. Clements Bay.

1. Colton Point (12286). On the Potomac behind St. Clements Island and at the western entrance of St. Clements Bay is a convenient place for gas, water, and supplies. This is at the long dock at Colton Point, to which 5 feet can be carried. The dock was bought from the government by Mary A. Butterfield after World War II and is a center of waterfront activity.

2. St. Patrick Creek (12286), West Shore of St. Clements Bay. A well-marked dredged channel, 60 feet wide and about 6 feet deep on our last visit, makes this creek accessible from the Bay. There are some boatyards in the coves along the north shore, and several anchorages beyond the channel.

3. Canoe Neck Creek (12286), West Shore of St. Clements Bay. This is large and wide with plenty of water well up and in various bights where good anchorages may be found. The best of these is in the cove south of Morris Point on the west shore near the entrance. If you want to avoid a large collection of houses and small motorboats you may prefer to anchor farther up the creek in the first cove on the east shore. This creek is not outstanding.

4. Deep Creek (12286), West Shore of St. Clements Bay. This is the best creek on St. Clements Bay, and compares favorably with some of the finest on the Chesapeake. While the chart shows 6 feet in the very narrow entrance, we were assured by a local authority who knows these waters well that there is more than that in the entrance channel. His own dock with the house behind it is just at the point to the starboard or north of the entrance, where the chart shows 6 feet. Our soundings showed 8 or 9 feet.

A fairly high wooded bluff marks the point to the left, or south, side of the entrance. Keep in the middle and go well up. The shore is steep and pretty and the shelter perfect.

5. *Mileys Creek (12286), West Shore of St. Clements Bay.* This creek, between Deep and Tomakokin, is not named on the chart, but is very snug, though not as pretty as Deep Creek. It is easily identified by the long wharf and white house just north of the entrance. Keep in the middle. Watch the overhead cable.

6. *Tomakokin Creek (12286), West Shore of St. Clements Bay.* This is open to easterlies for a mile or so and not nearly as snug as Deep Creek, but it has some good anchorages, nevertheless. Anchor in the middle in 7 feet just opposite the second cove to port. On the northern shore, just before the creek turns southwest, is a fine-looking white house with pillars. We were told that good-sized yachts sometimes anchor off this house.

X. Wicomico River (*12285, 12286*), Maryland Shore of the Potomac.

Here is one of the four Wicomico rivers on the Chesapeake, counting Great and Little Wicomico. This Wicomico is much less inviting to the cruising man than Breton or St. Clements Bay just below. It has only one good harbor, Neale Sound, or Cobb Island, no navigable creeks, and many outlying shoals. Furthermore, the shores are less attractive than those farther down or across the Potomac. However, some of the best duck shooting on the Potomac is said to be at the head of the Wicomico.

Neale Sound—Behind Cobb Island (12285, 12286), Maryland Shore. This is a very valuable harbor to yachtsmen going up the Potomac, for it is the last available port for some distance, except for Colonial Beach and Mattox Creek, across the river. It is also especially convenient for powerboats that don't draw more than 4 feet because they can enter from the east on the way upriver, and leave by the dredged northwest passage. But don't try leaving that way in a sailboat, unless you want to tangle with a fixed bridge (vertical clearance 18 feet).

The channels, particularly the upper one, are narrow and require caution since the water is very shoal on each side. In following the northwest channel remember that the beacons are colored with reference to Potomac River and not Neale Sound Harbor. In other words, leave red markers to starboard and green to port in going *out* of this channel toward Washington.

In entering from the east by the main and deeper channel, the usual procedure is followed on *entering* a harbor, leaving green to port and red to starboard. Swing wide to the north after passing the first green beacon east of Cobb Island and thus avoiding a 4-foot spot, which a prominent Potomac commodore remembers vividly.

The best anchorages are on the east side of the bridge. A dock with plenty of water for large boats is on the Cobb Island shore just east of the bridge. Here is the Cobb Island Marina, with gas, water, ice, and supplies. It operates a restaurant during the boating season. This is the most convenient place to tie up when coming from the southeast. A large "buy boat" ties up at an adjacent dock, which is also used by the Maryland Marine Police. A good anchorage is off Cobb Island Marina, or anywhere east of the bridge and far enough off the channel to avoid the small-boat traffic.

The old swing bridge has given way to a new fixed structure with vertical clearance of 18 feet, which effectively prevents cruising sailboats from entering the harbor from the east and leaving by the western channel. However, the best anchorage and shore facilities for transient vessels are found in the wider basin east of the bridge. Power cruisers attempting to use the eastern channel should check carefully on the depth across the outside shoal, which has a tendency to silt up the dredged cut.

In earlier editions we took note of a tiny rectangle 1½ miles west-northwest from Cobb Point Light and 600 yards from shore, at the 10-foot sounding. It cost one luckless skipper a large boat repair bill to learn that the rectangle designated two bundles of nonresilient piles. The new charts say "subm. ruins."

XI. WESTMORELAND STATE PARK AND THE CLIFFS (*12285, 12286*), VIRGINIA SHORE.

Between Nomini Bay and Popes Creek, where Washington's birthplace is located, rise the high cliffs of Nomini, Stratford, and Horsehead, forming one of the most beautiful shorelines on the Chesapeake. Large fossilized scallop shells and other fossils make these cliffs interesting to the explorer as well as attractive to the long shore cruiser.

In back of "The Sands" of Horsehead Cliffs, lovely Westmoreland State Park rises from a picnic grove at the beach's edge to the cliffs above. Thirteen hundred acres in extent, this park is worth a visit and a climb. If you have a sharp-pointed hook (for the sand is very hard) you can anchor for lunch off "The Sands" and row ashore for a swim and picnic, or perhaps a walk in the park. It would be safer, however, to leave someone aboard ready to get more sea room if an onshore squall is impending, since this shore, with its bad holding ground, has been called a graveyard of ships. Leaving the boat at Mount Holly in Nomini Creek and then taking a taxi or bus to the park would be still better. You will find the superintendent of the park most hospitable. If you are energetic, you may feel like walking about 3 miles farther to Washington's birthplace at Wakefield on Popes Creek, which is too shallow to enter by boat.

XII. MATTOX CREEK (*12285, 12286*), VIRGINIA SHORE OF THE POTOMAC.

For those who prefer a quiet anchorage this is a much better place than back of Colonial Beach, a couple of miles to the north. Local fishermen insist that there is 6 feet of water all the way up past Wirt Wharf to Fox Point, where a marina was built in 1961. Known as the Outdoor World Harbor View Marina and Resort, this commercial enterprise offers open and covered slips, gas, water, ice, showers, and a snack bar; there is also shore storage and a launching ramp. There is 4½ feet at the fuel dock. The lower creek isn't snug in a blow but farther up it is better protected. Get your supplies at Colonial Beach but anchor here for the night. Swimming is good and the place is pretty.

XIII. COLONIAL BEACH—MONROE CREEK (*12285, 12286*), VIRGINIA SHORE OF THE POTOMAC.

The Bay Yacht Center, a commercial marina located around Gum Bar Point to starboard as you enter, has 4½ feet at the gas dock and 4 to 6 feet in the open and covered slips. There is a restaurant, and a motel nearby. Showers, ice, electricity, a store, and a large travel lift are among the facilities. Farther up creek, on Robin Grove Point, is the Stanford Marine Railway, with a few slips, a good machine shop, marine supply store, and a dock with slips facing the turning basin. Several other small marinas are on this creek.

While most of these docks are new and well kept up, visitors complain that the wash from passing motorboats in the heavy traffic in and out of the harbor makes a berth here for meals aboard, or for overnight, too uneasy for comfort. There is a strong current at the entrance. However, it is much pleasanter at the Bay Yacht Center than at Colonial Beach, a crowded resort spot with plenty of "cocktail cruising," as one visitor put it. While the Yacht Center site at Gum Bar Point is low and paved with oyster shells, the land across the harbor is nice-looking woodland, and there is a good sandy beach south of Sebastian Point.

Taxis can be obtained to take visitors to Washington's birthplace at Wakefield.

XIV. UPPER MACHODOC CREEK, DAHLGREN (*12285, 12286*), VIRGINIA SHORE.

This is occupied by the Navy, but is no longer a prohibited area. The creek shoals to 5 feet beyond the last marker but boats drawing less can go to Dahlgren Marina on the point north of the piles shown on the chart. Gas, water, ice, and slips are available and there is a launching ramp.

XV. Potomac River Bridge, Morgantown (*12285, 12286*).

The high-level fixed bridge that crosses the Potomac just north of Morgantown has a vertical clearance of 135 feet, more than enough for any masted vessel. The main channel runs close to the Morgantown shore.

If you are heading upriver toward Washington you will find a convenient overnight stopping point in a dredged basin at Aqua-Land Park, just north of the Governor Henry W. Nice Memorial Bridge on the Maryland shore. The Aqua-Land Marina has more than 150 open and covered slips, with all the usual facilities: gas and diesel fuel, ice, showers, snack bar, and restaurant. For an overnight stay, this is preferable to Morgantown, 1½ miles south of the bridge, where the dock area is exposed.

XVI. Port Tobacco River (*12285, 12286*), Maryland Shore of the Potomac.

In approaching Port Tobacco River from the south, another Popes Creek (not Washington's birthplace) appears on the starboard hand. This Popes Creek is best known for Robertson's Crab House, on the site formerly occupied by the Potomac Shipwrecking Company, open April through October. Dockage is available at the crab house, with 10 feet of water at the end of the dock. There is also room to anchor and dinghy in for a meal.

It is interesting to note, as Fred Tilp pointed out many years ago, that "Long before the white man came to Maryland, Indian tribes camped by Popes Creek annually to eat oysters; the shell heap that accumulated for centuries once covered 30 acres and at places was

15 feet high. In recent years most of this accumulation has been used for road building or for fertilizer."

Port Tobacco is a very pretty place, with high wooded shores on either side. However, it is open too far to the north and south to be comfortable in strong winds from either direction. In going in, keep east of the range of the two lights off Mathias Point. Goose Bay Marina, to port near the entrance, has slips with 4 feet at the dock and launching ramps. A safe anchorage for boats drawing under 5 feet is above Fourth Point.

Overlooking the river from a high hill is an impressively located brick Catholic church—St. Ignatius, which celebrated its 175th anniversary in 1973. The view of the river from the church is worth the hill climb. Beyond Chapel Point, across the river, is the Port Tobacco Marina, with 4 feet at the dock.

Port Tobacco, which is anything but a port, is situated a short distance beyond the upper end of the river. The Indian name was Pertafacco, meaning "in the hollow of the hills," and from this the present name was evolved, just as other names have evolved on the Chesapeake. The ubiquitous Captain John Smith visited here in 1608, and his map shows an Indian village called Potapaco. Thus, the weed we smoke apparently had nothing to do with the name. Among the hills are some fine old manor houses.

After leaving Port Tobacco River to continue up the Potomac, look out for some obstructions and submerged ruins south of the channel, between Mathias and Metompkin points.

XVII. NANJEMOY CREEK (*12285, 12288*), MARYLAND SHORE OF THE POTOMAC.

Nanjemoy is Indian for "poor fishing." From its inadequate charting, it looks like poor cruising also. However, we are told by yachtsmen who have been there that the depths are somewhat greater than the chart shows. Apparently, most yachts, or at least those drawing no more than 5 feet, can go all the way up to the entrance of Hilltop Fork, despite the charted depths. They will find deep water at the landing, good shelter, and pretty scenery.

If you like getting off the beaten track and poking into out-of-the-way places like Fred Tilp and his Sea Scouts, you will enjoy finding your way up here. But take it easy.

The current is strong off Maryland Point, and there are some wicked fish traps and rotten stakes off the shore just above.

John Wilkes Booth, while fleeing the capital southward, rowed across at Blossom Point.

XVIII. POTOMAC CREEK (*12285, 12288*), VIRGINIA SHORE OF THE POTOMAC.

This creek features a difficult entrance, fossilized sharks' teeth at Bull Bluff, and big mosquitoes. It is also one of the many supposed sites at which Pocahontas saved Captain John Smith from her father, the great Indian chief Powhatan. The chart gives few soundings beyond the entrance and the creek is too large for comfort. So, unless you like exploring uncharted waters and the above features appeal to you, we'd recommend going elsewhere.

XIX. AQUIA CREEK (*12285, 12288*), VIRGINIA SHORE OF THE POTOMAC.

We were advised by one of our Potomac authorities to recommend staying out of this creek. The channel is very narrow and there are extensive shoals on either side. Some rotten old piles project from the marshy point south of the entrance. Another authority calls the place interesting and beautiful, but with strong currents.

Boats drawing under 4 feet might enjoy going in. There are a couple of marinas. The shores are high and there are some very old wrecks near the head. The Confederates once had a strong battery on Brent Point.

XX. Mallows Bay (*12285, 12288*), Maryland Shore of the Potomac.

Not so many years ago the beach at Liverpool Point was a good place for swimming, but pollution from up river has made this and other beaches unusable from here to Washington. Perhaps the current campaign for a clean Potomac will bring them back in the not too distant future. Mallows Bay is a "foul bight," most of which is strewn with wrecks. The only possible anchorage is in 5 feet in the cove to the south. Even here you may foul your anchor. If you don't, it is easy to drag, since the bottom is hard and the anchorage is exposed to the northwest.

XXI. Quantico Basin and Creek (*12285, 12288*), Virginia Shore of the Potomac.

We were prepared to warn yachtsmen to keep out—the Marines "landed" here some time ago and this is their bailiwick. However, we have had nothing but favorable reports from boats which have made an emergency stop here and received a friendly reception from the Marines at the Quantico Basin. But don't abuse the privilege.

Permission to tie up or use a mooring must be obtained from the harbormaster in the basin, which is indicated on the chart by the word "bell." We are told that this permission is usually granted. Be on guard against a strong crosscurrent in approaching the basin.

There is a fleet of small racing sailboats and a yacht club inside. Water and ice are available, and there are stores, restaurants, etc., in the town of Quantico close by. "There are no mosquitoes," commented an old river sailor who knows the Potomac.

Don't try anchoring in Quantico Creek in the bight outside of the bridge above Shipping Point. Frequent railroad trains make sleep impossible.

XXII. CHICAMUXEN CREEK (*12285, 12288*), MARYLAND SHORE OF THE POTOMAC.

This is too large to be snug and too shallow to be comfortable, and there is nothing there except mosquitoes—in season. The creek isn't charted beyond the entrance, but we are told that 5 feet can be carried about halfway up. The chart reported "hrd" or "grs," which doesn't look inviting from a holding viewpoint.

XXIII. MATTAWOMAN CREEK (*12285, 12288*), MARYLAND SHORE OF THE POTOMAC.

This used to be a popular anchorage for weekend cruises from Washington. A few yachts continue to anchor in the wide mouth of the creek, south of Deep Point in 7 or 8 feet, but the area is exposed to winds from the northwest. This is no longer a restricted area, but better shelter can be found up the creek by following the winding channel in depths of 13 to 26 feet to the bend off Bullitt Neck about a mile above the entrance. Sweden Point, where we used to tie up when researching the first edition of this guide, can be reached today only by boats drawing less than 3 feet.

XXIV. OCCOQUAN CREEK (*12285, 12289*), VIRGINIA SHORE OF THE POTOMAC.

Due to the great increase in population in this area, marine facilities have appeared on this creek, both above and below the 65-foot vertical clearance fixed highway bridge. All services are available, including marinas and restaurants. Powerboats are predominant. The channel in is narrow and bordered by marshes. Local boaters estimate a minimum of 8 feet in the channel except at very low tides.

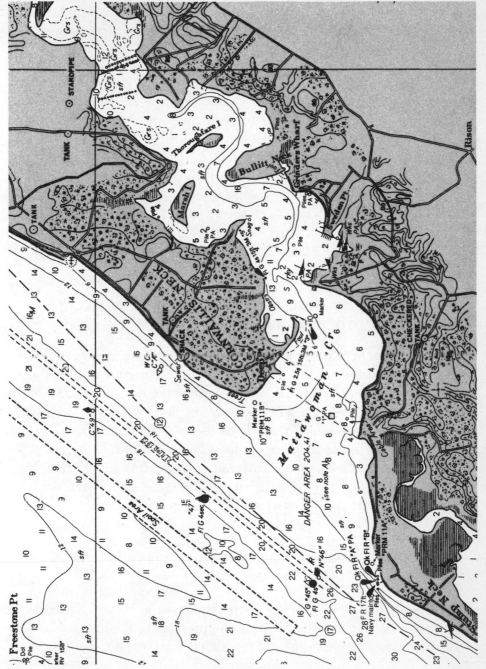

Mattawoman Creek on Potomac River (from chart 12288).

XXV. GUNSTON COVE (*12285, 12289*), VIRGINIA SHORE OF THE POTOMAC.

This is still a favorite weekend anchorage for Washingtonians, although the entrance channel shoals. Anchor anywhere in the middle, sounding carefully before you drop the hook. There are pretty, high bluffs on either side. Give Whitestone Point a wide berth.

Pohick Bay Regional Park is located on the east shore, south of Gunston Hall. There is a lot of activity here—swimming and board sailing in particular—on summer weekends. Gunston Hall, on the hill north of Kanes Creek, is an outstanding piece of colonial architecture, amidst hedges and large trees.

XXVI. MOUNT VERNON (*12285, 12289*), VIRGINIA SHORE OF THE POTOMAC.

The home of Washington is located on "Little Reach," a sailor's term for the stretch of the Potomac between Whitestone Point and Fort Washington. You can't tie up for long at the dock, but you'll be allowed to land crew members who want to visit Mount Vernon, provided you keep out of the way of the excursion steamers from Washington. This isn't a place for spending the night.

We don't need to advise yachtsmen to stop at Mount Vernon if they haven't been there already. It is, of course, one of the great historic places of our country, as beautiful as it is famous.

XXVII. PISCATAWAY CREEK (*12285, 12289*), MARYLAND SHORE.

Depths run from 3 to 5 feet and there is the Fort Washington Marina, with 5 feet at the dock and many slips. Gas, water, ice, and supplies are available. The fort for which the marina is named is just beyond. Built to protect Washington, D.C. (*after* the British burned the city during the War of 1812), the fort is open to the public as one of the National Capital Parks. In earlier editions we noted that the approach to Washington and Alexandria offered no safe anchorage or shore facilities before you reach the Woodrow Wilson Bridge (vertical clearance 50 feet). But now, in 1988, a major new development is being planned which will transform the waterfront south of the bridge on the Maryland shore. Called Port America, if built as planned, the development will include a marina, offices, retail shops, restaurants, and condominiums.

On the Virginia shore, in Alexandria, the Alexandria City Marina (opened in 1986) welcomes transients for a day or overnight, but does not allow long-term berthing. The marina does not offer repair services or fuel, but does have water, electricity, etc. Holding tanks are required; no consumption of alcoholic beverages is allowed. The location is very convenient for visiting the historic town and, in particular, the renovated Torpedo Factory, which now houses 200 arts and crafts studios where you may see the artists work. The *Alexandria*, a three-masted topsail schooner, is docked nearby at the foot of King Street. It is a sail training vessel which is available for charter and which acts as an ambassador for the city.

Don't anchor between Piscataway Creek and Haines Point. The river is narrow, the traffic heavy, and the current strong.

The river divides into three forks, just below Washington.

(1) Anacostia River, sometimes known as the Eastern Branch of the Potomac.
(2) Washington Channel, where most of the yachts, yacht clubs, and marinas are located.
(3) The Virginia Channel, west of Potomac Park.

Of these three, Washington Channel is by far the most important and usually the best place to go. A good deal of the Anacostia River is monopolized by the Navy and is unattractive, with few facilities for yachts, except at the Fort McNair Yacht Basin, which is a large

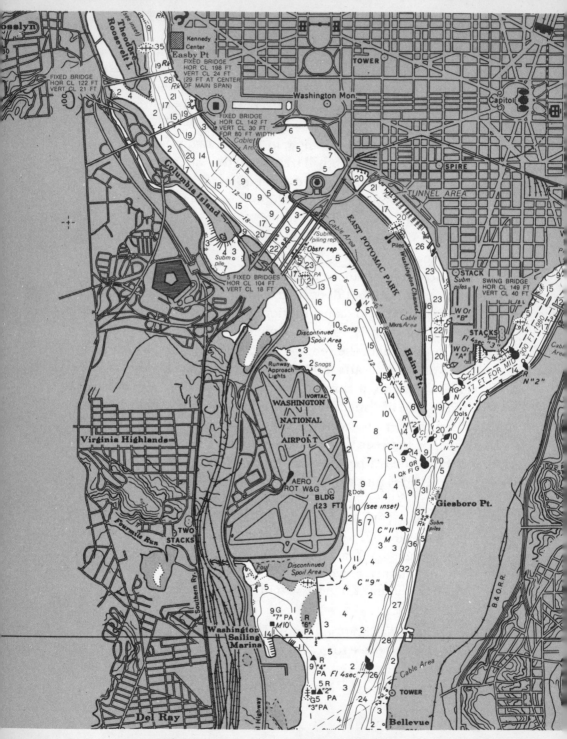

Washington Channel, Potomac River (from chart 12289).

public marina on the site of the old Corinthian Yacht Club, just back of the National War College on the point. If the Washington Channel facilities are crowded, the McNair Basin could be the best place to look for an overnight berth. The Virginia Channel has the Pentagon Lagoon, but the depths shown on the chart or the 18-foot vertical clearance of the fixed bridge eliminates this area for most cruising boats. The Washington Sailing Marina, south of the National Airport, may have mooring facilities for smaller cruising auxiliaries. The mean tidal range at Washington, as pointed out earlier, is 3 feet.

The Washington waterfront has been entirely rebuilt since the early 1970's as part of a major redevelopment program that has changed the skyline of southwest Washington. Entering Washington Channel from the river, you pass high-rise luxury apartments behind a broad pedestrian mall that extends from the steamer piers to the marinas and waterfront restaurants at the upper end, where highway and railroad bridges cut across the channel. Here, at the upper end, the Capital Yacht Club has built an attractive clubhouse near its old location, retaining its own slips in the channel.

The Gangplank Restaurant and Marina has floating docks where you may tie up. If you opt to anchor out, notify the Metropolitan Police Marine Branch either by going to their headquarters ashore opposite the anchorage or calling them on your VHF radio, Channel 16. You may land your dinghy at the Gangplank.

The Washington Marina, farther up, on Maine Avenue, beyond a fixed bridge with a vertical clearance of 37 feet, also has limited dock space.

Hogates and Flagship restaurants are housed in luxurious surroundings on the mall, but you may have to anchor out in the channel and come in by dinghy to savor their fine meals.

CHAPTER EIGHT

HARBORS OF THE LOWER EASTERN SHORE—BELOW CHOPTANK RIVER TO CAPE CHARLES

I. LITTLE CHOPTANK RIVER (*12266, 12264*).

This river is especially important to cruising yachtsmen because it is opposite the middle of the long, forbidding, and almost unbroken stretch of the Western Shore from Herring Bay to Patuxent River. The first snug harbors are about 5 miles above its mouth, but you can anchor in deep water sheltered from the west and south just inside James Island, the southern lip of the mouth. Convenience aside, the Little Choptank is well worth visiting, especially for cruising skippers who like to get off the beaten track. Most of its shore is unspoiled; it is not crowded, and it has an astonishing number of good anchorages, several of them among the best on the Lower Eastern Shore.

Because its shores and the shores to the north are low and irregular, its mouth is hard to make out from a distance. But if visibility is

306

average or better, you can sight James Island from 5 miles or more. Approached from the north, it is the westernmost land on the Eastern Shore, and you can head a little east of it till you pick up the entrance buoys. From the south, it is the northern tip of the unbroken shore running north from Hoopers Island, and you can head a little north of it till you pick up the buoys. The entrance is well buoyed, and it is not difficult to find your way in.

For about 5 miles, from Fl. G1 to Fl. G5, the channel is wide and marked adequately. Beyond that point it narrows but is well marked for 2 more miles. On an unusually low tide (drawing 4 feet) we had no trouble tacking all the way up to where the river divides into Gary and Lee creeks. Where the main channel is marked, the entrances to its tributaries are also marked.

The only villages along the river are Taylors Island, on Slaughter Creek; Hudson, on Hudson Creek; and Church Creek, on Church Creek. None of these can be reached by boats drawing more than 3 or 4 feet, but deeper boats can get within dinghy distance. It may be possible to arrange transportation to Cambridge, which is 16 miles from Taylors Island and fewer than 10 miles from Church Creek and Hudson.

1. Slaughter Creek (12264). This is the nearest anchorage to the Bay, and its entrance is lighted, but the bar midway between beacons 2 and 4 has only 4 feet at mean low water. With our draft of 4 feet we just managed to drag across it on an unusually low tide. So if you draw more than 3 feet and the wind is northerly, don't count on this anchorage. Once over the bar, you are okay and can go 2 miles up the creek and anchor in 6 feet below the bridge at Taylors Island or tie up at Taylors Island Marina on the east shore. This anchorage is attractive because it is "country," but the shores are low and marshy and it is not well sheltered to the north.

The marina has slips, gas, ice, and other supplies. On the other side of the creek, at the shore end of the bridge, is a general store, complete with loafers' benches. It's about a half mile from the marina by road. It can also be reached by boats drawing less than 3 feet. Near the general store are the Becky-Phipps cannon, a memento of the War of 1812, and Taylors Island Post Office.

The area has the following possibilities.

Want to try something? There is one place to test the mettle of the amateur, dinghy-borne explorer. Go under the bridge and continue up the creek. After a while you'll find yourself in Upper Keene Broad, after which you'll either get lost and starve to death while furnishing fare for the mosquitoes, find yourself in Lower Keene Broad and be just as lost, or maybe make it into the Honga River, from which you'll have to return, or suddenly burst out into the Chesapeake. Maybe we're doing wrong in provoking the exploring yen in you.

Few places this far up the Bay appear so isolated, yet nature here is bountiful. In summer the flats are alive with crabs; here you catch a bucketful of peelers in no time while amateur fishermen are unable to purchase them in bait stores in cities across the Bay. Weakfish, croakers, and spot abound in season. Early in November ducks by the hundred thousands come in here accompanied by geese and brant, and even a few wild swan alight here from their last stopping place on the Susquehanna River flats. Summer mosquitoes are bad at times, but seldom except in the evenings. But if it's solitude you want, you'll get plenty right here. It's a foretaste of what you'll get farther south in the Honga River and Tangier Sound country and the streams going inland from there.

2. _Brooks Creek_ (_12266_). This creek has a narrow entrance marked by a pair of day beacons. Beyond them you'll find only one more beacon and stakes marking the end of shoals. But with careful piloting you can carry a 6-foot draft up the creek for 1½ miles, where you will see two small marinas on the west shore that serve local watermen and small craft primarily. Just above beacon 3 on the western shore you will find the first of two pretty, tree-lined coves. We poked into both of these on our last visit and found more than 5 feet well on in. Either is a snug and attractive anchorage, except in a hard blow, when all of these creeks become uncomfortable as the wind sweeps across the lowland and bordering marshes.

3. Hudson Creek (12266). This is one of the best creeks on the Eastern Shore. Vessels drawing 5 feet can go as far as Speddens Wharf, a broken-down affair, within half a mile of the village of Hudson. With not over 4 feet, you can go still closer to the village, a little over 3 miles up the creek.

We first saw Hudson Creek in the early morning calm at sunrise, when every tree and the picturesque old wharf were reflected clearly on the mirrorlike surface. In the early 1970's, we went with Howard I. Chapelle (whose home was on Church Creek) and explored the whole length of the creek from the branch near Hudson. We liked it both times. But it takes some care and attentive watching of the water depths to make it.

In entering from Little Choptank River, swing wide around beacon 7 to avoid the shoal between there and beacon 1 at the creek entrance. The most convenient anchorage is behind Casson Point south of 2. We found a large auxiliary riding comfortably here, though it was blowing strongly from the southwest. The next anchorage is in the cove shown on the chart between the words "Hudson" and "Creek." Swing wide around the prominent point, leaving a duck blind to port, and anchor near the south shore. Another, less snug possibility is in the next cove beyond.

While there are no facilities for yachts on the creek, it is possible to continue almost to Hudson by keeping in the middle, leaving stakes to port and anchoring about halfway up the northwest fork in 4 feet, where the crabbing fleet rides. You can land a dinghy at a small dock and walk to a garage for a can of gas, or get supplies in Hudson. When we were there last a bugeye lay moored at the entrance of the northeast fork and we felt we were far from the yachting world so much in evidence at Oxford and Cambridge.

Long before there were any markers in the creek, a Chesapeake cruising man wrote that he piloted his boat "around the hook of a shoal at the entrance of Hudson Creek and anchored in a beautiful, peaceful cove close to its verdant shore." When swimming, he found the water almost fresh and in a thunder squall discovered the holding to be good. When a spectacular sunset followed the squall he became eloquent about Hudson Creek.

Back Creek offers a possible anchorage if you follow the chart carefully or have local pilotage.

4. Madison Bay (12266). The entrance to Madison Bay lies southeast of Hudson Creek and is marked by a lighted beacon. Inside the narrow entrance the channel opens up into a wide anchorage at least 7 feet deep. It is sheltered on all sides but the northwest, yet is too large to be snug. There is a small dock at Madison on the east shore where you can get gasoline, and some supplies are available in the village but you will probably have to use your dinghy to reach them. There is a launching ramp across the creek on the east shore.

5. Fishing Creek (12266). This is another interesting creek, though farther from the Bay and harder to navigate than Hudson. The entrance is marked by a day beacon, and there are two beacons inside, the last less than a mile from the entrance. Thereafter you must rely on your chart. After rounding Cherry Point, just past beacon 4, stay close to it and go well toward the south shore of the creek to avoid the shoal coming off Windmill Point to the north. From there on, if you can stay in the middle of the creek, you will have plenty of water.

On Town Point and the shore southeast of it so many houses are built close together that a skipper looking for a tranquil harbor may be discouraged from entering Fishing Creek. Don't be; this shore is not typical. Most of the creek runs through lovely farmland. Except in the pretty village of Church Creek, the only houses are (or were) solitary farmhouses.

The first snug anchorage is south of Cherry Point, opposite Windmill Point. Farther on, the bights east of Windmill Point offer good, though less snug, anchorages. Opposite Church Creek and beyond are three coves where you can anchor in 4 or 5 feet. If you draw 4 feet or less, you can poke your way up into Northeast or Southeast Branch, 4½ miles above the entrance. Or you can anchor in the channel without bothering anybody, as we did on a calm September afternoon in 1972.

Church Creek, off Fishing Creek. This spot is interesting chiefly because the lovely buildings and grounds of "Historic Old Trinity Church, circa 1675, America's oldest church now in active use" are on the south shore about ½ mile from its head. You can carry 6 feet for 1½ miles up the creek, and in 1975 at high tide we carried 4 feet past Old Trinity to Allen Parker's. But usually you need a dinghy to go ashore.

6. Other Little Choptank Creeks (12266). We said above that we had no trouble sailing up to the mouths of Gary and Lee creeks. According to the chart these creeks are too shoal for boats drawing over 3 feet, but you can anchor in the river, and it's a delightful sail between tree-lined shores with only a few houses visible. The other two creeks—Beckwith and Phillips—are somewhat deeper. According to the chart, you can carry 4 fcct almost 2 miles from beacon 13 up Beckwith Creek and 5 feet for about 1½ miles from beacon 13 up Phillips Creek. For those who don't mind grounding occasionally this is exciting sailing through lovely country.

II. FISHING CREEK, HONGA RIVER, AND HOOPER STRAIT (12261, 12264).

1. Fishing Creek (12261). Don't confuse this with the Fishing Creek on the Little Choptank. This creek leads directly into the open Chesapeake. The original author of this guide, Fess Blanchard, learned something about Eastern shoremen, as well as Fishing Creek, when he first walked into the store at Honga on a cold morning in November, 1948. The fishing gang was gathered about the stove, while several of the younger members played pool.

"I'm anxious to get some information about Fishing Creek and the dredged channel for a cruising guide I am writing" was the author's opening remark. "Do you know of anyone who might be willing to take me out in the channel in his motorboat. I'd, of course, be glad to pay what is fair."

No answer. Dead silence from the gallery on the wooden boxes. Finally, one of the men spoke up.

"Harry here has a boat; maybe he'll take you out."

More silence from Harry, broken only by the sound of billiard balls clicking. It lasted three or four minutes and seemed longer. Blanchard sat down and started off on a new tack.

"Could any of you tell me how much water there is in the channel at low tide? The chart says only four feet."

That broke the ice. An argument started. Everybody agreed that there was about 8 feet, but nobody could agree on whether it was 8 feet at low or medium tide. Also, what was low tide? We talked almost 15 minutes about depths, about the Honga River, and what was wrong with the oyster business. Finally the author got up to go.

"Thanks a lot for all the dope. I think I'll take a look around. If anybody turns up who will take me out, I'd appreciate your letting me know."

Harry got up. "Come on," he said, "let's go. My boat is just across the bridge."

We had learned a valuable lesson of the Chesapeake. Take it easy. Don't try to hurry anyone too much.

We went out in the channel. The bottom was a light green compared to a darker green water beyond the edges. Around Cape Cod, it is the shoalest water which looks light green. The channel looked to us more like 4 feet than 8 feet in depth. But Harry had said it was 8 feet and it wouldn't do to doubt his word. So we suggested: "You know, I am sure nobody at home will believe me when I tell them it is eight feet deep here. Do you mind if I sound, so I can tell them I saw it myself?"

"Oh no, I'll help you" was the reply.

We sounded and found 8 feet throughout the channel at about half tide. As the rise and fall is only 1 1/2 feet normally, this meant a depth of at least 7 feet. The reason for the lighter green inside the channel is that the dredging removed the darker weeded surface on the bottom.

But between Barren Island and Clay Point, Fishing Creek shoals up quickly after winter storms. So regardless of what the chart may say, the prudent skipper will take his own soundings when entering from either direction.

2. _Barren Island Gap_ (_12264_). A dredged channel marked by lighted beacons leads from the Bay into Fishing Creek and the north end of Honga River. It is much used by local fishing boats, but the channel is narrow, winding, and subject to constant shoalings. Over a period of 30 years we have never found channel depths to match Blanchard's soundings on his first visit, and only once have we taken our own boat (a 40-foot centerboard yawl drawing 4 feet with the board up) into the Honga by this route. But it can be done when the channel has been recently dredged, as it was in 1977. At that time, the controlling depth was reported as 7 feet. The swing bridge was in operation during daylight hours, and the overhead power cable had a clearance of 65 feet. So if you are intrigued by the thought of exploring Honga River by this northern route, be sure to check the latest depths with the Coast Guard.

On the south side of the creek just west of the bridge is a marina with gasoline, slips, and some supplies. On the north side, closer to the bridge, is Tyler Creek Cove. The channel in is marked by day beacons. This is the snuggest anchorage.

Honga is well worth a visit by yachtsmen wanting to see an unspoiled fishing village. For shoal-draft boats (or deeper craft if the channel is dredged, as it is periodically) Fishing Creek is a good shortcut to Honga River and an inland passage down Tangier Sound to some of the most interesting harbors in the Lower Eastern Shore—Deal Island, Crisfield, and Tangier.

3. _Honga River_ (_12264, 12261_). The Honga's shores are low and marshy, but it has a deep, wide channel and three harbors: Back Creek, on the west shore about 4 miles downriver from the bridge at

Honga; Muddy Hook Cove, on the west shore about 6 miles farther down; and Hearns Cove, on the east shore about 5 miles east of Muddy Hook Cove. All three are workboat harbors and have only small anchorages; but they all have dredged channels and basins with 6 or 7 feet and offer fuel, supplies, and shelter. In Back Creek there is a county wharf just southwest of the last mark (beacon 4), and just north of that mark is a crab house with a gasoline pump and about 5 feet of water. In Muddy Hook Cove and Hearns Cove gas pumps are right on the dredged basins. Back Creek is the snuggest of these harbors; Muddy Hook Cove is exposed to the east and northeast; and Hearns Cove to the west and southwest. At all three, supplies are within easy walking distance, and fresh seafood in season is right on the wharves.

The villages by these harbors—Fishing Creek, Hoopersville, and Wingate—seem hardly to have been touched by time. Fishing Creek and Hoopersville appear likely to change in the near future, but not Wingate, for it lies near the south corner of a large area of land so low that much is flooded whenever it rains hard. This land seems unlikely to attract either industry or permanent residents for some time to come. So, besides serving as a route from the Upper Chesapeake to Tangier Sound, the Honga will, we hope, continue to attract cruising people who enjoy looking for living enclaves from the past.

4. Hooper Strait (12261, 12230). This is by far the best of the two principal straits leading from the main Bay to Tangier Sound and harbors of the Lower Eastern Shore (the other is Kedges Strait, 15 miles farther south). Hooper Strait is the preferred route for vessels entering Tangier Sound from the north, and is used by local commercial traffic as well as pleasure boats. The natural channel merges with that of Honga River south of Hooper Island, and then swings southeasterly between Bishops Head and Bloodsworth Island into Fishing Bay and a dredged cut across the top of Sharkfin Shoal to the sound. The strait is about 7 nautical miles from the Bay to the sound, and is well marked all the way. The old Hooper Strait

Lighthouse (removed to the Maritime Museum at St. Michaels) has been replaced by a 41-foot light visible for 6 miles. The dredged cut has a controlling depth of 14 feet, according to the latest charts, but cruising boats can carry up to 7-foot draft directly across the north end of Sharkfin Shoal from N-6 to the 44-foot-high light on the sound side. Here you are close to Fishing Bay, Nanticoke River, and the harbors of Chance and of Wenona on Deal Island.

III. Fishing Bay (*12261, 12230*).

At the head of Tangier Sound, Fishing Bay is a wide, shallow estuary surrounded by low marshland through which several sluggish rivers and creeks wind their way, all looking alike and difficult to identify unless there are beacons. Dredged channels provide access to Tedious, Goose, Farm, and McReadys creeks. These are all workboat harbors and have gasoline docks and, in season, crushed ice. All but Goose Creek have some supplies nearby. Unless your draft is 3 feet or less, however, you can't count on docking in any of these harbors except Goose Creek, where the *Coast Pilot* reported a controlling depth of 6 feet in the channel in the 1980's; local fishermen assured us that in 1985 there was at least that. The harbor at Goose Creek is a mile southwest of a point called "Roasting Ear." Mr. Calvert Tolley, who owns the crab house on Farm Creek, says there is plenty of water in the entrance channel, the harbor, and on up the creek, and assures us that there is always a place for a visitor to anchor or tie up. The creek is certainly remarkably deep for its width.

Above Farm Creek there are no marks in Fishing Bay, and there is nothing to attract most cruising people. A really determined skipper with a draft of 4 feet or less might make his way up to Blackwater River, which is astonishingly deep. Like the Honga's, Fishing Bay's main attractions are its villages and people. They seem to exist in another time.

IV. NANTICOKE RIVER (*12261*).

Unless you like low, featureless marshland and narrow channels between extensive shoals, there is very little to appeal to the yachts-man on Nanticoke River, which can be navigated for 34 miles to Seaford, Del., with drafts up to 6½ feet. The principal ports on the lower river are as follows, and perhaps "port" is not the right word, except for shallow fishing craft.

1. Nanticoke (12261). This is a dredged-out fishing cove on the east bank of the river above Roaring Point. In 1984 the controlling depth in the entrance channel was reported to be 3 feet. The sheltered basin is not much deeper.

When we were last there the docks were crowded and it would have been difficult to find room to tie up. Gas and water are available at the docks; supplies are obtainable nearby.

2. Bivalve (12261). Bivalve is on the east bank 3 miles above Nan-ticoke. The entrance channel is short and clearly marked, with a controlling depth of 3 feet. The basin is well protected, except from the west-northwest. You can tie up to the county bulkhead, but no gas is available. We found several powerboats there on our last visit and it seemed a good place to lie overnight.

3. Tyaskin in Wetipquin Creek (12261). Here is found a good county wharf to which boats can tie up, preferably on the inner part. Boats can also anchor in the creek. However, the entrance channel, which is said to have about 4 feet, is unmarked and is difficult without local knowledge. The beacon off the entrance is poorly placed, either for going upriver (the shoal projects well beyond the beacon toward the channel) or for going into Tyaskin. A high bunch of trees on the west shore is about opposite the channel and gives a rough guide to the entrance. Keep about in line with this and head toward the right side of the wharf as you go in, on about a southeast course.

There is about 4¹/₂ feet at the dock, but no gas. A store is a short distance up the street. The place is exposed to the northwest for some distance across the river. There are better anchorages farther up the river, where the channel narrows but allows you to carry deep water close to the banks from Penknife Point to Vienna, and beyond.

V. WICOMICO RIVER (*12261*).

The banks of the Wicomico are chiefly low and marshy, and the water was yellow when we were there. This is a river with few features but important chiefly because Salisbury, the largest city on the Eastern Shore, is 20 miles upriver. A draft of at least 10 feet can be carried to Salisbury along a well-marked and well-charted channel, not difficult to follow but apt to be used by large commercial vessels.

The mean tidal range is 2¹/₂ feet at the entrance, 3 feet at Salisbury.

1. Webster Cove (12261). This is a good anchorage, about 3 miles above Great Shoals Light. It is on the south shore, entered through a narrow, dredged 6-foot channel between beacons leading into a man-made basin with a controlling depth of 3¹/₂ feet in 1984, used chiefly by local fishing and oyster boats. This is a county facility with some 25 slips around the basin. You might find a vacant slip for an overnight stop.

Tie up at the dock to the starboard as you go in. There you may find a depth of 6 feet alongside and in the basin, and also a conspicuous restaurant, with a dance floor, beer, showers, etc. Gas and water are obtainable at the dock and a few groceries nearby. Various supplies can be had at Mount Vernon, a short distance away.

The cove is easily identified by the group of houses and The Harbor restaurant at the entrance pier. This is the first of three ports on the river below Salisbury with any facilities for yachts.

2. *Whitehaven (12261).* Here is a tiny little town that was first settled in the mid-1600's. It lies on the north bank of the river, where the deep main channel runs close to the shore. Here you will find one of the oldest ferries in continual use on the Eastern Seaboard; today it's a free cable ferry, operated by the county during daylight hours in good weather. The crossing is not marked. Do not try to pass a moving cable ferry! You could snag the cable. A large marine railway can haul vessels up to 150 feet. Limited supplies are available in the town.

3. *Wicomico Creek (12261).* This creek lies on the south bank of the river about 2 miles above Whitehaven. The marked entrance has a controlling depth of about 4 feet, with deeper water inside leading to the Wikander Yacht Yard, with slips, gas, swimming pool, Laundromat, and facilities for hull and engine repairs. A small yacht club near the mouth of the creek has dockside ice and beverages.

4. *Upper Ferry (12261).* Boats proceeding up the river to Salisbury should keep a close watch for this second cable ferry 15 miles above the mouth. Unlike the Whitehaven ferry, the cable here is held taut by winches on both shores, and is close to the surface at all times. One blast on the horn is the signal for lowering the cable. Do not attempt to pass a moving cable ferry.

5. *Salisbury (12261).* This is a large commercial city with many docks, turning basins in both prongs of the river, and a large marine railway in the south prong. Gas and all kinds of supplies and shopping are available. Dockage, gas and diesel fuel, ice, and showers may be found at Port of Salisbury Marina.

VI. Deal Island Area: Chance and Wenona (*12231*).

To the north of Deal Island (once Devil's Island), Chance is one of the snuggest little harbors on the Lower Eastern Shore, and it is just off Tangier Sound. For some years a two-stack ferryboat lay beached on the north side of the harbor. Plans to turn it into a restaurant like the one across from Cambridge came to naught, and in 1974 it was cut up for scrap.

The entrance channel now has a lighted range that can be picked up as you approach buoys 3 and 4. The entrance channel was dredged in 1987 and depths were still 9 to 10 feet in 1988, with 6 feet in the basin. You get an extra 1½ or 2 feet with high tide.

This is still primarily a working and not a yacht harbor; yet the Chesapeake Station of the Cruising Club of America and the Sailing Club of the Chesapeake have held a rendezvous here. In the fall it is apt to be crowded with workboats. In the summer the workboats are fewer, and you are not likely to share the basin with more than half a dozen cruisers.

Two marinas and boatyards are on the north side of the turning basin: one, called Last Chance, has gas, water, ice, and a few transient slips; the second, Scotts Cove Marina, is entered through a dredged channel, leading to a bulkheaded yard basin with 100 slips and complete engine and hull repair shops.

Several other facilities are useful to cruising boats: Deal Island Hardware has a dockside wharf with gas and diesel; Island Seafood provides dockage for yachts in quest of fresh seafood. Groceries and other supplies are available nearby on the road to Wenona.

On our search for groceries we found two points of interest: first, just south of the harbor, a clearing with a sign announcing a skipjack museum; second, a little past the larger grocery, the grave of Joshua Thomas, "Parson of the Islands," and a chapel dedicated to him.

Wenona, at the south end of Deal Island, is even less affected by

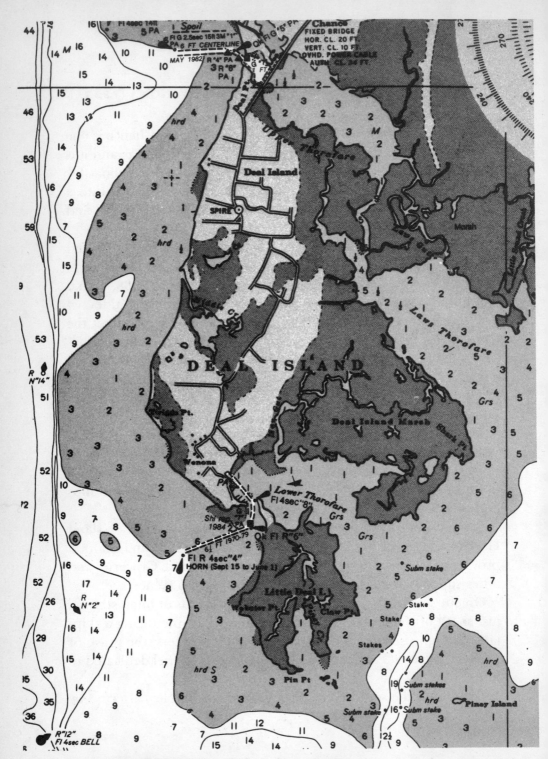

Deal Island in Tangier Sound (from chart 12231).

the yachting world than Chance. It is as close to Tangier Sound, and its entrance channel is almost as deep (6 feet in 1979, shoaling to an unknown extent reported in 1984).

Except for a narrow dredged channel, its harbor is very shoal. Fortunately a waterman hailed us as we entered and told us to stay close to the piers on our port. Another man told us that the channel along the piers was 8 feet deep but only 80 feet wide. The only anchorage for boats that draw more than a foot or two is in this channel.

Like all shore watermen, those of Wenona don't worry about appearances. The piers look rickety, and so does the rest of the town. The famous Brown sail loft, which had been making canvas working sails for skipjacks and bugeyes of Maryland's oyster fleet for over a century, was here. Henry Brown, the last sail maker, was the fourth generation of Browns to run the loft since it was established in 1870. But the piers are serviceable, the people are hospitable, and in the summer of 1982 the harbor still held 8 skipjacks, almost all in beautiful condition. Groceries and ice are available just off the piers.

Wenona offers an unequaled combination of convenience and tradition.

VII. MANOKIN RIVER (12231).

This river is wide, with extensive outlying shoals and no good anchorages; the only place which is at all passable is in Goose Creek. The docks are used by local fishermen and pleasure craft. The creek is exposed for several miles to the northwest.

It is possible to get shelter from northwesters east of Little Deal Island at the northern side of the entrance. With Deal Island and Chance so near there is no reason to go into the Manokin unless you have read about it in the *Entailed Hat, Patty Cannon's Times* or some other novel of the Eastern Shore and want to see for yourself what it is like.

VIII. BIG ANNEMESSEX RIVER (*12231*).

A little more than a mile above entrance buoys 1 and 2 is the approach to Daugherty Creek on the south shore, which leads into Annemessex Canal to Crisfield. In 1988, according to the *Coast Pilot,* the controlling depth in the canal (also known as Daugherty Creek Canal) was 5 feet; it shoals near Crisfield, however, so proceed with caution. If you don't want to go on to Crisfield, you can anchor in Daugherty Creek or in Jones Creek, just to the east. These anchorages are shoal, but sheltered from all points except the northwest.

The Big Annemessex is navigable for several miles above Daugherty Creek, but the only good anchorage is in Colbourn Creek, also on the south side. According to the *Coast Pilot,* this is an "excellent storm anchorage with good holding grounds . . . available in depths of 5 feet in midstream 0.3 miles above the entrance."

IX. CRISFIELD AND LITTLE ANNEMESSEX RIVER (*12231*).

The main entrance to Crisfield follows a well-marked dredged channel from deep water in Tangier Sound to the busy commercial docks of this "seafood capital." The mid-channel controlling depth was 7½ feet in 1982, making this approach essential for boats

Crisfield, Little Annemessex River.
(Photo courtesy of BaySailor.)

drawing over 5 feet. The spur channel to the commercial wharves reportedly carried 10 feet to Hop Point, and 6½ feet to the small basin beyond to the north, where the chart shows 10 feet.

A large marine railway is to the starboard on the point just before you reach the dock. Piles of oyster shells almost obscure the building. It is deep enough at the dock for big tankers, and the railway can haul vessels up to 100 feet long and 6-foot draft. There is also another marine railway, which can haul boats of similar size.

As you enter the main harbor, a large sign points the way to Somers Cove Marina, which is beyond the commercial docks. This large publicly owned facility is one of the finest to be found anywhere on the Chesapeake, with 325 slips, gas, diesel, propane, electric current, etc. A snack bar specializes in Crisfield's best-known produce—steamed crabs. Many stores are nearby on the main street, where restaurants and supplies are available.

X. SMITH ISLAND (*12231*).

This is one of the two most unusual and intriguing spots on the Chesapeake—the other is Tangier Island, just below. On our first visit, more than 30 years ago, we arrived at Crisfield by car on an early morning in late November after our sloop had been put into wet storage for the winter. Several men, carpenters, plumbers, and electricians were about to start across Tangier Sound in a small motorboat to do a day's work on one of the houses on Smith Island. They offered to take us along and we jumped aboard.

On the way out we were told that half of the population of 800 or 900 were named Evans, all of British descent. This seemed like another tall story until we counted the names on a memorial tablet outside the Methodist church of those who had served in both world wars. Forty names were listed: twenty-one of them were Evans. An interested bystander noted that two men had been left out and would have to be added.

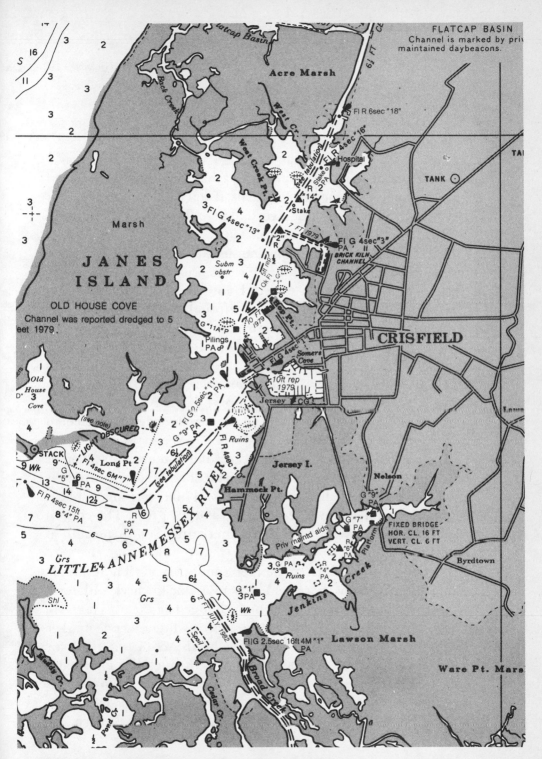

Crisfield and Little Annemessex River (from chart 12231).

"What are their names?" we asked, wondering if the 50-percent Evans average would be maintained.

"Tyler and Evans" was the reply.

"By the way," we asked, "what's your name?"

The answer—"Evans."

We were getting hungry as usual, so we asked if there was a restaurant on the island. There wasn't at that time, but a lady named Mrs. Kitching took in people for meals, if you let her know ahead of time. We went there and got a cordial reception and a good meal, with the best corn bread we ever tasted.

"How does it happen that your name isn't Evans?" we asked our hostess. "Everybody else seems to have that name."

The answer came with a smile: "I got married!" Mrs. Kitching gained great fame with her cooking through the years, but closed her popular establishment and retired in 1987.

There are two entrances to the Smith Island Harbor at Ewell, largest of the three villages on the island (the others are Rhodes Point and Tylerton). The principal entrance is the channel on the west side, approached from the main part of the Bay. According to the *Coast Pilot*, the dredged canal had a controlling depth of 5 feet in 1985, from Tangier Sound to Ewell.

Be sure to check your latest chart carefully, as the outer section of the dredged cut tends to shoal after storms. The western entrance is clearly marked by two lighted beacons, and after passing red beacon 4 the natural channel deepens to 12 and 14 feet. The church steeple in Ewell provides a good landmark after you turn south at beacon 10.

The other entrance is from Tangier Sound, via Big Thorofare. If you are entering from the Sound, it is advisable to check with local boatmen on controlling depths, which change from year to year. We have usually grounded lightly once or twice by hugging one marker too closely or giving another too wide a berth; so it's well to ask for advice if you have a chance before starting through the Thorofare. But the controlling depth is usually about 5 feet, and the passage is adventurous enough to make it interesting. Note that Ewell, unlike Tangier, is considered the head of navigation, and the western and

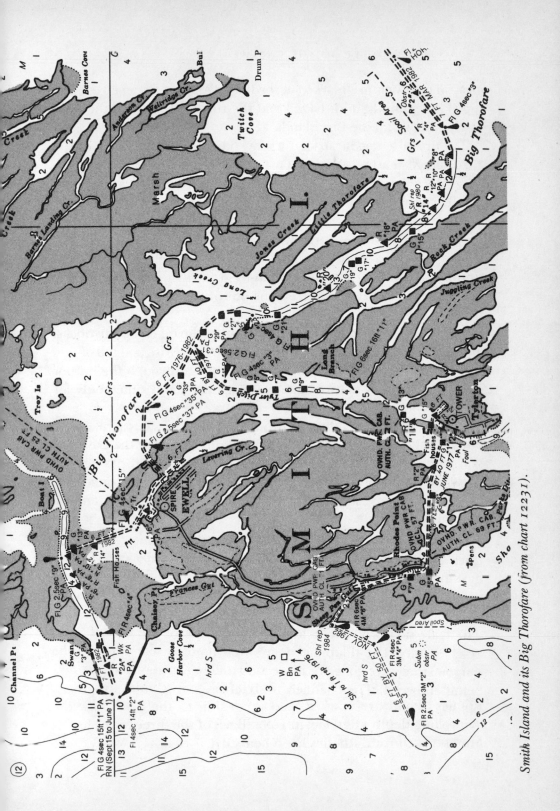

Smith Island and its Big Thorofare (from chart 12231).

eastern channels are marked accordingly. Many Chesapeake cruising skippers find Smith Island and the tiny port of Ewell the most fascinating of all the Bay islands.

Tie up in a vacant space (it may have to be two deep in the "drudging" season—November 1 to March 15) along the right-hand dock on the town side of the very narrow channel between Ewell and the marshy island across from it. If you want more privacy and less convenience, tie up at some piles across the channel. The harbor has perfect security from seas and from all directions, though the land is all very low and you can feel the wind. The unmarked channel east of the 90-degree turn is a comfortable anchorage unless the wind freshens out of the west, as it did when we were there.

Gas, diesel, and water can be obtained at the oil company docks, and ice and other supplies are found nearby. The rise and fall of tide is said to be about 2 feet. The ebb flows north through the harbor channel. The only marine railway is very small and suited only for fishing boats.

A good plan in heading southward along the Chesapeake is to enter Smith Island by the west channel directly from the Bay, or if you have been following Honga River–Tangier Sound passage, go through Kedges Straits first. Then, after a stop at Smith Island, you can get the latest information on the southeast channel and be guided accordingly.

Almost the entire island is low marshland, with a few clumps of trees here and there. Good-looking children were everywhere, dashing around on bicycles and scooters, many of them wearing rubber boots, though it was a fine day. There are no policemen, only a deputy sheriff who also crabs and whose official duties are few. There are no town officers and no jail; the towns are part of Somerset County. The dilapidated cars that used to roar through the narrow streets are gone, for inspection and registration laws are now being enforced. The channels to Tylerton and Rhodes (originally Rogues') Point are marked, and according to the Coast Pilot the controlling depth was 6 feet in 1982. Each of the three towns has its Methodist church. Rhodes has a boatyard.

The people are friendly, with nice voices and an accent that is neither Southern nor Yankee. Houses seem clean and neat, though there is much rubbish in the vacant lots.

Crabbing in summer, oystering in winter—these are the island's business. A mail boat used to be the only transportation route between the island and the mainland. Today several cruise boats carry passengers from Crisfield to Ewell, operating on a daily schedule.

One yachtsman called the New Jersey mosquitoes "sissies" compared to those at Smith Island. Another, whose cruiser was well screened, said he hadn't been bothered much by mosquitoes. However, don't go there in summer if you can make it in the fall or spring. But go there, somehow. We like it at least as well as Tangier, and it is just as interesting.

The fleet of skipjacks loaded with oysters, sails full, which we met when we went out of the channel toward Tangier Sound as the sun went down was one of the many things which made our visit to Smith Island a memorable one.

A developer was causing considerable controversy by proposing to build condominiums on Smith Island in 1988.

XI. TANGIER ISLAND (*12228*).

Tangier will always mean to me
A sandy spit set in the sea,
One narrow street all picket-fenced,
Front yard graves; the dead can sense
The news, as gay sunbonnets sway
Or sniff the salt air from the bay;
Children who swarm about like flies,
Quaint Cornish talk and curious eyes;
Brown, blue-eyed men who scull and pole;
Gaunt little boats that have a soul!*

* From "Tangier" by Gilbert Byron, in *These Chesapeake Men*, published by the Draftwind Press.

For more than 250 years successive generations of Tangier Island fishermen had only one narrow entrance leading in to their tight little harbor from Tangier Sound to the east. However, a dredged entrance from the west has been open since 1966, making it possible to approach the island directly from the Bay. Shoal-draft cruising boats drawing less than 4 feet may still prefer the Tangier Sound entrance, as it is often difficult to avoid the extensive restricted and prohibited areas maintained by the Navy for bombing practice around the old San Marcos wreck, southwest of the island, and a buoy testing area to the north. The numerous Navy-maintained markers are not easy to identify when entering from the Bay, and the island itself has few conspicuous landmarks. On our last visit we came in from Tangier Sound after a fine sail from Crisfield in a fresh westerly, picking up a tall clump of trees in the town of Tangier and a church spire close by. Then the island seemed to rise rapidly from the sea as the low marshlands alongshore came into view.

The main entrance to Tangier now leads from the open Chesapeake, however, and the channel is well marked and maintained. In 1985 it had a controlling depth of 7 feet from the lighted marker at the entrance to a new "yacht" landing in the harbor. A cruising yachtsman who visited the island reported the channel was easy to follow, with no bumps. "We were led in," he reported, "by a procession of tow-headed boys in outboard skiffs who took us to the yacht dock." Proceed cautiously from the sound side, because the channel constantly shoals to less than the 8 feet reported in 1985.

The anchorage basin is crowded with local fishing boats moored bow and stern to stakes, leaving little room for anchoring. Gas is obtainable at Tangier Oil Company's dock, but you are not encouraged to tie up there or at other nearby docks used by the local fishermen. Visiting yachts are not always welcome when the harbor is crowded. But the people are friendly and also curious about visitors from the outside world.

Wherever you go, it will be very snug and quiet so far as wind and waves are concerned, but not in any other respect. You will be

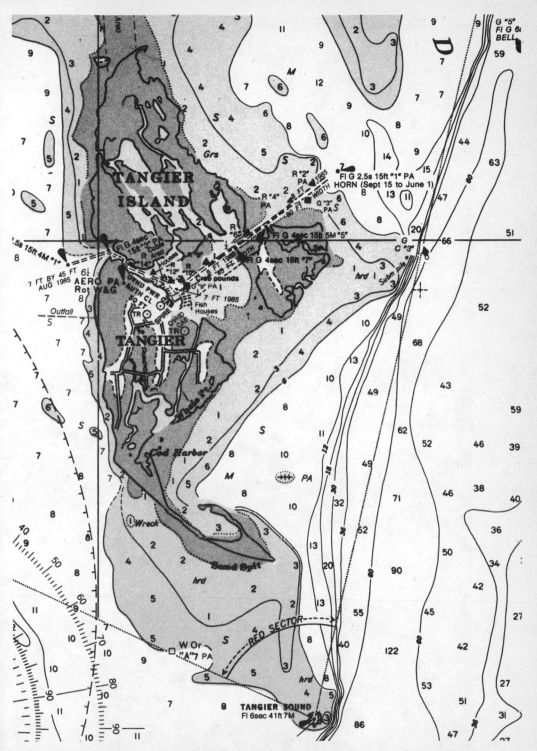

Tangier Island and entrance to Tangier Sound (from chart 12228).

Tangier Island workboats bob at their moorings on a brisk day.

inspected by swarms of nice-looking, active, and curious children. We discovered they were well behaved and less in evidence after their curiosity had been satisfied. If the basin is too crowded you may be able to poke your way around into a snug anchorage inside Sand Spit, the fishhook at the southern tip of Tangier Island, as we managed to do some years ago.

To us, the Tangier Island children seemed like other normal children, only much more good-looking than most, and the people like the people of any other fishing village on the Chesapeake. Perhaps the talk of quaintness has been a bit overdone, though the place is one of the most interesting on the Bay. Now that communication with the mainland is more easy and frequent, and visiting yachts may number six or seven in a day, Tangier Islanders, of whom there are 1,100, live less unto themselves alone and are very much like other people. About half of them are said to be named Crockett, with Pruitt and Parks next in line. At the time of our last visit there were several piers for visiting boats, one with a sign "Boat Parking," and a hotel which has rooms for the night and serves wonderful seafood meals. Mrs. Hilda Crockett, who ran the Chesapeake House for many years, has since been succeeded by other Crocketts, but if you want to partake of their meals, plan to get in early enough to "sit down" about 5 P.M. or earlier if the excursion boat is in the harbor. Ice may not be obtainable except on order from the mainland, though small quantities might be had. Groceries and various supplies are near at hand, some at Williams and Wheatley's dock. Don't depend on buying things on a Sunday, as everything is closed down tight. An excursion boat now makes a daily trip from Crisfield, and in summer a boat comes over regularly from Reedville, Va., on the Western Shore.

It is fun to wander along the narrow main street, to see the large crab traps along the channel, and to talk with the oystermen and crabbers. Tangier Island, bought from the Indians for a couple of overcoats, is one of the unique spots on the Chesapeake and worth going a long way to see. But don't go looking for quaint and queer people; you'll find them very normal. Don't get run over by a bicycle.

XII. POCOMOKE SOUND AND RIVER (12228, 12230).

The Pocomoke isn't for cruising skippers in a hurry. If you are going somewhere, don't stop; it is too far out of the way. If you are looking for comfortable marinas or the company of other yachts, stay away. You probably won't find any of either. The chart doesn't tell very much about what you will find, except a narrow, deep channel, winding between apparently featureless marshy shores, and ending at the town of Pocomoke. On the way are the hamlets of Shelltown and Rehobeth. Above Pocomoke there is nothing much for the yachtsman—or so it would appear.

But the yachtsman who believes in appearances and plans his cruises accordingly will miss a good deal that is fascinating, especially on the Pocomoke, if he hurries by.

There are two entrances to Pocomoke Sound. For boats proceeding southward down Tangier Sound, or stopping at Crisfield, by far the shortest route is through the dredged cut south of Crisfield from Little Annemessex River into Broad Creek to the sound. Depths are uncertain in this cut; the controlling depth was reported to be 2 feet in 1982. This passage saves many miles and, with a mean range of tide of 2 feet, it is practical for some cruising vessels at flood tides. The passage is subject to constant shoaling, and should be entered with due caution.

For yachts heading northward along the Chesapeake, the southerly entrance of Pocomoke Sound gives the most convenient access to the river, though it is 16 miles away—much too far, unless the Pocomoke is one of your major objectives. Perhaps it should be. Since talking with Corwith Cramer about his experience in "Poking up the Pocomoke"* and reading what he had to say, our vote would be for poking.

After dodging innumerable crab pots, fish stakes, and nets—many of them where they shouldn't be—you will arrive at the

---

* "Poking up the Pocomoke" by Corwith Cramer, in the *Chesapeake Skipper*, has provided much valuable material and all of the quotations in this section.

dredged cut, which, according to the latest published report, had a controlling depth of 7 feet. Enter through the cut. Except for "Beverly, a lovely old eighteenth-century house and plantation known by the odd name of Thrumcapped," there is little below Rehobeth, over 8 miles up, to relieve the monotony of the marsh grasses, except occasional oases of thick foliage. But at Beverly, about 4 miles upriver and just above the Maryland state line, two giant cypress trees, appearing to grow out of deep water, and with roots over 30 feet in circumference, give a hint of what to expect farther up.

> A short distance above Rehobeth, the river begins to flow between higher banks lined with towering trees, the water assuming a darker, more blackish tinge—the result of stains from cypress bark. Now fresh—pesky summer sea nettles, torredoes and barnacles can no longer survive. Huge cypress trees rise up from the watery roots on both sides of the weaving sluggish stream to confirm the end of saltwater life—a startling contrast to most other rivers on the Chesapeake.

This is said to be the most northerly cypress forest in the United States, and its tall trees are equal to the best you'll find in the Carolina cypress swamps.

> From here on up to Snow Hill might be called the heart of the Pocomoke. Deep, black, and perhaps more primitive in aspect than anything bordering on the Bay, it winds gracefully through almost all points of the compass. Here and there a break in the thick forests that line both banks reveals tidy farms with usually a small "bateau" or two tied up at the water's edge; but for the most part the dense foliage of poplar, maple, pine, dogwood and predominating cypress gave us the impression of wilderness.

Pocomoke City, 14 miles above the river mouth, is the terminus for most of the commercial traffic—petroleum products, sand and gravel barges, pulpwood, and some fish products from the Bay. There are public bulkhead landings near the two bridges, with provisions of all kinds available in the town. Boats planning to continue up the river should check the *Coast Pilot* for special regulations governing the Pocomoke City bridges. There is also an overhead power cable with a reported clearance of 57 feet, and a fixed bridge with clearance of 35 feet 1 mile north of the highway and railroad bridges.

> There is no reassuring chart to refer to beyond Pocomoke City, but infrequent shoals near mid-channel are marked by stakes and the river remains navigable and sufficiently deep for vessels drawing at least 10 feet as far as Snow Hill, a quaint and charming community some 28 nautical miles above the Tangier Sound . . . and 6 miles as the crow flies from Chincoteague Sound on the Atlantic seaboard.

Above Snow Hill navigation becomes so difficult with unmarked shoals and hidden stumps that we suggest calling it a day at that point and perhaps taking a ride over to the ocean before turning back for the voyage down this intriguing river.

The principal stopping places on entering Pocomoke Sound and River are as follows:

1. Starling Creek and Saxis (12228, 12230). This is a little snug harbor, on the south shore of Pocomoke Sound, much used by fishing craft. Like other dredged entrance channels, depths are subject to frequent change; according to our latest chart and the *Coast Pilot,* in 1982 the controlling depth was only 1 foot in the channel and about 5 feet in the basin. The passage is well marked by beacons.

Saxis is identified by many white buildings. Gas is obtainable in the turning basin and provisions in the town.

2. Shelltown, Va. (12228, 12230). A road runs down to the west bank between a shingle house with a windmill below the road, and a conspicuous white house with a large tree above the road. Just off the white house are some piles and a somewhat dilapidated bulkhead, where the water is very deep and a yacht can tie up. There is a small country store with a gas station a few yards up the road.

3. Rehobeth, Md. (*12230*). This is typical of the Lower Pocomoke, with its marshes, broken-down wharf, and small country store and post office. You have to walk to get gas, water, and ice.

4. Pocomoke City, Md. (*12230*). About 14 miles from the mouth, Pocomoke City offers free dockage at the city-owned bulkhead, with water and electricity. The town is not pretentious, but its civic pride is evidenced in its spruced-up appearance, which earned it an honorable mention in the All-America City contest. All kinds of supplies are available. As you approach Pocomoke City there is an overhead power cable with a clearance of 57 feet and a swing bridge, vertical clearance 4 feet. Above Pocomoke City, there is a bascule bridge, vertical clearance 3 feet, and a fixed bridge with a vertical clearance of 35 feet.

5. Shad Landing State Park (*12230*). If you can clear the fixed bridge at Pocomoke City and have the determination to continue on for another 10 miles through the cypress swamps, you will arrive at Shad Landing State Park, an attractive riverfront park with a marina and turning basin at the head of a dredged channel, marked by privately maintained buoys. In 1983 there was 6 feet in the channel and basin. Here you are only 4 miles from the town of Snow Hill.

XIII. Deep Creek (*12228, 12230*).

This Deep Creek might better be called "Long Creek," for the distance from its entrance on Pocomoke Sound to the village of Deep Creek is 8 miles. The outer channel meanders but is wide, deep, and fairly well marked almost to can 7. The dredged inner channel starts at lighted beacon 11 and is narrow and straight between marks. The chart says a controlling depth of 3 feet was reported, the *Coast Pilot* says it is 4 feet, and local watermen say it is 8 feet at high tide. A small fleet of workboats drawing up to 4½ feet uses the channel regularly.

After you pass beacon 15, you will see crab houses to the right, and just beyond them, the county wharf, which is crowded with workboats after working hours. You may tie up here wherever you can find a place, possibly alongside workboats. Here, as at other fishing ports, the waterman's code prevails: boats tied at public landings may be boarded if necessary in tying up and getting ashore. Gasoline and groceries can be had at a little store a short distance from the wharf.

Surprisingly, Deep Creek is the busiest Bay fishing port on Virginia's Eastern Shore. The buildings near the wharf—including a railway and a fish house—are sadly dilapidated, but the boats are many and their condition is excellent. The condition of the houses nearby further testifies to the port's prosperity. This is as truly a fishing village as Ewell, Tangier, or Chesconessex, 1½ miles to the south.

XIV. CHESCONESSEX CREEK (*12228*).

One of the watermen here told us that 2 years before, two motorboats bound for the Crisfield Crab Derby had come into Chesconessex instead and when they left they were glad they had made the mistake. Having spent an afternoon and morning there, we know why.

The channel is wide and well enough marked to beacon 6, but from there to beacon 8 it is narrower, shoaler, and tricky. On one passage in the 1970's, a little after low water, we sounded all the way and found nothing less than 6½ feet. But on two of our three other passages we either touched or grounded between beacons 6 and 8 (4-foot draft). The trick is to avoid the 2-foot shoal to the west by staying east of a line between beacon 6 and beacon 8 for a third of the distance, and then to avoid the 1-foot shoal to the east by staying west of this line for the rest of the distance. The narrowest place is by beacon 8; passage is made easier by stakes that mark the 1-foot shoal opposite the beacon.

As you approach beacon 10, you see crab houses to port. Almost opposite the beacon is an opening through which you can reach the county wharf of North Chesconessex. The watermen say there is 12 feet at its face but little water on either side of it or the approach. So the only way to dock is to head right into the face. The wharf has no public water or telephone, but we were welcomed so warmly that we borrowed both in the village without feeling embarrassed. On the south side of the creek are another public wharf, a gasoline pump, a launching ramp, and a small store. The channel dredged from the ramp runs alongside the wharf; so if you stay 4 or 5 feet away from the wharf you can carry 5 feet halfway into shore at low water—far enough to use the gas pump.

When we tied up to the county wharf in the 1970's, we asked for a mechanic. One waterman told us that Gene Tinzer would be glad to come over after work in Onancock; another offered us his car to drive to Onancock. When we asked about a place to anchor, the first man, pointing to beacon 1 (which is the last black beacon and ought to be 15), said, "Tie up to that mark. The Coast Guard doesn't mind. The line on it's mine. Use it." Besides these men, we talked to a nurseryman who moved down from New York in 1945 and to a man who lives nearby and publishes a newspaper in the suburbs of Washington. If we had not been preoccupied with the motor, our visit would have been even more enjoyable.

The anchorage there is snug but not at all secluded, and there are no other good snug anchorages in the creek. For a calm summer night there's a good anchorage 200 to 400 yards south of beacon 3; but as we learned the hard way, it is open to the west and northwest.

XV. ONANCOCK CREEK (*12228*).

This is our favorite creek on the Eastern Shore of Virginia. On its banks are handsome houses and lovely natural scenery. The entrance and the rest of the channel are well marked, and you can

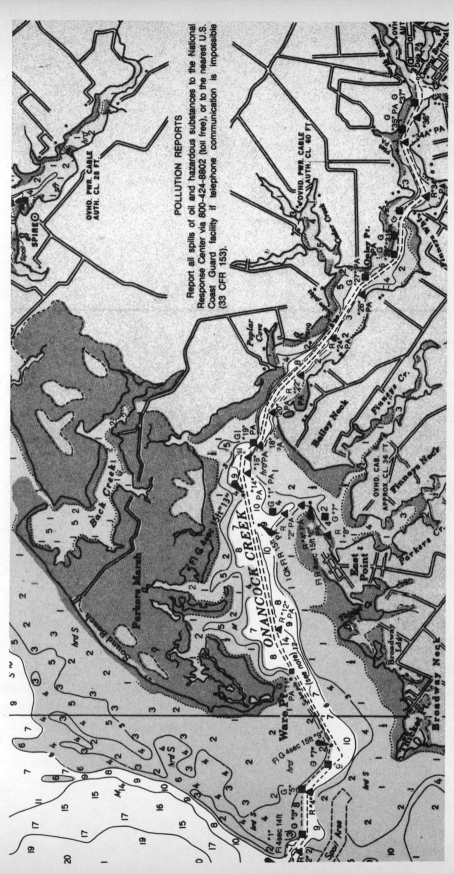

Onancock Creek leading to the village of Onancock (from chart 12228).

carry 11 feet to the turning basin in North Branch. Because small tankers and freighters use it, the channel is well maintained. The anchorage at Onancock is snug, and the dockside facilities are good for this area. If you are heading south down Tangier Sound and have paid a daytime visit to Tangier, Onancock provides a fine overnight stopping place. If you are heading north, Onancock is a convenient place to lie over before heading up through Tangier Sound.

As you enter North Branch, you head toward the large public wharf, which displays the sign "Onancock, the Cobia Capital of the World." Just off the wharf is a large brown building which is the Hopkins and Brothers Store, where transients can get a slip and some prepared food and groceries. You can anchor in the North Branch or in the mouth of Titlow Creek.

Onancock is one of the two or three historic towns on Virginia's Eastern Shore. Its center is a short walk from the wharf. There are many shops, a post office, and two drugstores that serve meals. The nearest real grocery is a mile farther on, and the ice house—a busy place that serves all the Lower Eastern Shore and has astonishingly low prices—is yet a mile farther. Gasoline is available within a mile. Except for Cape Charles, this is the best port for supplies on Virginia's Eastern Shore. In addition, it has many handsome old buildings and is a pleasant place just to walk around in.

For those in a hurry there's a snug anchorage in Parkers Creek, on the south side of Onancock Creek about 2 miles above the entrance. We found 6½ feet up to the last mark and 5½ feet a little above it.

XVI. PUNGOTEAGUE CREEK (*12226*).

The entrance and channel are well marked up to the public wharf at Harborton. Above that (beacons 15 and 16) there are no marks, but if you follow the chart carefully, you can carry 6 feet for 2 more miles and find pleasant, secluded anchorages. There are few houses; this is real country. All that is left of the once considerable commercial traffic are the ruins of Evans and Boggs wharves and the wharf on Warehouse Point, where pulpwood is stored and shipped to West Point on the York.

There is 6 or 7 feet of water at the face of the wharf at Harborton. At the land end is a gasoline pump, and after 1 P.M. crushed ice is available. Near the wharf is the Harborton post office, and about a mile down the road is a grocery. The village extends only about a quarter of a mile along the road. Watermen and pleasure boatmen use the wharf, and pleasure boatmen use the launching ramp beside it. Gasoline is available also at the Eastern Shore Yacht and Country Club (which has a golf course), on Taylors Creek just above Harborton.

In Pungoteague Creek we noticed square-bow, flat-bottom boats of the kind called "garveys" in New Jersey. Here they are called "scows."

If you are looking for a quiet, snug place with some conveniences, this creek will suit you. It is preferable to Nandua, the next creek south.

XVII. NANDUA CREEK (*12226*).

The dredged outer channel of this creek is well enough marked by day beacons, and you probably can carry 4 to 5 feet, as the most recent chart and the *Coast Pilot* says; but it is very narrow, and the soundings shown on the shoals are not always dependable (drawing 4 feet, we grounded just north of the channel where the chart shows 6). You can usually see the shoal to the north after beacon 7, and after beacon 14 piloting is easier. But beware the shoal off Monadox Point: it extends farther west than the chart shows.

Like Pungoteague, Nandua Creek is rural. It has even less traffic and no longer has a public wharf. Above beacon 17 are many anchorages. On the north side are several large, handsome houses; on the south side are the smaller houses of the village of Nandua. In a pinch, water and probably supplies can be obtained there by going ashore in a dinghy.

The name of the creek is pronounced with the accent on the second syllable. We once had trouble making ourselves understood when we accented it on the first. According to Colonel Birnn it was originally "Andua," after an Indian queen.

XVIII. Occohannock Creek (12226).

Except for Onancock, this is the easiest of Virginia's Eastern Shore creeks to enter, although careful piloting is required. The outer channel has 3 lighted beacons, and except between beacons 5 and 6 is reasonably deep and wide. Farther up, the marks are far apart, and may not be dependable. Drawing 4 feet, we hit bottom 20 yards south of beacon 15, where the chart shows 26 feet! Above the last beacon (19), the ends of shoals are marked by stakes, and it may be possible to carry 4 feet to the fixed bridge at Belle Haven.

For boats drawing 4 or perhaps 5 feet, there are two snug anchorages just inside the creek on the north side: one west of beacon 6, inside Powells Bluff; the other in the mouth of Tawes Creek. A third is near beacon 10 in the bight east of Pons Point. Farther up the creek are other anchorages, sheltered by banks unusually high for the Eastern Shore.

The only place where you can dock is Davis Wharf, one-quarter of a mile above beacon 11. There are a gasoline pump and a post office and a store run by the daughter of the Captain Davis the original wharf (long gone) was named for. The depth at the end of the pier is about 5 feet. You may be able to get ice cubes from Belle Haven, 5 miles away. Opposite Davis Wharf, on the south side, are the remains of Morleys Wharf, a public launching ramp, and a beach. There you can land a dinghy and perhaps catch a ride into Exmore (about 3 miles) with one of the many people who use the ramp.

Like Pungoteague, Occohannock Creek once had much commercial traffic, of which only a few traces remain, and it's now a quiet place, pleasant to visit if you don't need much ashore.

XIX. NASSAWADOX CREEK (*12226*).

The entrance to this creek is marked by a lighted beacon. Both chart 12226 and the *Coast Pilot* say the controlling depth at the entrance bar is 1 foot. But a local authority says, "The channel at entrance varies in depth from year to year. For the past several years it has been three to four feet deep . . . [and] has been well marked by local boat owners." The tidal range is 1.8 feet. If you can enter, you can go most anywhere inside, and chart 12226 shows many snug anchorages.

At Bayford, 1½ miles up on the southeast side, are a private wharf, a store, and a post office. At the Salt Works, on the north side a mile farther up, is a yard with a railway which can handle boats up to 50 feet.

This is a tricky creek to enter, and looks it on the chart. If you have the boat and temperament for it, you may find it worth trying.

XX. HUNGARS AND MATTAWOMAN CREEKS (*12226*).

These creeks have a common entrance, which is marked by 4 lighted beacons. According to the chart, you can carry 7 feet for 1½ miles up Hungars Creek and 4 feet for ¾ of a mile more. But the channel is narrow and meandering, and above it the creek is very shoal.

The entrance to Mattawoman Creek recommended by the *Coast Pilot* is between the fourth beacon and Wilsonia Neck. But according to the chart, this—like the other possible entrance—has a controlling depth of 1 foot, which we have found to be quite accurate.

No supplies are available on either of these creeks. If you can negotiate the narrow channel, Hungars Creek offers shelter in an emergency. Otherwise, it and Mattawoman appear attractive only to the inveterate pioneer with a shoal-draft boat.

XXI. CAPE CHARLES HARBOR (*12224*).

This harbor, about 10 miles north of Cape Charles, is the southernmost on the Eastern Shore. We are discussing it before Kings Creek and Cherrystone Inlet, both north of it, because it is on the way to them.

Approaching from the north, you can save some time by picking up nun C-10 and laying a course from there to a point a little south of R-4 in Cape Charles Harbor Channel. Approaching from the south, just keep about a mile offshore and you will run right into the channel. Approaching at night, pick up the flashing green light at the entrance. A lighted range takes you from there to R-2, and another lighted range from there into the harbor.

As you turn east from the channel into the harbor, you see on the south side a concrete plant, on the north a forbidding bulkhead and ferry slips, and beyond them the buildings of Cape Charles' main street; ahead is a Coast Guard Station on a point dividing the municipal harbor, called the Harbor of Refuge, from the turning basin on the south side. Slips are usually available in the municipal harbor for a modest fee, and should be arranged for at the gas dock. There is a grocery store nearby, as well as a small restaurant and most of the other shops you would expect in an active small town.

The town was built as a ferry terminus for the railroad, and for many years before the bridge across the mouth of the Bay was built, trains ran to Cape Charles, then were put aboard ferries to continue their trip south to Norfolk and beyond. In the 1950's, when the railroad closed its headquarters there and stopped the ferry service, the town went into a decline. It is currently enjoying a small boom,

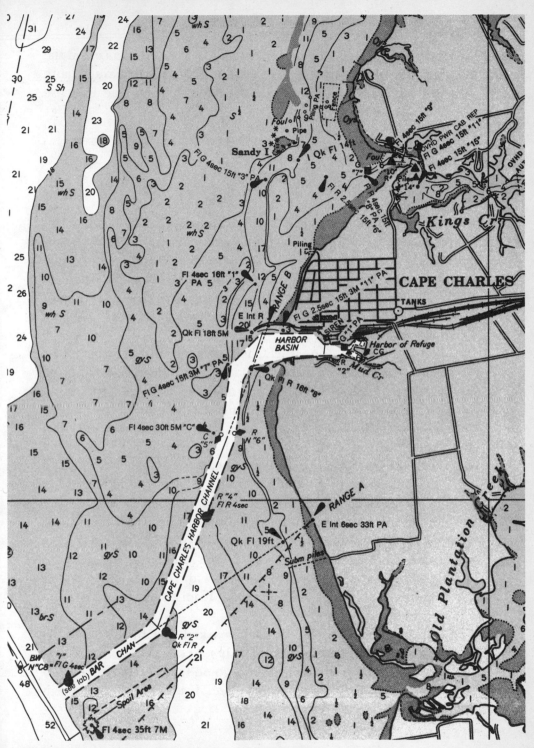

Cape Charles and Kings Creek (from chart 12224).

thanks to retired people who are attracted by the ambience and the recreational possibilities. It is a very popular port during drum season, from late April through June, when fishermen line up to use the two boat ramps.

XXII. KINGS CREEK (*12224*).

If you don't draw over 5 feet and the tide isn't unusually low, this is the place to go. It is used by both workboats and pleasure boats, and a yard here can haul vessels up to 60 feet. On our visit in 1972 we were piloted by Allison Mills, ardent fisherman and native of Cape Charles; but we are convinced that in a boat drawing 5 feet or less a stranger can make his way up to the two marinas by following the marks and chart 12224.

Coming up Cherrystone Inlet Channel, leave the northern break-water of Cape Charles Harbor to starboard and continue approximately north until you pass flashing red beacon 6. Then turn right about 45 degrees and head for the quick-flashing dividing-channel beacon. Leave this to port, turn right about 90 degrees, and head for flashing beacon 6. Leave this to starboard, turn left about 70 degrees, and head between the day beacon and the flashing red beacon. After you pass beacon 6, head for beacons 7 and 8 marking the narrow creek entrance. Disregard the pilings on the way in; they are not channel marks but moorings. The approach to the marina is shoaler than the creek channel at this point. So if you've had trouble in the channel, you probably won't be able to get in.

Kings Creek Marina caters to transients and offers many services and comforts. It is well sheltered, except from easterly breezes coming down King Creek.

Above beacon 15 the creek is not marked, but by watching the crab floats and the chart and using your sounding pole (known here as a Chincoteague compass), you can go on up to beautiful anchorages with 4 or 5 feet. As yet Kings Creek is unspoiled. Its shore is fringed with marsh; behind the marsh is high ground with many pines and only a few houses built among them. It is only a short distance from Cape Charles Harbor but seems a world away.

XXIII. CHERRYSTONE INLET (*12224*).

The channel is the same as for Kings Creek until you reach the channel-dividing beacon northeast of beacon 18 and just east of Cherrystone Island. Pass this beacon close on either side and keep well off the island. According to Mr. Mills, a shoal that is neither marked nor charted extends to the east of it. After clearing Cherrystone Island, head for Wescoat Point and keep in close to the spit above it where the chart shows the deep water. If there are bush stakes, they mark shoals to the east; leave them to starboard.

Any anchorage above Wescoat Point is reasonably snug. On the shore opposite the point is a camp ground which, we were told, can accommodate 7,600 people, twice the population of Cape Charles. So, if you like seclusion, it may be worth the trouble to work your way up above Mill Point. According to the chart you can carry 7 feet for 2 miles above Cherrystone Island. Cherrystone Inlet is deeper and simpler to navigate than Kings Creek, but it is less snug and much less interesting.

XXIV. KIPTOPEKE (*12224*).

At Kiptopeke, about 7 miles south of Cape Charles Harbor, is the last slip used by the Cape Charles ferry before the bridge-tunnel replaced it. To protect this slip, the ferry company sank nine concrete ships in two lines roughly parallel to the shore. The anchorage between the ships and the shore is sheltered from the east and west but not from north and south. If you need shelter from either direction, you can anchor just north or south of the ferry slip. There

Chesapeake Bay and the 17.6-mile Chesapeake Bay Bridge-Tunnel connecting Virginia's Lower Eastern and Western shores.

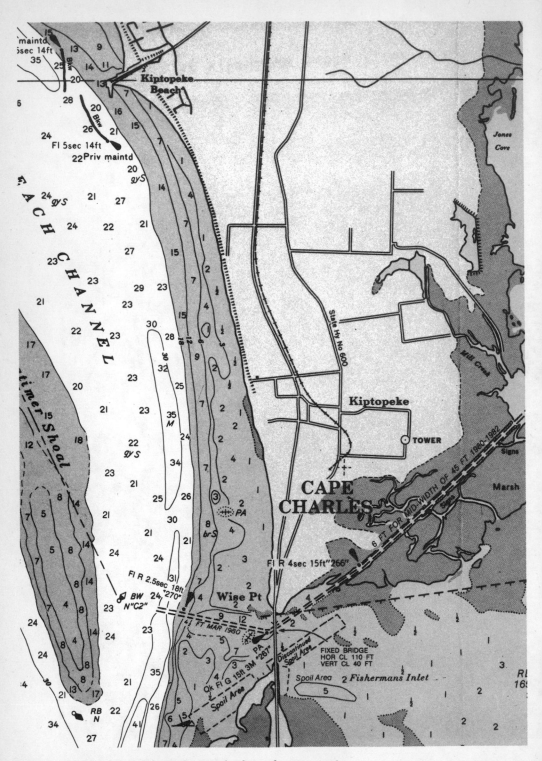

The harbor at Kiptopeke Beach (from chart 12224).

is plenty of water so long as you stay a reasonable distance off the beach. This can provide a snug, if unattractive, harbor of refuge.

The main advantage of Kiptopeke is that it takes almost no time to get in or out. Another advantage is that it is easy to find and enter at night. There is a white flasher at the north end of the northern line of ships and another at the south end of the southern line, and there are no other navigation lights nearby. No supplies or services are available; in fact, we were told that the present owner of the breakwater and slip does not welcome people ashore.

If you are entering the Chesapeake from sea, and planning to head up the Eastern Shore, Kiptopeke is the first harbor on this side of the Bay. Of course, if you are departing through the eastern channel off Cape Charles, this is a convenient jumping-off point.

CHAPTER NINE

HARBORS OF THE LOWER WESTERN SHORE—BELOW POTOMAC RIVER TO CAPE HENRY

I. GREAT WICOMICO RIVER (*12235*).

The largest river between the Potomac and the Rappahannock, the Great Wicomico provides a number of convenient and attractive anchorages for vessels cruising the mid-Bay area. The old familiar lighthouse at the entrance has been replaced by a new lighted steel structure (much harder to see from a distance) and the channels beyond are well marked. But don't be guided entirely by the chart in selecting an anchorage or overnight berth, because some of the choicest spots are not immediately apparent.

1. Cockrell Creek (12235), Fairport, and Reedville. Although this convenient creek looks inviting on the chart, it has several disadvan-

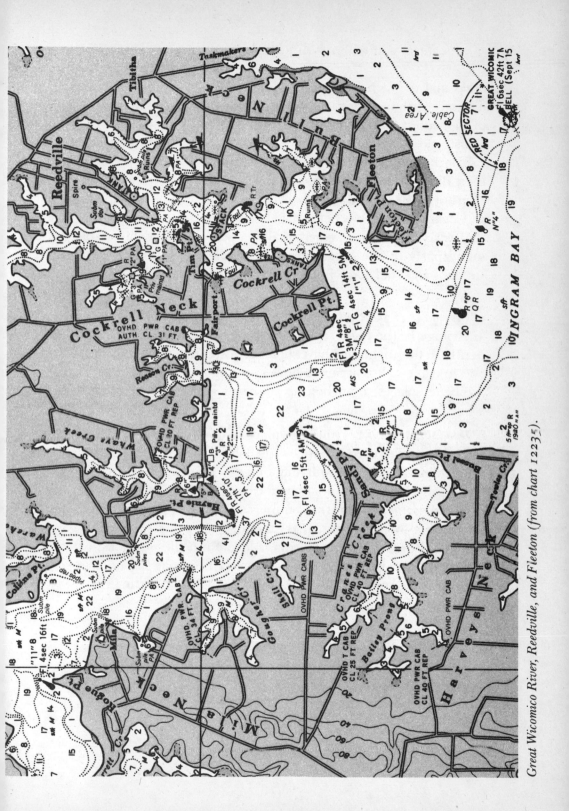

Great Wicomico River, Reedville, and Fleeton (from chart 12235).

tages and is much less attractive than the Great Wicomico above. The large fish factories at Fairport and Reedville have made this one of the busiest (and richest) commercial fishing ports on the Atlantic Coast, and you will usually find a fleet of seagoing purse seiners in the harbor. Reedville is home port for the menhaden vessels, with their distinctive rigs and crow's nests; but if the fertilizer plants are operating, the smoke and smell can be disagreeable. The pollution of Cockrell Creek has been largely cleared up in recent years, but the wake of passing vessels makes anchoring uncomfortable in many parts of the creek below Reedville. However, if you need supplies and fuel you will find them at Reedville.

a. Fleeton (12235). Some years ago we occasionally found overnight anchorage in the bight just inside Fleeton Point in 9 feet. But the depths in the anchorage have shoaled. You can get ice, beer, and bait and find a few slips at Steam Boat Landing on Fleeton Point. There are better places to anchor, up the river if not in Cockrell Creek.

b. Reedville (12235). This is the place to go for supplies. The docks are commercial, used chiefly by the fishing fleet, but gas and diesel are obtainable, and you will find an icehouse nearby. Weaver's Food Store is just back of the docks, and carries a good line of supplies. It is not advisable to lie at the commercial docks overnight, but if you are looking for an anchorage try the fork to the east in 10 or 12 feet of water. Buzzard's Point Marina is located in the west fork, where gas and diesel fuel are available. The cruise boat *Captain Thomas* runs from Buzzard's Point to Tangier Island daily during the summer months.

c. Fairport (12235). Here you will find a number of large marine railways crowded in between the fish factories and fertilizer plants. It's another commercial area without much to attract cruising boats. However, Jennings Boatyard can haul yachts up to 80-footers with 8-foot draft, at prices which compare very favorably with those charged by yards in most Chesapeake yachting centers. The Jennings yard has also built trawler-type yachts.

2. *Cranes Creek* (*12235*). Located on the southwest side of the Great Wicomico opposite the entrance to Cockrell Creek, this little creek offers peace and quiet in rural surroundings. The approach is tricky, despite two channel markers in the entrance, and should not be attempted if your boat draws over 5 feet. But for shoal-draft craft it offers fine protection.

3. *Great Wicomico River above Cockrell Creek* (*12235*). "This is one of my favorite rivers on the Western Shore," writes an experienced Chesapeake cruising man. " 'Delightful' best describes the anchorages. It is much to be preferred to Cockrell Creek." The most convenient anchorage for boats cruising the Bay is in the bight north of Sandy Point, with deep water close up to the sandy beach. You will find this less exposed than it looks on the chart, with enough room for a large rendezvous of deep-draft sailing vessels.

Farther up the river, which is well worth leisurely exploring if you have the time, you will find 15- to 20-feet mid-channel depths to Glebe Point, where an overhead power cable crossing with 54-foot vertical clearance at mid-channel, just above the swing bridge, prevents further navigation by larger-masted sailing craft. The shores are high and wooded, with two or three delightful creeks and gunkholes. One of our favorites is Horn Harbor, on the north shore just before you reach Ferry Point. The narrow entrance is unmarked, but can be approached safely by favoring the starboard side. Once inside, you can anchor in 7 or 8 feet in a landlocked basin surrounded by fields and woodland rising to 80 feet near the upper end of the creek.

Tiffany Yachts, builders of inboard powerboats, provides excellent engine and hull repairs. Glebe Point Market has 100 feet of dockage and a launching ramp. If you can clear the 54-foot overhead cable crossing above the bridge, there are good anchorages for another 2 miles upstream. Take a look.

II. Mill Creek, Va. (*12235*), Between Great Wicomico and Rappahannock Rivers.

A yachtsman, who knows this creek well, writes us as follows:

Easy refuge passage from Great Wicomico River Light. The creek is fairly wide, quite deep, as charted, and very attractive, being lined with nice trees, etc. The bottom is mud-sand, fairly good holding.

The entrance from the Bay is clearly marked by red-and-black buoys, but proceed cautiously as you approach red nun 4, and don't swing too sharply around that mark as the ¹/₂-foot shoal now extends farther east than shown on the chart.

On entering, a few stakes suggest giving the sandbar on the right a fairly wide berth. Same with next point on left, though not as wide a berth is needed.

No docks are to be seen, except small private ones of small capacity. Some of the land on the left side is divided up and is for sale to water lovers. Anchorage anywhere is o.k. The nearest large general store or good restaurant is at Wicomico Church, three miles away.

The above was written for an earlier edition some 20 years ago. Most of it is still true today, though you will see more piers and houses along the shores. We don't know many navigable waterways in other parts of the country where you will find less evidence of encroaching civilization.

III. Dividing Creek, Va. (*12236*), Between Great Wicomico and Rappahannock Rivers.

This creek is wide, with long sweeps to the southeast and north-west, though good shelter can be found in the various coves and tributaries. Give the shoals off Kent Point and the point north of it to port a wide berth. There is a bush stake on the shoal just north of

Prentice Creek and at the ends of some of the other prominent shoals, but stay in the middle and play safe.

A Chesapeake cruising man wrote us some years ago: "The last time we visited this creek a farmer and his two small sons rowed out after supper to look over our 36-foot cutter, which he said was only the second sailboat he had seen all year. After returning to milk his cows, our farmer came back with a quart of strawberries, and a pitcher of thick cream. Friendly folk, these Virginia tidewater farmers!"

Good anchorages abound and some of the most convenient are in Prentice Creek. One of the best is the cove on the south side just above the brick ruins.

IV. INDIAN CREEK, VA. (*12235*).

This is one of the best of the creeks—all things considered—emptying into the Chesapeake between the Potomac and the Rappahannock. It is easy to enter, well marked with beacons and private stakes, attractive, deep, and with many snug anchorages. In addition, a fine marina has been established there by William B. Walker, a northern yachtsman, who came down to the Chesapeake after World War II and picked out the location for his Chesapeake Boat Basin after considerable exploration of this part of the Bay.

It is located at Kilmarnock Landing about 2 miles up the creek, as shown on the chart, at the end of a road from Kilmarnock, a mile and three-quarters away and one of the finest towns on this part of the Chesapeake. Supermarkets, a Laundromat, and other facilities appreciated by yachtsmen make Kilmarnock the best shopping center in these parts.

The Chesapeake Boat Basin has many deep-water, sheltered slips, showers, rest rooms, a Laundromat, gas, charts, ice, marine supplies, and repair service, and may also provide transportation to Kilmarnock. The Indian Creek Yacht and Country Club, to starboard on entering, and a short distance above Bells Creek, has a few guest slips. Make arrangements to rent one through the manager, (804) 435-3136, or the current commodore. The club has a good restaurant, and a very snug cove in which to tie up.

In entering the creek from out in the Bay, the Kilmarnock water tank (shown on the chart) is visible for some miles. Two flashing red beacons show the way in, and two more red flashers and some unlit marks show the way up the creek. Don't mistake several duck blinds for beacons. Keep in the middle of the creek as you go up.

Henrys Creek is a small, fairly deep harbor, with a couple of small private docks. The principal bar on the left at the first turn has a stake to be left to port. Other stakes show the starboard side of the channel.

Pitmans Cove, on the left farther up Indian Creek, offers the most attractive anchorage and has an easy entrance. Keep in the center—it is very snug.

A yachtsman wrote, "We found over 12 feet all the way in and 100 yards to the right, with channel at least $^2/_3$ the width of the water area. An old usable dock in 10 feet of water lies on southwest shore with road leading towards town. Anchorage seemed o.k. (mud), with plenty of room to swing, yet fully protected."

Despite the presence of an Esso bulk fuel plant near Kilmarnock Landing, Bill Walker's Boat Basin provides snug berthing, with little traffic. Transportation is available to Kilmarnock, and you'll find Bill a knowledgeable guide for land or water exploration.

V. DYMER CREEK, VA. (12235).

Several experienced Chesapeake yachtsmen have helped us update our information about areas they know intimately; one of them, who lives on Dymer Creek, has been particularly helpful in pointing out some fine anchorages we have overlooked or neglected in earlier editions.

For instance, we failed to mention a particularly attractive anchorage in a protected basin which is visible on the north shore just inside Grog Island. Known locally as the Grog Island anchorage, it provides clear water with depths of 9 to 13 feet and a nice sandy beach. It provides a convenient anchoring place for vessels sailing up and down the Bay, but you may find it crowded on summer weekends or holidays.

Farther up the creek you will find a choice of fine, tight little coves on both the south and north shores. The best on the south bank are: Ashley's Cove, with a pretty and well-protected anchoring spot, and George's Cove just above it, with two well-run boat repair facilities as well as good anchorages.

The marine railway formerly operated by Dave Winegar continues under the efficient management of his daughter, Cathy Winegar Davenport, at the same location in George's Cove, near the Ocran Boat Shop, another locally operated facility.

Hunt's Cove on the north shore of Dymer (to starboard on entering) is the best of several snug anchorages on that side of the creek.

VI. Tabbs Creeks, Va. (*12235*).

The entrance to this little creek just south of Dymer has been dredged, a local yachtsman reports, and it is sometimes accessible to boats of as much as 6-foot draft. The channel is privately marked, and once inside you can anchor in 10 to 12 feet with complete protection in a landlocked basin.

VII. Antipoison Creek, Va. (*12235*).

According to local legend, Indians living on this creek at the time of Captain John Smith's exploration of the Bay supplied the "antipoison" which enabled that doughty explorer to recover from a stingray bite. (The captain's version of this encounter is told on page

364.) The entrance between outlying shoals is marked, and inside there are several pleasant anchorages in rural surroundings that haven't changed very much over the years.

VIII. RAPPAHANNOCK RIVER (*12235, 12237*).

One of the great rivers of the Western Shore, the Rappahannock, like the Potomac to Washington, is navigable for 95 nautical miles to its leading city—Fredericksburg. As in the Potomac, the best cruising waters are in the lower reaches; in fact, all of the best harbors are within 16 miles of Windmill Point Light at the entrance of the river. On Windmill Point itself there is the well-equipped Windmill Point Marine Resort, a most impressive facility having a dredged basin 700 feet long by 250 feet wide with a dredged channel between rock jetties from the deep water in the river. The entrance is marked by privately maintained lighted beacons about ¹/₂ mile southwest of Windmill Point. Inside are many slips, gas, diesel fuel, water, ice, a restaurant, a snack bar, a store, a motel, a lounge room, etc. This man-made harbor provides a splendid and easily accessible stopover for longshore Bay cruisers, but yachts drawing 5 feet or more should not attempt the channel without first checking the depths, as it is apt to shoal after heavy storms. A yachtsman who "commutes" to Florida each year rates Windmill Point one of the very best marinas on the entire waterway.

The best deep-water anchorages are in Carter Creek (11 miles upriver), Corrotoman River (12 miles), and Urbanna (16 miles)—three estuaries which rival in appeal any on the Bay. Cruisers wishing to go farther can continue to Tappahannock, 39 miles upriver and just below the bridge. However, extensive marshes begin just below there and become more prevalent as the river gets narrower.

Gas, ice, and provisions can be obtained at Irvington and Weems on Carter Creek, at Urbanna, and Tappahannock. Above the bridge they can be found at Port Royal and Fredericksburg. The

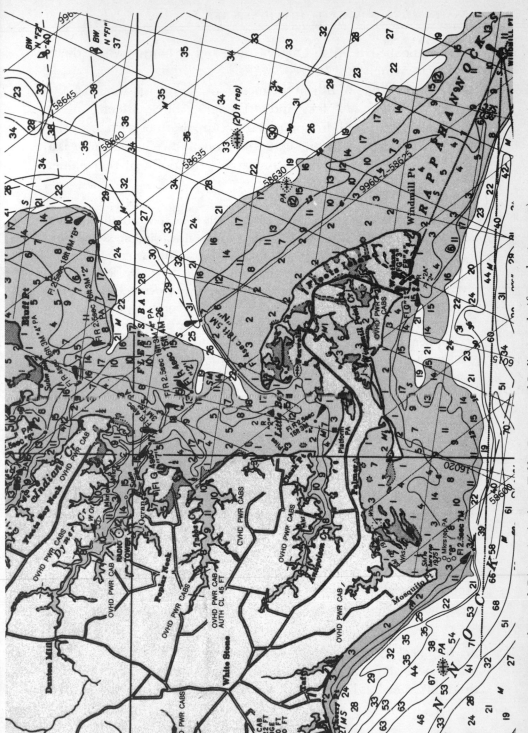

Entrance to Rappahannock River, Antipoison, Tubbs, Dymer, and Indian creeks (from chart 12225).

principal boatyards are at Carter Creek and Urbanna, where there are also thriving yacht clubs.

The mean range of tide at the mouth of the river is about 1 foot; at Tappahannock, 1½ feet; and at Fredericksburg, 2 feet.

Captain John Smith first visited the Rappahannock while a prisoner of the Indians, but later explored it on his own hook. There is a story that he got stung by a stingray off the point of that name, whereon, as the ancient story goes:

> No blood nor wound was seen, but a little blew spot, but the torment was instantly so extreame, that in foure houres, had so swollen his hand, arms and shoulder, we all with much sorrow concluded his funerall, and prepared his grave in an Ile hard by, as himselfe directed: yet it pleased God by a precious oyle Doctor Russell at the first plyed to it when he sounded it with a probe (ere night) his tormenting paine was so well asswaged that he ate of the fish for his supper, which gave no less joy and content to us than ease to himselfe, for which he called the Island Stingray Ile after the name of the fish.

It wasn't really an island, or at least it isn't one now, but rather is the point that separates two of the finest rivers for cruising on the Western Shore: the Rappahannock and the Piankatank.

1. Broad Creek (12235, 12237), Deltaville, Rappahannock River. Across the river from Windmill Point, on the southwest shore of the Rappahannock, is the well-marked channel to a busy Broad Creek. Lighted beacons mark the outer and inner ends of the 7-foot dredged channel, leading into a small harbor lined with boatyards and marinas. Several of the larger marinas have 150 slips or more, occupied mostly by powerboats and local fishing craft. A local yachtsman writes that good repair facilities are available.

2. Mill Creek (12235, 12237), Rappahannock River. Located on the south shore about 2 miles east of the Rappahannock River bridge, this Mill Creek has little to attract visiting cruising boats, and is used chiefly by local fishing craft. The entrance is tricky, despite the two lighted beacons, and it is shoal inside. If you must go in, start from the outer light and head for the three remaining piles at the end of what is left of Mill Creek Wharf. Then follow the channel to the turning basin and wharf southwest of the second light. The passage beyond there into the creek winds between shoals and should not be attempted without local knowledge. There are no supplies in the creek.

3. Locklies Creek (*12235*, *12237*). This creek can be negotiated through the entrance between the light off Grey Point and Parrott Island, heading midway between them. Then swing southward with the light dead astern and leave red nun 2 well to starboard. After that head for the mouth of the creek, giving the red mark a good berth. The creek is poorly charted but boats drawing under 5 feet should have no difficulty. There are 3 marine facilities, and gas and most services are available.

4. Carter Creek—Weems and Irvington (*12235*, *12237*). About 11 miles above Windmill Point Light at the entrance of the Rappahannock, Carter Creek is one of the finest creeks on the Chesapeake, with everything that a yachtsman can—or should—desire. Beauty, complete security, privacy if you want it, a fine yacht club, one of the finest inns on the Bay, supplies and facilities of all kinds, plus hospitable people. What more do you want?

a. Carter Cove and Weems. This cove is somewhat commercial and less attractive than the other branches. In entering Carter Cove, keep to the port shore; there is a long shoal south of the point to starboard. There are three marinas in the cove which usually have transient slips available, as well as a good launching ramp. The large marine railway across the creek is Humphries Railway. It can and does haul the largest yachts, and its hull and engine repair facilities are excellent.

Carter Creek and Irvington. (Photo courtesy of Backus Aerial Photography.)

b. East Branch and Irvington. Off Irvington the creek is too cluttered to be attractive, though the south shore across the creek is wooded and pretty. The best plan is to pick up your fuel and supplies at Irvington and then go farther up the east branch to the fork just after the creek turns to the northeast. There it is snug and attractive. Another good anchorage is in the lower fork of this branch, behind the entrance point.

c. Carter Creek, Main or North Branch. This is the best branch of all. Just beyond the point to starboard, where the east branch separates from the main creek, is the Rappahannock Yacht Club, a friendly place, with 8 feet at the dock and Rappahannock Yachts next door, which may have a spare slip. The first conspicuous landmark on entering is the Irvington Marina on the point at West Irvington just above the yacht club. Here are slips, gas, diesel fuel, water, ice, and a marine store.

Farther up the creek, on a point to starboard just below the first fork to the right, situated on a lovely wooded hill overlooking the creek, is perhaps the finest resort inn on the Bay—the well-known Tides Inn. Here are a number of slips, gas, water, and other facilities and the Tides Lodge and Marina across the creek. Beyond the Inn, in the fork to the right near the 7-foot depth mark, is one of the most perfect anchorages on the Chesapeake. Drop your hook there in perfect peace and security and then climb the hill. Through the trees between Tides Inn and the creek you will look down on a scene of rare beauty.

5. Corrotoman River (12235). Those who know the Chesapeake, as did Dr. Walter C. Tilden, member of the Cruising Club of America who lived for many years on the Rappahannock, rate the Corrotoman in the top bracket of fine cruising areas. Its unspoiled, thickly wooded shoreline is an invitation to the venturesome skipper who likes to explore strange creeks following the contours of the chart. If you stick in the middle you will avoid the outlying shoals and find delightful snug anchorages in both eastern and western branches. A few supplies are obtainable at Millenbeck. Various waterfront "improvements" have begun to appear along the shoreline, but the character of the place remains unspoiled. Tilden's "favorite anchorage" here was in the east branch, opposite the mouth of Bells Creek, in 10 feet near a "sandy beach and lovely point."

You can no longer poke into Taylor Creek (where Doc Tilden lived) with a keelboat drawing 6 feet. The entrance channel, which lies 1 1/2 miles northeasterly of the Corrotoman River entrance beacon, has shoaled to less than 4 feet and cannot be safely entered by keelboats.

The entrance to the Corrotoman is marked by a red lighted beacon off Millenbeck, and most of the outlying shoals beyond are clearly indicated on the chart. Take a day for leisurely gunkholing, and you will be well rewarded. "Here is tranquility," as Doc Tilden used to say, "deep and clean water, and that most elusive element, peace."

6. *Urbanna Creek, Urbanna* (*12237*). Here is another fine sail-in harbor, with a dredged channel and controlling depth of 9 feet to the docks on the west shore. The entrance has a 4-second red light on the outer end of the breakwater and the channel is clearly marked. There are no shoals inside the harbor to the fixed bridge ahead.

Take your choice among four marine facilities, all on the west bank, where you will find most necessities and some frivolities. Or anchor out. A restaurant called Windows is on the waterfront. Town is a short walk up the hill. You will find an establishment called The Town House there which offers bed and breakfast. The town turns out for two big events—the Folklore Festival at the beginning of the boating season and the Oyster Festival toward the end.

British privateers entered the creek in 1781 and pillaged Urbanna and Rosegill, the famous old estate on the hill between Rosegill Lake and Urbanna. This estate is certainly worth a visit, if we are to believe the eloquent words of several authorities on the subject, but it is not accessible from the water.

7. *Urbanna to Tappahannock* (*12237*). On this section of the river channels have been dredged to open up several small creeks which previously were inaccessible to most cruising boats. Here are two worth mention:

a. Robinson Creek. About 1 mile above Urbanna Creek on the west side of the river, a dredged channel provides 9-feet depths to Robinson Creek. There is one marina, Burrell's, on the creek offering slips, repairs, and many services.

b. Greenvale Creek. Two miles farther upriver on the opposite (east) shore, a clearly marked 6-foot deep-dredged channel leads to the narrow entrance of Greenvale Creek. Inside are Greenvale Creek Marina with slips and a ramp, and Conrad's Seafood, also with slips, a ramp, and a restaurant. The creek widens, allowing room for those who choose to anchor.

8. *Tappahannock* (*12237*). This town is on the west shore of the Rappahannock, some 39 miles upriver and just below the new highway bridge. Although the river is navigable for another 50 miles to Fredericksburg, this is as far as most cruising boats go. Tappahannock is becoming an active boating center, with several good marinas and modern launching facilities for cruiser-size trailer craft. Hoskins Creek Channel was dredged to a depth of 10 feet several years ago, and the best facilities and anchorages are inside the creek. Slips and gas, diesel, lifts, etc., are available at the Haven, on the town side of the creek. Shoal-draft boats can usually find a berth at the Tappahannock Marina, with 4 feet at the docks. There are both state- and town-maintained launching ramps.

IX. PIANKATANK RIVER (*12235*).

The old Stingray Point Lighthouse has been replaced by a steel structure that is not easy to pick up from a distance on entering from the Bay. Leaving the light to starboard, you come to the entrance of the Piankatank, one of the most delightful rivers on the

Chesapeake, pleasantly winding its way between fairly high tree-clad banks, and offering good harbors on either shore. A river to write home about! It is nearly 15 miles upriver to Freeport from the lighthouse, but watch for outlying shoals, some marked by bush stakes. The best harbors are below the fixed bridge (43-foot clearance), two of them on opposite sides of the entrance. Watch for fish traps as you go in. Mean tidal range is 1 foot at the mouth.

1. Jackson Creek and Deltaville (12235), North Shore of the Piankatank. "They don't know nuttin'," a scornful young fisherman told us when he described the number of careless yachtsmen who had tried to cut corners at the entrance and had come to grief. If you forget to look north for the string of green beacons (3 through 9) close to the shore and head cheerfully from the lighted entrance beacon roughly northwest to the red one at the creek's mouth, you'll be in trouble quick and our fishing friend's opinion of yachtsmen will go even lower. Follow the chart carefully, with some channel stakes to help, heading about north and then swing sharply to a course south of west, after passing green 9.

You will then soon be past the third red beacon at the mouth of a first-rate little harbor, with a fine yacht club and a nice town in which to stock up.

On the narrow neck of land connecting Stove Point Neck with the mainland is the Fishing Bay Yacht Club, "the most active and enterprising sailing organization in the Middle Bay area." There is a growing fleet of fine cruising yachts and visiting yachtsmen are welcome. You may be able to find a slip at the Yacht Club or at the Deltaville Marina or at one of the other facilities which have been developed in both branches of this active boating center.

Although Jackson Creek is an interesting and busy little harbor, we prefer Fishing Bay on the south side of the peninsula, where you will have more room in equally pleasant surroundings.

2. Fishing Bay (12236), North Shore of the Piankatank. On the other side of the narrow strip connecting Stove Point Neck to the main shore in Fishing Bay, at the back (or front) entrance of the yacht club

Fishing Bay, on Piankatank River. (Photo courtesy of Backus Aerial Photography.)

of that name. Don't confuse this with the other Fishing Bay, on Tangier Sound. One of our cruising friends wrote:

> One of the nicest anchorages I know is Fishing Bay, which you'll find inside Stove Point Neck at the mouth of the Piankatank River. It is perfectly protected from the north and east, and we went in there one afternoon when the N.E. wind was freshening to disturb the waters of many less protected spots. The scenery is beautiful; lovely big estates line the shores, and we were the only boat in there.

There is a sandy beach at the head of the bay and a cove in which protection can also be found from the northwest. In strong winds from south to west it can be uncomfortable, but on a hot summer night a light southwesterly across the water is refreshing.

Deagle and Sons Marine Railway, Inc., operates two marine railways on the northwest corner of Fishing Bay, just north of the place where the chart shows Grinels Wharf. Next door is Deagle's Marina, run by Larry Arnold and Randy Dunn, with a dredged basin, and covered and open slips, used mostly by power cruisers; next door to that is Ruark's Marina, with many sailboats at its slips. An Annapolis yachtsman friend of ours takes his boat to Gene Ruark every year for his spring hauling, and has high praise for the work of this yard.

3. *Milford Haven (12235), South Shore of the Piankatank*. On the south side of the entrance to the Piankatank, helping to form the harbor of Milford Haven, is Gwynn Island, nursery for the Merchant Marine.

> There is an old saying along the waterfront, said the *Baltimore Sun,* to the effect that when the men-children of Matthews County first learn to toddle, their mothers take their hands, lead them out to Cherry Point on Gwynn Island, where the Piankatank and Chesapeake Bay meet, wait until a Bull Line ship heaves in sight and say:
> "Son, there is your future home."

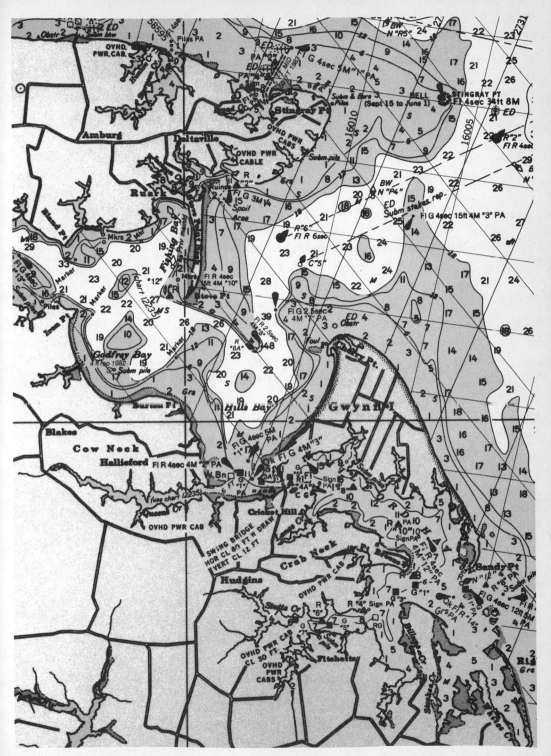

Piankatank River and Milford Haven (from chart 12225).

According to a local authority on the fish wharf who talked convincingly, 5 of the first 61 merchant marine captains whose ships were torpedoed in World War II came from Gwynn Island—out of a population of 700. Before that, in 1942, there were 57 men from the Island serving the nation in some capacity, including 19 sea captains. Many of the islanders bear the appropriate name of "Mariner."

Milford Haven is easily accessible through its western entrance, and interesting; it's an authentic fishing and seafaring community, as may have been gathered from the above stories. Don't try the southeast entrance without a local pilot.

The main entrance channel from Hills Bay is simple until you pass through the drawbridge. Just watch the chart and follow the buoys and beacons. As you pass through the draw, swing wide around the green beacon, leaving it well to port, since the shoal projects beyond it. The next marker is red and on the end of Middle Ground Shoal. Give this a good berth also. After that, the going in is clear if you watch for the shoal to the west of Callis Wharf and others on the various points.

> Nobody need go aground at Milford Haven, says Howard Bloomfield. With a deep and wide channel that hardly needs a marker because through the clear water you look down at the shelving edges, any excuse is lacking. But we did it on our way out in the morning. There was a moment of sun glare on the water ahead and "Kittiwake" stopped. She wanted to stay there too. Then an oyster boat with a husky engine and the name "Myrna Loy" came along, tossed us a line, and jerked us back into the channel.

Many new facilities have been developed in recent years. A Coast Guard Station is located just inside the drawbridge as you enter Milford Haven. Here also is the Narrows Marina, owned and operated by W. D. Jenkins, with dockage on the dredged entrance channel, covered slips, and ramp; it is associated with the Islander Motel and Restaurant next door.

The best anchorages are as follows:

(1) In the center, southeast of Callis Wharf, east of the Middle Grounds beacon. This is convenient to the wharf, but a bit large, with a sweep from northwest to southeast.
(2) In the northwest corner between the 1-foot spots.
(3) In Edwards or Barn creeks, much snugger but less convenient.
(4) Tie up at Callis Wharf, if there is room. There is 10 feet of water, gas, diesel fuel, water, ice, fish, and groceries nearby.
(5) Stutts Creek at the southeast end of Milford Haven has several good anchorages close to the entrance from the Bay. Local fishermen use the Bay entrance, but cruising yachts drawing more than 4 feet should not use this entrance without local knowledge.

4. Porpoise Creek (12235), North Shore of the Piankatank. Not even named on the chart, this is a little pond behind the beach dunes just above Fishing Bay, with a privately marked dredged channel (6 feet deep) between wooded breakwaters. You can spot a large gas sign from the river, with the roof of the covered slips of Porpoise Cove Marina visible inside. The pond provides good small-boat shelter in a blow.

5. Healy Creek (12235). This is another of those delightful hideouts you encounter so often on the Chesapeake, but seldom find elsewhere. Sailing up the river you may spot a few tall masts which look as though they were rising from a field back of Horse Point. Actually, they are probably the masts of auxiliaries tied up behind the "Sandy Hook" entrance to Healy Creek. The entrance is marked. Once you clear the hook and bear hard to port you will find yourself in a tight little basin, with slips of 5- to 6-feet depth maintained by the Horse Point Marina.

6. Cobbs Creek (12235), South Shore of the Piankatank. There is a quiet, sheltered anchorage in 8 feet behind the sandy spit.

7. *Wilton Creek* (*12235*), *North Shore of the Piankatank*. This is one of the loveliest and snuggest anchorages on the Chesapeake—the kind you dream about on a stormy night on wide waters. It ranked high on Walter Tilden's list of "favorite anchorages," and many other yachtsmen agree. Keep in the middle and anchor around the first bend to the right in 7 or 8 feet. The land is high and thickly wooded and you feel as if you were floating in an Adirondack lake. Perhaps it would be hot in summer, and there are no facilities or supplies. Otherwise, we'd call it perfect.

The bridge, with 43-foot vertical clearance, keeps larger masted vessels from the upper river, which is worth exploring at least as far as Berkley Island, if you can get under the bridge.

8. *The Piankatank above Dixie* (*12235*). There is good anchorage north of Berkley Island, off Stampers Wharf in the large bight between Wilton Point and Doctor Point in 8 and 9 feet, and farther up the river off the wharf at Freeport, on the south shore, with 6 feet.

X. HORN HARBOR (*12238*).

Between Stingray Point Light at the mouth of the Piankatank and the next harbor to the south is a 15-mile stretch of marshy, inhospitable shore without a harbor but with the famous Wolf Trap Light as a warning of outlying shoals. This light was named after a British frigate, H.M.S. *Wolf*, which was trapped on the shoals and captured by local watermen in the American Revolution.

Then you come to Horn Harbor, a handy little refuge because it is the only one in some miles, and an interesting one besides. Don't be discouraged by the long entrance with the shoal spots—that is, if your boat draws under 5½ feet. But proceed with the utmost caution, because the chart and the channel may not always be in complete accord. They weren't when a fisherman first showed us the way in and out. Since then the channel has been dredged, perhaps three or four times. An experienced Chesapeake yachtsman advises not attempting the channel in yachts drawing over 5 feet; and even that may be too much by the time you get there.

The best plan is to follow the chart and buoys carefully but also watch water depths from the bow—not always taking the chart too literally. If you are lucky enough to find a local fisherman going in when you are, perhaps you can persuade him to go in slowly and act as your pilot without attempting any shortcuts which might be all right with him but not for you. If no local pilot turns up, you'll have to feel your way. But don't even consider trying it after dark.

Once inside you can go 3 miles or so to the westward if your craft doesn't draw too much, and find snug shelter in one of the many arms which are so characteristic of Chesapeake creeks. As you go along, keep near the middle of the harbor. The deep water is made easier to follow by rows of oyster stakes on each side as you pass between. There is reported to be 6 feet of water all the way up to the boatyard. Even if you touch, the bottom is soft and you will probably keep moving.

The farther up you go the more attractive and snug the harbor becomes. When we explored the creek for the first edition of this guide, we went all the way up to the last 6-foot spot on the chart, where the harbor turns sharply to the west around a wooded point. Here we found a dock and small boatyard run by Charles Diggs, one of the most hospitable people we had ever met on the Chesapeake.

On our last visit we failed to find Mr. Diggs, but found the Horn Harbor Marina, with open and covered slips, a marine railway capable of hauling vessels up to 80 tons, and complete repair facilities. The yard builds cruisers and fishing boats.

The best anchorage is off the yard docks or, if you don't want to go that far, anchor almost anywhere beyond the staked channel on the way up. In stormy weather Mobjack Bay is a better objective.

XI. MOBJACK BAY (12238).

This is a cruising ground all of itself and days can be spent poking around its four tributary rivers and the creeks which flow into them. It is óne of the few large areas which has remained almost untouched by "civilization." Life along these tidewater shores is almost the same as it was in the nineteenth century, except that local fishermen now use power. There is a Deep Creek with only a foot in it. Watch for fish stakes off New Point Comfort; a long detour may be necessary.

When we cruised this historic area for the third time, we found it even more rewarding than on our first visit 20 years earlier. Fish traps are still something of a hazard, particularly at night, but there are not so many of them, and the fairways (marked by painted spar buoys) take you through without trouble. There are good anchorages in each of the four rivers, and in most of the creeks as well, so we won't try to rank them in order of preference. Gloucester County had some of the earliest English settlements in the New World, and many of its historic houses are close to the shores of Mobjack Bay. If you poke up the creeks, you will find an old mill, or a farmhouse, or cattle grazing in wide meadows that reach to the water's edge. And everywhere you go, you will find friendly people, ready to help a stranger.

1. East River (12238), East Shore of Mobjack Bay. This is perhaps the easiest river to reach from the main Bay, and is visited frequently by cruising boats passing up and down the Chesapeake. The town of Mobjack is on the west side of the entrance, where the Tidewater Oil Company has some conspicuous tanks and a large fuel dock.

About 2 miles up the East River on the right bank you will see one of the last tide mills on the Chesapeake. It is no longer in operation, and the millrace has been closed to allow passage into the tidal pond; but the waterwheel and original grinding wheels have been preserved. They are well worth a visit.

On the west bank about a mile above the old tide mill, and opposite Williams Wharf, was a unique yard formerly operated by Thomas Colvin, a naval architect who designed and built steel-hulled yachts for delivery in all parts of the world. At the time of our visit in 1972, Mr. Colvin had several seagoing sailing vessels under construction in his yard. Since then he has been cruising one of his own boats in the Caribbean, and the yard has been operated by another custom boat builder, named David Dana, who builds sailboats, auxiliaries, and workboats.

Williams Wharf is a bulk fuel depot, and gas was not available for yachts when we were there. There is a fair anchorage between Williams Wharf and Bohannon. A better place is farther up in "Put In" Creek, or below Woodas Point.

Wooded shores and farms, in typical Chesapeake style, give this part of the river a pleasantly restful character.

2. North River (12238), North Shore of Mobjack Bay. This is too large for comfort until you get well up. There is an attractive anchorage off Dixondale in 9 or 10 feet, though exposed to the north and southeast for a way. The wharf there has almost disappeared, but south of the spot where the wharf shows on the chart is a private wharf and one of the most beautiful houses and estates we have seen on the Chesapeake. It is known as Elmington and belonged to a man named Rhodes. Across the river is a pretty wooded point.

In approaching, keep well over to the west shore, as the chart indicates. No supplies or public landing facilities are available. Blackwater Creek has several good anchorages. The Mobjack Bay Marina there has gas, diesel, hardware, ice, and showers.

3. Ware River (12238), Northwest Shore of Mobjack Bay. This is another interesting river, wide at the entrance with outlying shoals, but with protected anchorages above the green beacon off Baileys Point and in Wilson Creek. We have found Wilson Creek delightful. There you can anchor in 9 feet between two private wharves and be very comfortable except in northeasters. In that case, a run farther up the creek will give good shelter in 6 feet. Nicholson's Marina has a few slips, usually occupied by local boats.

Captain Clark, a retired naval officer, then living in the house behind the dock on the south bank, greeted us hospitably when we arrived and gave us instructions for entering the creek—one of the most attractive and sheltered anchorages we have found on Mobjack Bay. Dr. and Mrs. Robert Armstrong, formerly active sailors in the Annapolis area, had a home and pier on the north shore near the 6-foot spot shown on the chart.

Run in close to the wharf shown by the chart where the road from Zanoni comes down to the water, north of the creek. Follow this shore closely so as to clear the long shoal projecting north-northwest from the lower entrance point. There is, or was when we were there, an oyster stake on the end of this point, which is to be left to port. After passing this stake, swing gradually, but not too soon, to the port and give the tiny, marshy nub to your starboard a reasonable berth. Then keep slightly to the starboard, or north of the middle and anchor between the two private docks, favoring the northern one.

Except for Nicholson's, no facilities are available. Toward the head of Ware River, where Route 261 runs down to the bank, is a state-owned launch ramp. The Ware River Yacht Club, on Ware Neck near the entrance to the river, has no public facilities.

4. Severn River (12238), West Shore of Mobjack Bay. This river on the southwest shore is favored by many Chesapeake cruising skippers because of its good anchorages and easy access from the Bay. The entrance is well marked, but after passing flashing beacon 3, take note that the nearby day beacon 1 marks the entrance to S. W. Branch, and leave it to port.

One of the anchorages is in the Southwest Branch between "Glass" and "Lady" in 7 feet. In entering give the southeast point of Bar Neck a wide berth. Near the anchorage is Glass Marine, a builder of fiberglass workboats. There is 8 feet at the dock, where gas, diesel, water, ice, and marine supplies may be obtained. A store is nearby. The railway can haul boats up to 75 feet in length and 7-foot draft. You can follow stakes which mark the channel to the southeast, leading to the Holiday Marina, which has dockside slips and a travel lift.

In the Northwest Branch, there is an anchorage in 9 to 12 feet, but without the facilities available in the Southwest Branch.

Before leaving Mobjack Bay we must mention a phenomenon often observed by cruising boats in this part of the Chesapeake, but seldom elsewhere. We refer to the strange crackling sound heard when you are lying quietly at anchor in a still creek or cove. Carson Gibb reported hearing it when he anchored in the Ware River in 1972, giving us this account:

> When I went below I became aware of a light crackling sound that seemed to come from the bilge. I looked around, but found nothing to explain the noise. Later, when I went to bed, the crackling sound became louder and seemed to originate in or on the hull, but a few inches from my ear. This time I began to fear my boat was infested with noisy insects; but a thorough search of cabin and bilge again turned up nothing.
>
> The next day my wife joined me on the boat and we moved over to Put-In Creek off the East River, where I again heard the strange sound. My wife did too; so I could discount the possibility that it was an hallucination. This time I went overboard and felt over the bottom to be sure a float or Clorox bottle wasn't tapping against the hull. Nothing there. Then, finally, I swam off fifty yards and ducked my head under the surface; there it was again, the same crackling sound, but coming from the water and not connected with the boat.

Mr. Gibb's curiosity was aroused, and he later wrote the Virginia Institute of Marine Science, at Gloucester Point, Va., to see if they could solve the mystery. In due course he received a letter, suggesting several possible explanations of "the crackling noise," the most likely of which appears to be "the pistol, or snapping shrimp (two species of the genus *Alpheus* are found in this area), which are one to two inches in length and are capable of producing a snapping or popping noise with a specially developed, enlarged claw. Although *Alpheus* has been seen stunning small shrimps with this pop, the sound is apparently used more often to frighten away predators. In other words, the 'pistol' is more defensive than offensive in nature."

Another possible explanation advanced by the Virginia Institute is "the oyster toadfish (*Opsanus tau*), which also makes sounds which have been heard above the surface of the water. These grunts are low in pitch, however, and probably would not be described as a 'crackling noise.' "

XII. YORK RIVER (*12241, 12238, 12243*).

York River is wide and deep in its lower reaches. Its shores are high in many places and most attractive. Above Yorktown the shore becomes generally lower, though there are some heights back from the river. Marshes and outlying shoals are frequent, and there are no harbors, except anchorages along the marshland far upriver. The tidal range is 2¹/₂ feet at the entrance and at Yorktown, 3 feet at West Point.

There is a large space reserved for Naval Anchorage at the mouth of the York. Since depths range from 26 to 81 feet, it will never be missed as a yacht anchorage.

Unlike its famous namesake on the Hudson, the West Point on York River, 35 miles above the entrance, is low, commercial, and unattractive. A paper and pulp plant is said to "emit a foul odor" at times, which even floats down the river a way on northwesterly winds.

We'd strongly recommend that yachtsmen do not spend much time above Yorktown and Gloucester Point. There is more that is worthwhile near at hand.

On historic Gloucester Peninsula, formed by the York and James rivers, are three famous places: Yorktown on the York, Jamestown on the James, and Williamsburg on the road between. Connecting Yorktown and Williamsburg is the Colonial National Historical Park, through which winds a beautiful drive that follows the heights above the river for part of the distance. How best can the cruising yachtsman take in these three centers of historical lore? We tried to figure this out and were getting nowhere until we found the answer in Sarah Creek.

The docks at Yorktown and Jamestown are very exposed and

facilities for tying up are so poor that no skipper would feel safe in leaving his boat for any length of time. But, on the north shore of the river, not far from the bridge that connects Gloucester Point with Yorktown, is one of the finest and most convenient small creeks on the Chesapeake: Sarah Creek. There, a yacht can be left in perfect security while her skipper and crew are driven (or walk) to the bridge, go across to Yorktown, and take a car or bus for a tour of the historic triangle—or just of Yorktown itself.

1. Perrin River (12238), North Shore of York River. The entrance is through a narrow, winding 6½-foot channel, marked by lighted beacons and buoys, but said often to be obstructed by oyster stakes. Keep close to the line of the green cans, or away from the east shore, after rounding the inner lighted marker. Cook's Landing Marina, with slips, ramp, gas, diesel, two lifts, engine and hull repairs, marine store and pool, as well as other more usual facilities and services, is just beyond the last buoy at the end of the road leading to Perrin. There is a store at which gas, diesel oil, food, and fishermen's supplies are obtainable. A marine railway, said to be able to haul boats 100 feet long with 7-foot draft is nearby, but it has no slips and only 3½ feet. This is the nearest harbor to the main Bay on York River. Sarah Creek is 4 miles farther.

2. Sarah Creek (12238), North Shore of York River. Here is the best small-boat harbor on York River, with facilities that rate among the very finest anywhere on the Chesapeake.

The entrance is well marked and lighted so that by following the chart closely any draft under 8 feet can be taken inside to a completely landlocked anchorage off Yacht Haven on the second point to port inside of the entrance. A "sandy hook" marks the right side of the narrow entrance and a white house is on the point to the left. Hug this last point closely and then either tie up at the marina in 9 feet or anchor just off it.

The York River Yacht Haven provides complete facilities, with 75 modern open slips, gas, diesel, ice, water, electricity, etc., and a good

Sarah Creek, on York River. (Photo courtesy of Backus Aerial Photography.)

dockside restaurant. Part of the facilities are occupied by the York River Yacht Club, which has a swimming pool (private) open to visiting yachtsmen by invitation and a nominal fee. Covered slips and wet storage are available, along with hull and engine repairs. There are a crane and a lift. Two smaller facilities—Jordan Marine Service and Gloucester Point Marina—are farther up the creek on the northwest branch.

Sarah Creek provides a good answer to the sightseeing problem of those who want to take in the historic triangle. Through the Yacht Haven, transportation can be arranged for trips to Yorktown, Jamestown, and Williamsburg across the river by the bridge which has replaced the old ferry. The marina will help with planning and take good care of the boat in the absence of skipper and crew. A walk around the battlefield at Yorktown or through the revival of a colonial community at Williamsburg are rewarding experiences, and Sarah Creek is a fine starting point for cruising yachtsmen.

There are no marshes around, and the shores, though not high, are very pleasant. Though the anchorage is well protected, a cooling breeze from the southwest may come across the water on a hot summer night.

The brick house among the cedars on the point to the east is called Little England, as its bricks are said to have come from old England.

"We were extremely dubious about the tiny twisting channel into the creek," wrote one yachtsman, "but found it to be one of the most delightful little harbors we had ever seen. . . . The manager came down to the dock to greet us, and I asked him if it was a club. He said that it was not. Just a group of people who like boating and like to be together, a distinction that was not too fine for me to grasp."

3. *Yorktown* (*12238*), *South Shore of York River.* As every schoolboy knows, or should know, this is the spot where the surrender of Cornwallis, on October 19, 1781, virtually ended the Revolutionary War. Most yachtsmen entering York River will of course want to go here, climb the heights, and carry their minds back to those stirring times.

There are no docks suitable for tying up here. Should you have a chance to visit the waterfront by some other means than your boat, you will find a small restaurant and the rather new Watermen's Museum.

Arrangements can be made at the Information Center for tours of Yorktown or possibly for a more extended trip to Williamsburg and Jamestown.

The view of the river from the heights is very lovely. Perhaps someone will be smart enough some day to arrange facilities at Yorktown which will be inviting to yachtsmen.

XIII. BACK CREEK (*12238*) AND THE THOROFARE NEAR YORK RIVER.

This Back Creek is out of the way for most cruising boats, and less appealing than Sarah Creek, but it provides a useful harbor of refuge in stormy weather and the Thorofare is used as a shortcut behind the Goodwin Islands marsh for small craft entering or leaving York River from the south. Entering from the Bay, pick up the 4-second flasher R-2 southeast of Goodwin Islands and head westerly for the three lighted beacons marking the entrance channel. Thereafter, the channel winds westerly, but there's plenty of water where the chart says it is. Controlling depths in the Thorofare may change from year to year, but are seldom less—and sometimes more—than indicated on the latest chart (3¹/₂ feet). The Thorofare is marked as a continuous channel, entering from the south; so if you are approaching from the north or York River side be careful to leave the first lighted beacon 16 to port and green markers to starboard.

If you are entering Back Creek from either the Thorofare (Belvin Marine is on the west bank) or the Bay be careful to keep clear of the shoal with only 2 feet to the southeast before swinging southwest after passing G-7 and R-8. If you keep in the middle and follow the markers and the chart carefully, you can carry at least 6 feet to the dock at Mills Marina about ³/₄ of a mile from beacons 7 and 8. The

Seaford Scallop plant is nearby. The village of Seaford is a short distance inland. Farther up Back Creek are the Seaford Yacht Club and Back Creek Park, a 26-acre state-administered park with floating docks, tennis courts, and picnic and play areas. You can find room to anchor in several places in Back Creek and in Claxton Creek.

XIV. POQUOSON RIVER (*12238*).

As the broad mouth of the Poquoson River narrows, three options are presented to the cruiser. To the south is Bennett Creek, where there is a good daytime anchorage near a beach on the southwest side of the marshy Cow Island wildlife refuge as you enter, and three marinas and a ramp farther up in White House Cove. To the north is Chisman Creek, with three more marine facilities and many opportunities to anchor. Straight ahead the southwest branch of the river carries good water but offers little protection in its anchorages from northerly winds. There is a public launching ramp in the southwest branch but no other public facilities.

XV. BACK RIVER (*12238*), LOWER WESTERN SHORE.

This is one of the 15 "Back" rivers, creeks, coves, thorofares, and landings on the Chesapeake, reported in the *Coast Pilot*. There are probably more.

While "the place is large, the shores low and marshy, the shelter poor," as one yachtsman reported, the facilities are now good, with several boatyards and marinas having gas, water, slips, etc. "Furthermore," says our authority, "Langley Field is back of Willoughby Point and the noise of planes is incessant. But there are times when this Back River can provide a welcome harbor of refuge for yachts heading up the Bay in stormy weather."

The only practical way ashore to see the NASA/Langley Visitors Center is to take a shuttle bus from the Langley Air Force Base Yacht Club, which is open to active-duty and retired military personnel.

XVI. HAMPTON ROADS (*12245, 12253, 12222*).

Hampton Roads, where the James, Nansemond, and Elizabeth rivers meet to flow into Lower Chesapeake Bay, is one of the world's greatest natural harbors. Large enough to hold many vessels of the deepest draft, it has around its borders and in its rivers, creeks, and bays a wide selection of yacht harbors varied enough to meet every taste, except that of the person who yearns to be "away from it all." Even such a person can find more peace and privacy than he might expect in such a crowded area, if he picks the right places to go.

In the bewildering array of busy ports around Hampton Roads, Norfolk and Portsmouth, Hampton and Newport News, it is easy to get mixed up and find yourself anchored in a spot about as out of everyone's way as the middle of Grand Central Terminal would be to a camper.

As in earlier editions of the Guide, we urge you to check carefully the pages of the *Coast Pilot,* wherein harbor and anchorage regulations are given for Hampton Roads. The chart also indicates restricted and prohibited areas. Hampton Roads is a great naval base, as well as a harbor with several great commercial ports. It is also the location, at Newport News, of one of the largest shipbuilding companies in the United States.

The mean range of tide is 2 ¹/₂ feet. Currents, as given in the Atlantic Coast Current Tables, vary considerably with the wind and at times are much stronger than those given in the tables. Along the wharves at Old Point Comfort, the current turns about an hour earlier than in mid-channel to the southward. Thus, there is about an hour preceding each mid-channel slack when the currents near the wharves and in the channel set in opposite directions.

In approaching Hampton Roads, the most prominent objects, as the *Coast Pilot* amply describes, are: Thimble Shoal Light (red conical tower on pier); Old Point Comfort Light (white tower); Fort Wool (flashing light on north searchlight tower); the Chamberlain Hotel at Old Point Comfort (twin towers on colonial brick building) and Fort Monroe behind it; a low gray structure on the south side of the entrance abreast Old Point Comfort; and a large group of buildings at Ocean View, a summer resort on the beach leading to Willoughby Spit.

Storm warnings are displayed on a tower at the south waterfront of Old Point Comfort. A National Ocean Service office, where charts, etc., are obtainable, is located at the U.S. Post Office and Court House Building in Norfolk. Chart agencies are in both Norfolk and Newport News.

On March 8, 1862, the *Monitor* and the *Merrimac* had their famous battle in Hampton Roads, which changed the course of naval warfare. Blackbeards Point, in Hampton, was so named because here, in 1718, Captain Henry Maynard set on a pole the head of Blackbeard, whom he had just personally beheaded in a sea battle. With Blackbeard's death, organized piracy ended.

1. *Mother Hawkins Hole* (*12245*), *Phoebus*. This is an anchorage exposed to wind if not sea from west to south, close to the west wall of Old Point Comfort, between the channel to the wharves at Phoebus and the Point. Except during a brief stop for a meal at the hotel, or perhaps after dark, we'd recommend going on into Hampton Creek. The Hole can be very uncomfortable in southwesters, but gives good protection from the northeast.

2. *Hampton River* (*12245*), *Hampton*. In our opinion this is by far the best yacht harbor on Hampton Roads. It is also one of the most accessible from the Bay, well marked, attractive and snug, with facilities readily available. The Kechoughtan Veterans Hospital is conspicuous to the east of the entrance. Beyond, and on the east shore of the river, are the tree-shaded grounds and buildings of the famous Hampton Institute.

Gas and diesel fuel are obtainable at the large wharf at the entrance to port. The current in the river is strong at times. Speed in the creek is restricted to 4 knots, though there is some complaint that this regulation is not enforced.

The harbor is too small and boat traffic too heavy for anchoring in the channel. Proceed upstream to a spot near the Settlers Landing Bridge to anchor or look for a slip at one of the following.

(1) In Sunset Creek, to port as you enter Hampton Reach. Follow carefully the charted channel. Bluewater Yacht Sales to port on the south shore has 60 or more slips, electricity, water, ice, showers, and other facilities. The Sunset Yachting Center, with gas and diesel fuel, slips, etc., is farther up the creek on the same side.

Supplies, or a shore meal or bed, are obtainable about half a mile away. The surroundings on Sunset Creek are pleasant and the commercial traffic less in evidence than on Hampton River. Feel your way in slowly because the water is shoal outside of the channel.

(2) At the Hampton Yacht Club, with its clubhouse on the west shore above Sunset Creek. There is deep water at the dock and the club is most hospitable to members of other recognized yacht clubs. The club will try to help visiting yachts find a berth, even if its own slips are full. It has gas, water, electricity, showers, and other facilities. Both groceries and marine supplies are close by and so is a marine railway. The Hampton Roads Marina on the river has slips and other facilities. However, as stated, the waters are apt to be quieter in Sunset Creek.

The Symes Eaton Public School at Hampton is said to be the oldest public school in the country, built in 1634. The splendid Mariners Museum, rivaled only by the museum of Mystic Seaport in Connecticut, is only 15 minutes away by car.

Note the tabulation on the chart of latest depths in Hampton River and Sunset Creek.

Sunset Creek and Hampton. (Photo courtesy of Backus Aerial Photography.)

3. Newport News (12245). At the end of the point at Newport News is Newport News Creek. Here there is protection from wind and sea but the place is narrow, commercial, crowded, and unattractive. There is much traffic of fishing craft but few yachts. The Hampton Roads tunnel has replaced the old ferries.

It used to be possible to tie up along the wall to starboard of the entrance, but the place is crowded and the wash of passing boats makes it uncomfortable. Little Boat Harbor Supply, a base for charter fishing boats, has diesel fuel and gas, groceries, and a restaurant. Davis Boat Works has a lift and can repair boats up to 130 feet. The U.S. Coast Guard has a station in the middle of the east bank, but Willoughby Bay and Norfolk have more to offer.

4. Willoughby Bay (12245, 12222). Most cruising boats find Hampton or Norfolk more convenient for an overnight stopping place, but Willoughby Bay provides a harbor of refuge just inside the Spit. There is a depth of at least 6 feet in the dredged channel leading across the bay to the Willoughby Bay Marina, the Willoughby Harbor Marina, and Rebel Marine Service, which have slips, gas, diesel, showers, and engine repairs. A good restaurant is close by, and groceries ¹/₂ mile away. If the tide is running hard you may have trouble staying in the channel, so check your course carefully and watch the markers forward and aft. Once inside you will find a tight little basin fully protected in all weather. In addition, you are close to the entrance to Chesapeake Bay if you are making an early morning start up the Bay.

5. Lafayette River (12245), Norfolk. This river, formerly called Tanner Creek, is popular with the Norfolk yachting fraternity. The dredged channel offers no particular difficulties. Just outside of the first bridge and on the north shore are the attractive grounds and clubhouse of the Norfolk Yacht and Country Club, with a well-kept dock with at least 14 feet of water at the end. Though open a way to the southwest, this is a fine place.

The facilities of the club are open to members of recognized clubs, who are naturally expected to observe the same regulations as those in effect for the club's own members. There is a sign on the dock welcoming such visiting yachtsmen, who are asked to report to the man at the dock. Twenty-four hour service is maintained and often slips are available.

Gas, oil, water, and ice can be obtained at the dock, and supplies by telephone in half an hour. The use of the club, its showers, dining room, and other privileges are all open to members of recognized clubs, with the approval of the club manager. The club wants to keep the place attractive to members, and all visitors are asked to cooperate to this end.

The friendly atmosphere of this club has always appealed to us. On one visit the manager even drove us to town to get a new key to a locked car!

Farther upriver are the Tidewater Boat Club and Morgan's Snug Harbor. But the first bridge is a fixed structure with only 26 feet clearance, so don't try to go up the river if your boat requires more clearance than that.

6. *Elizabeth River* (*12253*), *Port Norfolk Beach*. The most convenient overnight stopping point in Norfolk Harbor is the Tidewater Yacht Agency, located on the southwest point where the Intracoastal Waterway leaves the Eastern Branch, just beyond red nun 38. This is a large modern facility, with 325 dockside slips, fuel, marine supplies, swimming pool, and restaurant, adjacent to the Holiday Inn. Here you are close to the heart of downtown Norfolk, with a good view of the busy harbor, yet protected from the wash of passing tugs and steamers.

Waterside, Norfolk's waterfront "festival marketplace," is located almost directly across the river from Portsmouth's Holiday Inn. The slips for transients at Waterside will appeal to the boater who likes to be in the midst of activity. Tours of the city leave Waterside frequently during the day and it is an interesting place to visit. A bus makes a loop every hour and you can get off anyplace along the line

The American Rover, *a reproduction of a Chesapeake Bay cargo schooner, departs from The Waterside Marina, taking visitors on a three-day cruise of Norfolk's harbor. (Photo courtesy of Norfolk Convention and Visitors' Bureau.)*

to visit various attractions and get back on again to complete your journey. Next to Waterside is Town Point Park, a good place to stretch your legs if you have been on your boat for a while. Waterside is a popular place, and you might be wise to call ahead for a reservation, during a weekend especially, (804) 441-2152.

Facilities for hauling and repairing larger yachts are available at Norfolk Shipbuilding and Drydock Corp., on the eastern branch, and at several yards on the western branch.

7. Elizabeth River, Western Branch (12253). This branch of the river is somewhat less convenient, and more commercial, than the other parts of the Norfolk-Hampton area, but three marinas and boatyards provide slips and repair facilities in West Norfolk.

The entrance channel to the western branch is difficult to see until after you have passed Lambert Point and the numerous piles and dolphins on the south side of Lambert Bend; then you swing to starboard just before reaching Qk. Fl. red 30, which you leave to port, entering a clearly marked dredged cut leading to the swing bridge about 1 mile to the west. All of the marinas and yards are located just beyond the bridge. The Virginia Boat and Yacht Service provides slips, with gas, diesel, propane, etc., and has a 100-ton lift capable of handling yachts up to 80 feet. Engine and hull repairs are available. Western Ranch Diesel, Inc., has a 300-foot dock (formerly the Dunn yard) and is a good place to go for propeller and engine work. Lee's Yachting Center, at the bridge, has open and covered slips, and limited marine supplies.

XVII. NANSEMOND RIVER (*12248*).

This river, which empties into Hampton Roads opposite Newport News, has almost no facilities for cruising boats. There is room to anchor below the bridge, where the river is wide and open, but it is too shoal outside the channel for most boats in the more protected water above the bridge (fixed, vertical clearance 65 feet).

399

XVIII. JAMES RIVER (*12248, 12251*).

Except historically, James River in our opinion is less attractive for cruising than most of the other important rivers on the Bay. While the northern shore from Newport News to Deep Creek is lovely, with the Mariners Museum and its beautiful park, along the remaining shores, across and above, shoals and marshland are extensive; the land is low and good harbors rare. Almost every river and creek emptying into the James is fringed with marshes on at least one side and usually on both. Unlike some of the other Chesapeake rivers, the shores become higher farther up, but not until near Richmond do the marshes end. There the hills become higher and the shore more steep. It is 77 nautical miles by river from Newport News to Richmond.

For the cruiser who likes to wind a circuitous path along tiny placid streams between the marshes, and who avoids the mosquito season, the James may have a strong appeal. Creeks can be found which are too deep for a 12-foot pole and too narrow for turning around; they follow a snakelike course for miles between low banks, all looking very much alike, until perhaps at last a little pond opens up and the hook goes down in a solitude of marsh and water.

For the lover of history and antiquity and for one who enjoys the search for old houses and historic spots, a trip up the James offers rich rewards. About 6 miles above the southern tip of Newport News and 4 miles below Deep Creek, in a lovely park on Lake Maury, is the outstanding Mariners Museum, most easily reached from Deep Creek and not to be missed. Twenty-seven miles upriver is famous Jamestown Island, now a National Historic Monument. Along both sides of the James are some noted old houses. We shall mention a few, several of which are shown on the chart.

Near Sandy Point, just above the Chickahominy River on the north shore of the James, is Tettington, with a boxwood garden for which $4,000 is said to have been refused at the time of the Jamestown Exposition in 1906. Above Tettington, on the other shore are two famous homes, Upper and Lower Brandon. After turning first southwest and then northwest, Windmill Point is rounded, until just beyond Herring Creek, on the north shore is one of the most imposing colonial houses of Virginia, Westover, of deep red brick, home of the Byrd family. Just above the point where the Appomattox River enters the James is Shirley, "four square to the world and three stories high . . . in the midst of a lawn shaded by giant oaks." At Richmond, there is an old house (1737) known as "Washington's Headquarters," now an Edgar Allan Poe shrine.

Across the James River just above Newport News is a highway bridge about 4 miles long. The left draw has a vertical clearance of 50 feet when closed and 145 feet when open. Green lights at night indicate that the span is up; red lights that it's down. One long and one short blast of a whistle is the signal for opening.

The mean tidal range at Newport News is 2 1/2 feet, and at Richmond 3 1/2 feet. In mid-channel average velocities of the current at strength of flood or ebb run from 1 1/2 knots near Newport News to 1 knot at Dutch Gap.

1. Pagan River (12248), Southwest Shore of James. Unless you are addicted to ham and want to see the home of Smithfield hams so much that you won't mind dodging tugs and other commercial vessels, we'd suggest staying out. There is, however, a deep channel to Smithfield through marsh-lined banks.

2. Deep Creek (12248), Northeast Shore of James. This is not to be confused with the creek of the same name near the entrance of the Dismal Swamp Canal; neither is it to be confused with two other "Deep" creeks which we have mentioned, which have 1-foot depths. This creek has 6 feet according to the chart and 10 feet according to a local authority. It is the first good anchorage above Newport News. It also has the advantage of being only 2 or 3 miles by land from the Mariners Museum.

The entrance to the creek is easily identified by the lighted beacon, and by a white one-story house on the left, or Menchville, shore.

Deep Creek, off James River. (Photo courtesy of Stephen Knox.)

Turn to starboard around the beacon on the entrance point and anchor or tie up at one of the three marinas in the creek.

In the mosquito season you may not want to linger long on deck, for marshes are near at hand.

Don't miss the Mariners Museum. If you telephone them at Newport News, you may get a ride over there—provided the museum is open, and a car available. It is located in a lovely park along the shores of Lake Maury. The museum has a world-famous maritime collection, with a splendid library and a most accommodating staff, who are interested in helping yachtsmen. It is open on weekdays from 9 A.M. to 5 P.M., and on Sundays from 2 P.M. to 5 P.M.

3. Warwick River (12248), East Shore of the James. The river is shoal, with a narrow and difficult channel and no good anchorage or facilities.

4. Skiffes Creek (12248), East Shore of the James. Take a look at the "idle fleet" anchored off this creek and don't stop. We understand that the area is restricted for government use.

5. Jamestown Island (12248, 12251), East Shore of the James. "Jamestown, the first permanent colony of the English people. The birthplace of Virginia and of the United States, May 13, 1607."

So it says at the base of the monument erected 300 years afterward on the western end of Jamestown Island. This end of the island is attractive with its tall pines, and teems with historic interest. There is a statue of Captain John Smith and a monument to the Indian princess who saved his life: Pocahontas. The Jamestown Church Tower, long the only visible relic of old Jamestown, dates from 1639, perhaps earlier. Try to look back nearly 350 years and imagine the *Sarah Constant,* the *Goodspeed,* and the *Discovery* moored, or tied to trees, off the island while the first white Virginians—105 of them—landed and "set to work about the fortification."

The island is administered by the National Park Service as a National Monument. During the Jamestown Exposition of 1957 the

State of Virginia built a number of exposition buildings and a reconstruction of the first stockade built by the Jamestown colonists. These have remained open to visitors. The exposition grounds are located along the riverbank just north of the island and adjacent to the government dock. A smaller pier and breakwater have been built south of the government dock, where full-sized replicas of the three Jamestown ships are permanently moored. The boats were built by Dunn's yard at Norfolk and are faithful reproductions based on the best design information available. They are indeed worth a visit.

So, as you sail up the James today, your imagination gets more assistance than if you had made the trip when our first edition was published. You can rub your eyes and see the three old ships. But there are no facilities for berthing your yacht or lying alongside, as there were in earlier years.

Two channels with privately maintained markers lead in from the river, but there is still no adequate protected harbor for keel yachts. A facility is located on Powhatan Creek, which can be reached only by shoal-draft cruisers, entering either through the Thorofare behind Jamestown Island, or under the fixed bridge with 12-feet vertical clearance over Back Creek. This is the Jamestown Yacht Basin, with open slips, fuel, and repair facilities.

Don't miss Jamestown. If you can't get there by boat, drive over by car from Yorktown or Sarah Creek.

6. *Grays Creek (12251), West Shore of the James*. Unless you draw not much more than $3^1/_2$ feet and the tide is halfway above mean low water, don't try to go into Grays Creek. If, however, the above conditions are favorable, it is possible to obtain a marshy shelter in plenty of water around the bend of this narrow stream. This would be a much safer place to leave the boat than the Jamestown dock, and Jamestown could then be reached by ferry from Scotland.

7. *Chickahominy River (12251)*. This is the place for winding along narrow deep streams among the marshes. Some of these streams look fascinating on the chart, though we haven't been able to get there yet in our own boat. The river is used by only a few local fishermen and pleasure boatmen. The channel through the broad flats is marked by day beacons at critical points.

a. Gordon Creek. First to the starboard as you go up the Chickahominy, it has depths from 5 to 11 feet and yet is so narrow that its width is difficult to measure on the chart. This creek stops briefly in Nayses Bay, where the chart shows 8 to 6 feet on the east side, and then goes on, becoming still more narrow but remaining deep for some distance.

b. Morris Creek. On the west shore of the Chickahominy, this is another, even narrower creek, yet it has depths of not less than 8 feet for nearly 2 miles of meandering through the marshes.

c. Yarmouth Creek. Farther up this creek is another of the same kind—long, winding, very narrow, and deep. There is a 24-foot spot about 2 miles up and, except for a 4-foot spot, nothing less than 5 feet appears on the chart all the way up.

If you don't get stuck or lost in one of the creeks, you can zigzag, wind, and at times almost retrace your course all the way up the Chickahominy to Walker Dam, about 19 miles above the mouth, but not much more than half of that as the crow flies.

The Barretts Ferry Bridge, a swing bridge near the entrance, has a vertical clearance at mean high water of 12 feet through the westerly opening. The fish wharf at Shipyard Landing has 14 feet, and the buildings there are prominent from downstream. Lanexa is 15 miles above the entrance. Gas, fresh water, and supplies can be obtained. There are small marinas and campgrounds on both banks of the river all the way up to Chickahominy Lake.

8. James River above the Chickahominy (12251). Above the Chickahominy the James becomes narrow and winding, with many miles of marshland, ending in the rolling hills near Richmond. Outside of

An old cypress tree on the upper Chickahominy River makes a good home for an osprey. (Photo courtesy of the Chesapeake Bay Foundation.)

the James itself, or in the tributary, Appomattox River, there are no outstanding harbors, though anchorages along the river are many.

XIX. LITTLE CREEK (*12254*), NEAR CHESAPEAKE BAY ENTRANCE.

For cruising boats entering or leaving the Chesapeake by sea, Little Creek provides the first (or last) good harbor within the shelter of the Bay. Eight miles west of Cape Henry, and about 3½ miles south of Thimble Shoal ship channel inside the Chesapeake Bay Bridge-Tunnel, this offers a convenient stopping place and a safe harbor of refuge for offshore cruisers and deep-sea fishermen. The dredged entrance channel is clearly marked by a 70-foot lighted beacon on the eastern jetty.

As you approach the entrance, Little Creek appears dominated by the big ships and landing craft of the Naval Amphibious Base. You may also see a Coast Guard cutter or two and a freight car ferry on its route to or from Cape Charles. But don't be intimidated. In fact, the chance to see these vessels so near is one of the attractions of Little Creek. The deep channel is well marked by lighted beacons. About ¾ of a mile from the entrance, swing hard right around the red beacons and continue into the western branch, keeping fairly close to the landing craft berthed on the south side. Past the landing craft and before the fixed bridge are six marinas offering a variety of services and facilities. Two are on the south side of the creek, the rest on the north. If you are heading for one of the marinas above beacon 3, hug beacon 5 and the docks above it on the south side. On our visit a few years ago we found very shallow water and grounded briefly even though we thought we were reasonably close to beacon 5.

Most of the marinas serve primarily the local boats that are based there, but among them they offer all the services and most of the supplies you're likely to need: fuel, slips or dockside berths, ice, and repair facilities. Groceries are available at Jack's nearby, and a large

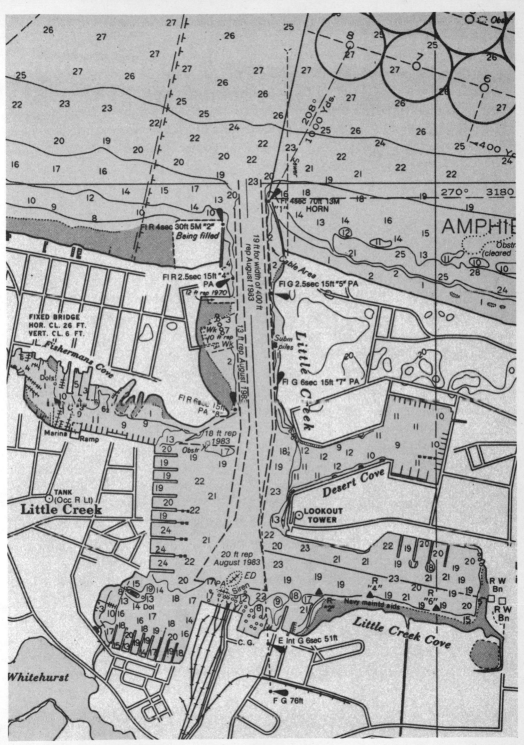

Little Creek, near the Chesapeake Bay entrance (from chart 12254).

shopping center with supermarket, department store, and small shops is about a mile from the north-side marinas and somewhat closer to those on the south. Transportation can easily be arranged.

Anchoring in Little Creek is not advisable, but it should always be possible to find an overnight berth at one of the marinas. Cobb's Marina and the Taylor's Landing Marina, both on the south side, have the largest number of slips.

XX. Lynnhaven Inlet (*12254, 12223*).

This is the first inlet west of Cape Henry, leading into Lynnhaven Bay and a protected waterway route to the back door of famous Virginia Beach. It is extensively used by sport fishing boats, charter boats, and power cruising yachts which can make the entrance bar and get under the two fixed bridges with 35-foot vertical clearance at mean high water. The entrance is subject to continual change. Six feet can usually be carried across the bar, but we don't recommend trying it in a strong onshore wind or rough sea conditions. The channel has been improved in recent years, and vessels drawing up to 6 feet can safely navigate the inlet and canal leading to Long Creek, Broad Bay, and Linkhorn Bay behind Virginia Beach.

After passing under the first highway bridge and the lighted beacons beyond, turn sharply to port into Long Creek and the Beach Canal leading toward Broad Bay. Tidal currents run strongly through the narrow cut by the bridge, but inside you'll find protected waters in the canal and along the creek where charter boats are moored and several marinas are located. The Lynnhaven Municipal Marina, with 50 slips, holds 4 for transient boats. Other docks and facilities are available at Long Creek Marina farther up that creek.

If you want to visit Virginia Beach, you can continue through the dredged and well-marked waterway past the Virginia State highway bridge (vertical clearance 35 feet) into Broad Bay, where you can carry 6 to 8 feet to the narrows. An improved channel now provides a project depth of 6 feet for a width of 90 feet, but you should check current depths with the marinas at the inlet before making this passage. When you reach Linkhorn Bay, which has 10- to 11-foot depths, swing to port at lighted beacon 23 into the eastern branch that leads closest to the beach and docks of the Cavalier Yacht and Country Club. The club, which is separate from the Cavalier Hotel, has facilities for transient yachts, and visitors may use the 18-hole golf course with payment of greens fees. The surroundings are attractive, and close by you can hear the breakers roll in Virginia Beach. The Barco Marine Railway, on the west side of Bird Neck Point, has slips and complete engine and hull repair facilities.

APPENDIX A

COASTWISE AND CHESAPEAKE BAY DISTANCES

NEW YORK, N. Y., TO CHESAPEAKE BAY ENTRANCE, VA.

COASTWISE DISTANCES

Figure at intersection of columns opposite ports in question is the nautical mileage between the two. Example: New York, N. Y., is 240 nautical miles from Philadelphia, Pa.

	NANTUCKET SHOALS 40°30.0'N., 69°25.0'W.	MONTAUK POINT, N.Y. 41°01.7'N., 71°47.3'W.	NEW YORK, N.Y. 40°42.0'N., 74°01.0'W.	Manasquan Inlet, N.J. 40°06.1'N., 74°01.9'W.	Barnegat Inlet, N.J. 39°46.0'N., 74°06.3'W.	Atlantic City, N.J. 39°22.6'N., 74°24.9'W.	Cape May Harbor, N.J. 38°57.1'N., 74°52.6'W.	DELAWARE BAY ENTRANCE 38°50.5'N., 75°03.3'W.	Harbor of Refuge, Del. 38°49.0'N., 75°05.2'W.	C. & D. CANAL E. ENT. 39°33.8'N., 75°32.8'W.	Wilmington, Del. 39°43.2'N., 75°31.5'W.	Marcus Hook, Pa. 39°48.2'N., 75°25.2'W.	Chester, Pa. 39°50.0'N., 75°22.0'W.	Philadelphia, Pa. 39°56.8'N., 75°08.3'W.	U.S. Steel Basin, Pa. 40°08.2'N., 74°45.3'W.	Trenton, N.J. 40°11.4'N., 74°45.4'W.	Indian River Inlet, Del. 38°36.5'N., 75°03.6'W.	Ocean City, Md. 38°19.6'N., 75°05.6'W.	Chincoteague, Va. 37°56.1'N., 75°22.8'W.
MONTAUK POINT, N.Y.	113																		
NEW YORK, N.Y.	223	122																	
Manasquan Inlet, N.J.	212	117	40																
Barnegat Inlet, N.J.	221	131	63	22															
Atlantic City, N.J.	242	159	94	52	32														
Cape May Harbor, N.J.	271	192	128	85	65	37													
DELAWARE BAY ENTRANCE	285	212	153	97	78	49	16												
Harbor of Refuge, Del.	285	212	153	98	79	50	17	2											
C. & D. CANAL E. ENT.	336	263	204	148	129	100	67	51	52										
Wilmington, Del.	347	274	215	159	140	111	78	62	63	11									
Marcus Hook, Pa.	353	280	221	165	146	117	84	68	69	17	8								
Chester, Pa.	356	283	224	169	150	121	88	72	73	21	11	3							
Philadelphia, Pa.	372	299	240	184	165	136	103	87	88	36	26	18	15						
U.S. Steel Basin, Pa.	395	322	263	207	188	159	126	110	111	59	49	41	38	23					
Trenton, N.J.	400	327	268	212	193	164	131	115	116	64	54	46	43	28	5				
Indian River Inlet, Del.	285	209	145	105	86	57	24	15	14	66	77	83	86	101	124	129			
Ocean City, Md.	295	227	161	121	101	73	40	32	31	83	95	101	104	119	142	147	20		
Chincoteague, Va.	328	262	201	161	141	113	80	72	71	123	134	140	144	159	182	187	60	41	
CHESAPEAKE BAY ENT. 36°56.3'N., 75°58.6'W.	381	322	267	219	199	171	141	155	155	206	218	224	227	242	265	270	118	100	69

Ambrose Light (40°27.5'N., 73°49.9'W.) to New York, 20.7 miles.
Five Fathom Bank Lighted Horn Buoy F (38°47.3'N., 74°34.6'W.) to Philadelphia, 111 miles.
Delaware Lighted Horn Buoy D (38°27.3'N., 74°41.8'W.) to Philadelphia, 116 miles.
Chesapeake Light (36°54.3'N., 75°42.8'W.) to Norfolk, 42 miles; Baltimore, 165 miles.

DISTANCES BY INTRACOASTAL WATERWAY
MANASQUAN INLET, N.J., TO CAPE MAY CANAL, N.J.
(Nautical Miles)

Figure at intersection of columns opposite ports in question is the nautical mileage between the two. Example: Atlantic City N.J., is 13 nautical miles from Ocean City, N.J.

Ports (with positions):

- CHES. & DEL CANAL E. ENT — 39°33.8'N., 75°32.8'W.
- Cape May Canal W Ent — 38°58.0'N. 74°58.0'W
- Cape May Harbor — 38°57.1'N. 74°52.6'W
- Wildwood — 39°00.5'N. 74°49.8'W
- Stone Harbor — 39°03.4'N. 74°46.0'W
- Avalon — 39°06.8'N. 74°44.0'W
- Sea Isle City — 39°09.4'N. 74°42.0'W
- Ocean City — 39°17.3'N. 74°34.4'W
- Mays Landing — 39°26.9'N. 74°43.4'W
- Atlantic City — 39°22.6'N. 74°24.9'W
- Beach Haven — 39°34.0'N. 74°14.8'W
- Barnegat Inlet — 39°46.0'N. 74°06.3'W
- Forked River (town) — 39°50.1'N. 74°11.7'W
- Seaside Park — 39°55.3'N. 74°05.0'W
- Toms River (town) — 39°56.9'N. 74°11.8'W
- Mantoloking — 40°02.2'N. 74°03.4'W
- Bay Head — 40°03.8'N. 74°03.1'W
- Manasquan Inlet — 40°06.1'N. 74°01.9'W
- Shark River Inlet — 40°11.2'N. 74°00.5'W
- NEW YORK, N.Y. (The Battery)* — 40°42.0'N. 74°01.0'W

Triangular distance table (each row lists the distances from the named port to the ports above it, reading toward CHES. & DEL CANAL E. ENT at the right end):

Cape May Harbor	48
Wildwood	4, 52
Stone Harbor	5, 9, 57
Avalon	5, 9, 14, 62
Sea Isle City	5, 10, 15, 19, 67
Ocean City	4, 9, 14, 18, 23, 71
Mays Landing	11, 15, 20, 25, 30, 34, 82
Atlantic City	18, 29, 33, 38, 43, 47, 52, 100
Beach Haven	30, 13, 25, 28, 34, 39, 43, 47, 95
Barnegat Inlet	18, 45, 29, 40, 44, 49, 54, 59, 63, 111
Forked River (town)	20, 38, 65, 49, 60, 64, 69, 74, 79, 83, 131
Seaside Park	8, 21, 39, 66, 50, 61, 65, 70, 75, 80, 84, 132
Toms River (town)	10, 13, 26, 44, 71, 55, 66, 70, 75, 80, 85, 89, 137
Mantoloking	7, 15, 18, 31, 49, 77, 60, 72, 75, 81, 86, 90, 94, 142
Bay Head	12, 9, 17, 20, 33, 51, 79, 63, 74, 77, 83, 88, 92, 96, 144
Manasquan Inlet	2, 14, 10, 19, 22, 35, 53, 80, 64, 76, 79, 85, 89, 94, 98, 146
Shark River Inlet	4, 6, 18, 14, 23, 26, 39, 57, 84, 68, 79, 83, 88, 93, 98, 102, 150
NEW YORK, N.Y. (The Battery)	34, 40, 44, 46, 58, 54, 63, 66, 79, 97, 124, 108, 74*, 119, 123, 128, 133, 138, 142, 190

* Outside distances between New York and Manasquan Inlet.

DISTANCES ON DELAWARE BAY AND RIVER
(Nautical Miles)

Figure at intersection of columns opposite ports in question is the nautical mileage between the two. Example: Salem, N.J., is 41 nautical miles from Philadelphia, Pa.

Location	Tren	Bord	USS	Burl	Phil	Schy	Ches	Brdg	Marc	Wilm	NewC	C&D	Salem	Smyr	Brdgt	Maur	StJo	CMay	Roos	DelBay
Trenton, N.J 40°11.4N 74°45.4W																				
Bordentown, N.J 40°09.1N 74°43.0W	4																			
US Steel Basin, Pa 40°08.2N 74°45.3W	5	2																		
Burlington, N.J 40°04.9N 74°51.8W	12	9	7																	
Philadelphia, Pa 39°56.8N 75°08.3W	28	25	23	16																
Schuylkill River Mouth, Pa 39°52.8N 75°11.9W	34	31	29	23	7															
Chester, Pa 39°50.0N 75°22.0W	43	40	38	31	15	9														
Bridgeport, N.J 39°48.0N 75°21.1W	49	46	44	37	22	14	6													
Marcus Hook, Pa 39°48.2N 75°25.2W	46	43	41	34	18	12	3	4												
Wilmington, Del 39°43.2N 75°31.5W	54	51	49	42	25	19	11	11	8											
New Castle, Del 39°39.4N 75°33.6W	58	55	53	46	30	23	15	15	12	5										
CHES. & DEL. CANAL, E ENT. 39°33.8N 75°32.8W	64	61	59	52	36	29	21	21	17	11	7									
Salem, N.J 39°34.6N 75°28.7W	69	66	64	57	41	34	26	26	22	16	12	5								
Smyrna River Mouth, Del 39°22.2N 75°30.2W	77	74	72	65	49	42	34	34	30	24	20	13	16							
Bridgeton, N.J 39°25.5N 75°14.2W	100	97	95	86	72	65	57	57	53	47	43	36	39	25						
Mauricetown, N.J 39°17.1N 74°59.5W	115	112	110	103	87	80	72	72	68	62	58	51	54	39	51					
St Jones River Mouth, Del 39°04.0N 75°02.5W	97	94	92	85	69	63	55	55	51	45	40	34	36	21	35	30				
Cape May Canal W Ent., N.J 38°58.0N 74°58.0W	112	109	107	100	84	77	69	69	65	59	59	55	51	36	47	26	21			
Roosevelt Inlet, Del 38°47.7N 75°09.4W	116	113	111	104	88	81	73	73	69	63	59	55	52	40	52	37	20	14		
DELAWARE BAY ENT. 38°50.5N 75°03.3W	115	112	110	103	87	80	72	72	68	62	58	51	54	39	51	33	20	9	6	

CHESAPEAKE BAY DISTANCES

Figure at intersection of columns opposite ports in question is the nautical mileage between the two. Example: Washington, D.C., is 155 nautical miles from Annapolis, Md.

Chesapeake Bay distance chart (triangular mileage table). Ports with coordinates, from top to bottom:

27	CHESAPEAKE BAY ENT.	36°56.3'N., 75°58.6'W.
	Norfolk, Va.	36°50.9'N., 76°17.9'W.
	Richmond, Va.	37°31.4'N., 77°25.2'W.
	Petersburg, Va.	37°14.1'N., 77°24.0'W.
	Hopewell, Va.	37°19.0'N., 77°16.4'W.
	Suffolk, Va.	36°44.3'N., 76°35.0'W.
	Newport News, Va.	36°58.0'N., 76°26.0'W.
	West Point, Va.	37°31.6'N., 76°48.1'W.
	Yorktown, Va.	37°14.4'N., 76°30.5'W.
	Cape Charles, Va.	37°15.9'N., 76°01.4'W.
	Fredericksburg, Va.	38°17.8'N., 77°27.2'W.
	Crisfield, Md.	37°58.6'N., 75°51.9'W.
	Washington, D.C.	38°52.4'N., 77°01.4'W.
	Potomac River Mouth	37°57.1'N., 76°16.1'W.
	Salisbury, Md.	38°21.9'N., 75°36.3'W.
	Solomons, Md.	38°19.2'N., 76°27.4'W.
	Cambridge, Md.	38°34.4'N., 76°04.3'W.
	St. Michaels, Md.	38°47.2'N., 76°13.2'W.
	Annapolis, Md.	38°59.0'N., 76°28.6'W.
	Chestertown, Md.	39°12.4'N., 76°03.8'W.
	Baltimore, Md.	39°16.0'N., 76°34.5'W.
	Havre de Grace, Md.	39°32.1'N., 76°05.0'W.
	Chesapeake City, Md.	39°31.8'N., 75°48.9'W.
	C. & D. CANAL E. ENT.	39°33.8'N., 75°32.8'W.

Distance values as read from the chart (nautical miles between ports). The following lists the distance figures appearing in each port's column of the triangular chart:

Port	Distance figures (as printed in chart)
Norfolk, Va.	27
Richmond, Va.	90, 101
Petersburg, Va.	28, 80, 92
Hopewell, Va.	10, 19, 70, 82
Suffolk, Va.	79, 89, 29, 98, 42
Newport News, Va.	21, 58, 77, 12, 24
West Point, Va.	63, 78, 66, 56
Yorktown, Va.	22, 35, 114, 122, 36, 34
Cape Charles, Va.	55, 101, 123, 66
Fredericksburg, Va.	48, 88, 132, 56
Crisfield, Md.	28, 50, 114, 201, 161
Washington, D.C.	122, 154, 143, 211
Potomac River Mouth	129, 51, 64, 86, 182
Salisbury, Md.	121, 221, 146, 164, 185
Solomons, Md.	96, 27, 125, 50, 186
Cambridge, Md.	49, 141, 43, 165, 240
St. Michaels, Md.	51, 27, 118, 150, 144
Annapolis, Md.	39, 81, 58, 149, 137
Chestertown, Md.	36, 89, 65, 156, 163
Baltimore, Md.	25, 39, 45, 155, 187
Havre de Grace, Md.	40, 59, 72, 187
Chesapeake City, Md.	45, 28, 45, 150
C. & D. CANAL E. ENT.	13, 33, 62, 78, 65, 83, 98, 85, 70, 90, 130, 124, 109, 200, 121, 230, 156, 149, 132, 155, 174, 201, 185

APPENDIX B

BASIC CHART COVERAGE REQUIREMENTS*

CHESAPEAKE AND DELAWARE BAYS
including major rivers and tidal estuaries to head of navigation,
and coastal areas between Sandy Hook and Cape Charles

I. The main bay of the Chesapeake, with principal rivers and tidal estuaries, arranged for planning and laying courses for cruising and long-distance racing

Area Coverage	Chart No.	Scale (000 omitted)
Upper Bay—C & D Canal to Point-No-Point	12260	1:197.2
Lower Bay—Point-No-Point to Chesapeake Bay entrance	12220	1:200
Head of Bay—Sandy Point to Susquehanna River	12273	1:80
Cove Point to Sandy Point	12263	1:80
Smith Point to Cove Point	12230	1:80
Wolf Trap to Smith Point	12225	1:80
Chesapeake Bay entrance	12221	1:80

*(†)denotes small-craft charts temporarily cancelled. "SC" indicates small craft.

II. Rivers and harbors of the Chesapeake, with principal bays, sounds, tributary creeks, and coves

Area Coverage	Chart No.	Scale (000 omitted)
Head of Bay—C & D Canal to Worton Point	12274	1:40
	†12275-SC	1:40
C & D Canal approaches	12277	1:20
Approaches to Baltimore Harbor	12278	1:40
	†12279-SC	1:40
Baltimore Inner Harbor	12281	1:15
Chester River	12272	1:40
Kent Island Narrows, Rock Hall Harbor		1:10
Severn and Magothy rivers	12282	1:25
Chesapeake Bay—Eastern Bay and South River	12270	1:40
Selby Bay		1:20
Annapolis Harbor	12283	1:10
Choptank River and Herring Bay	12266	1:40
Cambridge		1:10
Choptank River—Cambridge to Greensboro	12268	1:40
Chesapeake Bay—Patuxent River and vicinity	12264	1:40
Patuxent River—Solomons Island and vicinity	12284	1:10
Potomac River	12285-SC	1:80
Washington and vicinity		1:20
Chesapeake Bay to Piney Point	12233	1:40
Piney Point to Lower Cedar Point	12286	1:40
Dahlgren and vicinity	12287	1:20
Lower Cedar Point to Mattawoman Creek	12288	1:40
Mattawoman Creek to Georgetown	12289	1:40
Washington Harbor	12289	1:20
Honga—Nanticoke—Wicomico rivers	12261	1:40
Fishing Bay	12261	1:40
Tangier Sound—northern part	12231	1:40
Pocomoke and Tangier sounds	12228	1:40
Virginia Eastern Shore		
Cape Charles to Wolf Trap	12224	1:40
Wolf Trap to Pungoteague Creek	12226	1:40
Rappahannock River—Corrotoman River to Fredericksburg	12237-SC	1:20, 1:40
Rappahannock River entrance, Piankatank and Great Wicomico rivers	12235	1:40
York River entrance—Mobjack Bay	12238	1:40
York River—Yorktown and vicinity	12241	1:20
Yorktown to West Point	12243	

Area Coverage	Chart No.	Scale (000 omitted)
Cape Henry to Thimble Shoal Light	12254	1:20
Chesapeake Bay—Thimble Shoal	12256	1:20
Norfolk Harbor and Elizabeth River	12253	1:20
Hampton Roads	12245	1:20
James River—Newport News—Jamestown	12248	1:40
Jamestown Island to Jordon Point	12251	1:40
Jordan Point to Richmond	12251	1:20
Cape Charles to Norfolk Harbor	†12223-SC	1:40

DELAWARE BAY AND RIVER
Entrance to Chesapeake and Delaware Canal

Area Coverage	Chart No.	Scale (000 omitted)
Delaware Bay entrance	12304	1:80
Cape May Harbor	12317	1:10
Delaware River—Smyrna River to Wilmington	12311	1:40
Wilmington to Philadelphia	12312	1:40
Philadelphia and Camden waterfronts	12313	1:15
C & D Canal	12277	1:20

NEW JERSEY COAST AND INTRACOASTAL WATERWAY
Sandy Hook to Manasquan Inlet; Manasquan to Cape May; Delaware entrance to Virgina capes; and Chesapeake entrance

Area Coverage	Chart No.	Scale (000 omitted)
New York Harbor	†12328-SC	1:40
	12327	1:40
Sandy Hook to Little Egg Harbor	12324-SC	1:40
Little Egg Harbor to Cape May	12316-SC	1:40
Cape May Harbor	12317	1:10
Delaware Bay	12304	1:80
Delaware River—Smyrna River to Wilmington	12311	1:40
C & D Canal	12277	1:20
Cape Henlopen to Indian River Inlet	12216	1:40
Cape May to Fenwick Island	12214	1:80
Fenwick Island to Chincoteague Inlet	12211	1:80
Ocean City Inlet (inset)	12211	1:20

APPENDIX B

Area Coverage	Chart No.	Scale (000 omitted)
Chincoteague to Great Machipongo Inlet	12210	1:80
Chincoteague Inlet (inset)	12210	1:20
Chesapeake Bay entrance	12221	1:80
Cape Charles to Wolf Trap	12224	1:40
Cape Charles to Norfolk Harbor	†12223-SC	1:40
Norfolk Harbor and Elizabeth River	12253	1:20

NATIONAL WEATHER SERVICE OFFICES AND RADIO WEATHER BROADCASTS

National Weather Service Offices: The following offices will provide forecasts and climatological data or arrange to obtain these services from other offices. They will also check barometers in their offices or by telephone. (Consult the local telephone directories for telephone numbers.)

Atlantic City, N.J.: National Weather Service office, National Aviation Facilities Experimental Center.

Baltimore, Md.: National Weather Service office, Baltimore-Washington International Airport.

Newark, N.J.: National Weather Service office, Newark International Airport.

New York, N.Y.: National Weather Service office, 30 Rockefeller Plaza.

Norfolk, Va.: Norfolk Regional Airport; Atlantic Marine Center, NOS, 439 West York Street.

Philadelphia, Pa.: National Weather Service office, Terminal

Bldg., International Airport; National Weather Service Forecast office, Federal Bldg., 600 Arch Street.

Richmond, Va.: National Weather Service office, Byrd International Airport.

Washington, D.C.: National Weather Service Forecast Center, FOB 4, Suitland, Md.; National Weather Service office, Washington National Airport; National Weather Service office, Dulles International Airport.

Wilmington, Del.; National Weather Service office, Greater Wilmington Airport.

Radio Weather Broadcasts: Taped or direct broadcasts of forecasts and storm warnings are made by commercial and Coast Guard radio stations in the area covered by this guide. These broadcasts usually are made several times a day; the transmission schedules are shown on the Marine Weather Services Charts for the following areas:

Montauk Point, N.Y., to Manasquan, N.J.

Manasquan, N.J. to Cape Hatteras, N.C.

These charts are for sale by the National Ocean Service, Distribution Division (C44), 6501 Lafayette Avenue, Riverdale, Md. 20840, and its authorized sales agents.

The weather broadcast schedules of Coast Guard radio stations are also listed in the description of Coast Guard marine services found elsewhere in this appendix.

VHF-FM Weather Broadcasts: National Weather Service VHF-FM radio stations provide mariners with continuous FM broadcasts of weather warnings, forecasts, radar reports, and selected weather observations. These stations usually transmit on 162.55 or 162.40 MHz. Reception range is usually up to 40 miles from the antenna site, depending on terrain, type of receiver, and antenna used. The following VHF-FM radio stations with location of antenna are in or near the area covered by this guide.

KWO-35, New York, N.Y., 162.55 MHz. (40°46′N., 73°59′W.)

KIH-28, Philadelphia, Pa., 162.475 MHz. (40°04′N., 75°15′W.)

KHB-38, Atlantic City, N.J., 162.40 MHz. (39°23′N., 74°27′W.)

WXJ-94, Lewes, Del., 162.55 MHz. (38°47′N., 75°10′W.)
KEC-83, Baltimore, Md., 162.40 MHz. (39°11′N., 76°40′W.)
KHB-36, Manassas, Va., 162.55 MHz. (38°38′N., 77°26′W.)
KEC-92, Salisbury, Md., 162.40 MHz. (38°18′N., 75°40′W.)
KHB-37, Norfolk, Va., 162.55 MHz. (36°49′N., 76°28′W.)

APPENDIX D

AGENCIES
FOR GOVERNMENT PUBLICATIONS

Nautical charts and certain related publications, such as the *Coast Pilot*, Tide Tables, Current Tables, and Tidal Current Charts, may be purchased from the National Ocean Service (formerly Coast and Geodetic Survey) of the Department of Commerce, at 6501 Lafayette Ave., Riverdale, Md.; or from sales agents; or from the NOS district offices. Mail orders should be addressed to Distribution Branch N/CG33, National Ocean Service, Riverdale, Md. 20737. Mail orders should be accompanied by check or money order in U.S. funds and made payable to NOS, N/CG33.

Notice to Mariners is published by the Defense Mapping Agency, and is prepared jointly with the National Ocean Service and the U.S. Coast Guard. The Coast Guard's Fifth District, at Norfolk, Va., issues a local *Notice,* covering Chesapeake Bay, which is more useful to yachtsmen cruising this area. Request to be placed on the mailing list for this publication by writing to Aids to Navigation and Waterway Management Branch, Fifth Coast Guard District, 431 Crawford St., Portsmouth, Va. 23704-5004.

Light Lists may be purchased from the Superintendent of Documents, Washington, D.C.

The *Coast Pilot* covering the areas described in this guide is Vol. 3, "Sandy Hook to Cape Henry," and is now published annually in paperback editions that include corrections made by computer tape. Copies are available at most agencies handling charts and other navigation aids. An up-to-date edition of the *Coast Pilot* should, of course, be on board every cruising yacht.

NOTE: Government aids to navigation on Chesapeake Bay are being altered to be consistent with the International Association of Lighthouse Authorities (IALA) Maritime Buoyage System. The conversion is taking place over a period of 6 years to coincide with the usual maintenance schedule in order to minimize the cost of instituting the system. The conversion should be complete by 1989.

The major changes are the introduction of the yellow Special Mark, the replacement of the black and white mid-channel aids by the red and white Safe Water Mark, and the changing of some aids to navigation signals— most notably green marks, which replace the older black porthand marks.

APPENDIX E

SAVING THE CHESAPEAKE BAY— A NATIONAL PRIORITY

William C. Baker
President, Chesapeake Bay Foundation

April 1, 1988

In 1976, the United States Congress concluded that Chesapeake Bay was a natural resource of outstanding value to the nation. The Environmental Protection Agency (EPA) was, therefore, directed to conduct an in-depth investigation into the state of the Bay. EPA was to determine what major environmental problems the Bay faced and to explore management alternatives which would improve its condition. Congress allocated $25 million dollars over five years to carry out the study. On September 30, 1982, one year late and $2 million dollars over budget, a 625-page "synthesis" of some 40 research projects was presented to Congress. Thus the first phase had been completed. To fully meet the congressional mandate, however, EPA was required to correlate long-term water quality trends with living Bay resources and outline possible management strategies. Although a report was filed with Congress on September 30, 1983, this phase of the project is still ongoing. In essence, there remain more questions than answers.

The research documents two general categories of Bay pollution, one caused by an excessive inflow of "nutrients" (mainly nitrogen and phosphorus), and the other by toxic chemicals. Although a certain amount of nutrient enrichment is good for the Bay, too much "fertilization" causes an overproduction of algae. When these tiny plants die, the decay process uses up dissolved oxygen in the water, which is essential for all forms of life. In fact, during warm summer months, waters in deep, mid-Bay regions have historically experienced anoxia, a phenomenon in which the levels of dissolved oxygen reach zero. In recent years, however, the scope of anoxia has increased fifteenfold, and it now lasts far longer than before. During these times, no aquatic life can survive. In addition, the overabundance of free-floating algae prevents light from reaching vitally important underwater grass beds, the result of which has been a dramatic decline. In the past 20 years, up to 80 percent of these grasses have disappeared.

With toxic chemicals, the story is somewhat different. Even a small amount of them, one might suppose, is bad for life in and around the Chesapeake Bay. And certainly the types and quantities which are continually dumped into its waters are taking a toll on the delicate estuarine mechanism. Consider, for example, just *some* of the chemicals discharged *daily* from one large industrial installation as sanctioned by its legal permit: over 4,000 pounds of oil and grease, 15 pounds of cyanide, 40 pounds of zinc, and 3 pounds of chromium. And this does not even mention a whopping 18,000 pounds per day of toxic and oxygen-demanding ammonia.

The EPA study identifies certain "hot spots" of high toxicity, most notably Baltimore Harbor and Virginia's Elizabeth River, where bottom sediments are heavily contaminated. The report also notes, however, that even near the water's surface, an area of high organic activity, high concentrations of contaminants are present. Such a situation may be introducing pollutants to the Bay's food chain. Finally, laboratory tests on discharges from industrial plants show that up to half the waste water sampled may kill fish and invertebrates.

For years, toxic chemical pollution has received the predominant amount of public attention nationwide, and the Chesapeake has been no different. The overenrichment of the Bay from high nutrient inflow may, however, be an even more insidious killer. For while toxics are released primarily from individual discharge pipes which can be identified and, if the public demands, the effluent can be treated, nutrients enter the Bay primarily with storm water runoff from land. It is called nonpoint source pollution, because it does not come from an individual point. Naturally, the control of such runoff is difficult, yet it will be mandatory if the Bay is

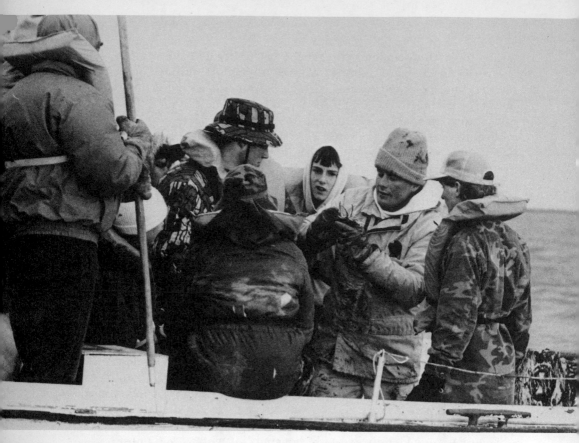

On Chesapeake Bay Foundation–sponsored trips like this one, everyone can get out on the Bay and examine Bay life. (Photo courtesy of the Chesapeake Bay Foundation.)

to survive, especially with surging regional populations. New and improved farming practices, better designs for subdivisions, the use of buffer strips near creeks and rivers, vegetated drainage ditches, and sediment control devices all will help. To further complicate matters, however, it has now become apparent that nonpoint source pollution may also contribute more toxics than scientists had previously realized. In addition, air pollution may also contribute toxics to the Bay, through a process known as atmospheric deposition.

The EPA's comprehensive Chesapeake Bay study has revealed an estuary that is suffering from a number of different ailments. It has documented massive pollution problems and drastically declining living aquatic resources. We no longer hear, for example, that underwater grasses or striped bass are simply on the "down side" of natural cycles. In the last few hundred years, just a wink in geologic time, modern man has left a sorry mark on the magnificent Chesapeake.

Yet, if it was man who polluted the Bay, it can be man who will clean it up. And the situation *can* be reversed. Thanks to years of scientific research and now the EPA study, we know more about the Bay than ever before. We have the "tools" needed to begin a broad and far-reaching restoration effort. To put such a strategy in place, however, will take a great deal of time, money, and sacrifice by all who have been using the Bay for so long. Fortunately, Governors Baliles, Schaefer, and Casey of Virginia, Maryland, and Pennsylvania, respectively, in conjunction with Washington Mayor Barry, have publicly committed themselves to making the Bay clean-up a high priority. In late 1987 they signed a document known simply as The Chesapeake Bay Agreement. It is a historic document that lays the foundation for an unprecedented level of cooperation between the Bay states. It sets forth a number of commitments for improvements in water quality, living resources, public access and education, growth and development pressures, and Bay governance.

Most important, however, the new agreement calls for a specific timetable to achieve the various goals and objectives. That is welcome news, because as the Bay has made abundantly clear, it cannot afford the luxury of time. We must move to Save the Bay today, for tomorrow may be too late.

BIBLIOGRAPHY

I. *Government Publications*
   U.S. Department of Commerce
     National Oceanic and Atmospheric Administration (NOAA)
     National Ocean Survey (NOS)
       Light List, Volume I, Atlantic and Gulf coasts (includes list of lights, fog-horns, buoys, day beacons, radio beacons, and Loran stations).
       National Chart Catalog. Atlantic and Gulf coasts.
       Tidal Current Tables. Atlantic Coast of North America.
       United States Coast Pilot, Volume 3, Atlantic and Gulf coasts.
   U.S. Government Printing Office
     Nautical Almanac, published jointly by the U.S. Naval Observatory, Washington, D.C., and H.M. Stationery Office, London, England.
II. *Privately Published Almanacs and Pilot Books*
   Eldridge *Tide and Pilot Book.* Tide and currents, Nova Scotia to Key West.
   Reed's *Nautical Almanac and Coast Pilot.* East Coast, Gulf Coast, and islands (U.S. distributor, Better Boating Association).
III. *Cruising Guides and Chart Kits*
Anderson, Elizabeth B. *Annapolis, A Walk Through History.* Centreville, Md.: Tidewater Publishers, 1967.
Barrie, Robert, and George, Jr. *Cruises: Mainly in the Bay of the Chesapeake.* Philadelphia: The Franklin Press, 1909.

Boating Almanac, Volume 4, covering Chesapeake Bay, Delaware, Maryland, Washington, D.C., and Virginia, with full information on marinas, boat facilities, launching ramps, etc. Published annually by Boating Almanac Company, Severna Park, Md. 21146.

Bodine, A. Aubrey. *Chesapeake Bay and Tidewater.* Baltimore, Md.: Bodine and Associates, Inc., 1954.

Bodine, A. Aubrey. *The Face of Maryland.* Baltimore, Md.: Bodine and Associates, Inc., 1961.

Brewington, M. V. *Chesapeake Bay, A Pictorial Maritime History.* Centreville, Md.: Cornell Maritime Press, 1953.

Bryon, Gilbert. *The Lord's Oysters.* Boston and Toronto: Little, Brown and Company, 1947.

Burgess, Robert H. *Chesapeake Circle.* Centreville, Md.: Cornell Maritime Press, 1965.

Burgess, Robert H. *This Was Chesapeake Bay.* Centreville, Md.: Cornell Maritime Press, 1963.

Chart Kit/BBA, Region 4, Chesapeake and Delaware bays. Includes photographic reproductions of U.S. Government charts, with courses and distances in both bays and coastal waters of the Delmarva Peninsula. Published by Better Boating Association, Inc., Box 407, Needham, Mass. 02192.

de Gast, Robert. *Lighthouses of the Chesapeake.* Baltimore, Md.: Johns Hopkins University Press, 1973.

Earle, Swepson. *Chesapeake Bay Country.* Baltimore, Md.: Remington-Putnam, 1938.

Footner, Hulbert. *Rivers of the Eastern Shore.* Reprinted Centreville, Md.: Tidewater Publishers, 1972.

Guide to Cruising the Chesapeake Bay. Includes sketch charts of popular harbors. Published by Chesapeake Bay Magazine, 1819 Bay Ridge Ave., Annapolis, Md. 21403.

Guide for Cruising Maryland Waters. Reproductions of U.S. Government charts, with courses and distances to major harbors in Maryland's part of the Chesapeake. Published by Maryland Department of Natural Resources, Annapolis, Md. 21401.

Gutheim, Frederick. *The Potomac.* New York: Rinehart & Company, 1941.

Hamer, Red. *Four Seasons of the Chesapeake.* West Chester, Pa.: Four Seasons Book Publishers, 1980.

Hays, Anne M., and Hazleton, Harriet R. *Chesapeake Kaleidoscope.* Centreville, Md.: Tidewater Publishers, 1975.

Hill, Norman Alan. *Chesapeake Cruise.* Baltimore, Md.: George W. King Printing Company, 1944.

Klingel, Gilbert. *The Bay.* New York: Dodd, Mead & Company, 1951.

Lang, Varley. *Follow The Water.* Winston-Salem, N.C.: John F. Blair, Publisher, 1961.

Michener, James A. *Chesapeake.* New York: Random House, 1978.

Middleton, Arthur Pierce, Ph.D. *Tobacco Coast.* Newport News, Va.: The Mariners Museum, 1953.

Sherwood, Arthur W. *Understanding the Chesapeake: A Layman's Guide.* Centreville, Md.: Tidewater Publishers, 1973.

Tawes, William I. *God, Man, Salt Water and the Eastern Shore.* Centreville, Md.: Tidewater Publishers, 1967.

Wallop, Douglass. *Regatta.* New York and London: W. W. Norton & Company, 1981.

Walsh, Harry M. *The Outlaw Gunner.* Centreville, Md.: Tidewater Publishers, 1971.

Warner, William W. *Beautiful Swimmers: Watermen, Crabs and the Chesapeake Bay.* Boston and Toronto: Little, Brown and Company, 1976.

Waterway Guide, Mid-Atlantic edition. Covers New Jersey, Delaware Bay, Chesapeake Bay, and Intracoastal Waterway to Florida. Published annually by Waterway Guide, Inc., 850 Third Ave., New York, N.Y. 10022.

Waterway Guide Charts, New York to Norfolk, including Chesapeake and Delaware bays, New Jersey, and Delmarva coasts; air photos, distance tables, etc. Published by Waterway Guide, Inc., 850 Third Ave., New York, N.Y. 10022.

Wennersten, John R. *The Oyster Wars of Chesapeake Bay.* Centreville, Md.: Tidewater Publishers, 1981.

INDEX

435

If you enjoyed this book, you'll want to order other titles in our series. The following titles are available:

A Cruising Guide to the Caribbean and the Bahamas
ISBN 0-399-15002-1 $29.95 ($41.95 CAN)
A Cruising Guide to the New England Coast
ISBN 0-399-15000-5 $29.95 ($41.95 CAN)

For your convenience, use the form below to order.
These books are available at your local bookstore or wherever books are sold.

The Putnam Publishing Group
390 Murray Hill Parkway, Dept. S.
East Rutherford, NJ 07073

Please send me the following books. I'm enclosing $_____ for books plus postage and handling and applicable sales tax (CA, NY, NJ, PA).

Enclosed is my ☐ check ☐ money order. Please charge my ☐ Visa ☐ MasterCard.
(Postage and handling: $1.50 for one book, $.50 for each additional book.)
Card #_____
Expiration date_____

ISBN	TITLE	PRICE

Name_____

Address_____

City_____ State_____ Zip_____

Subtotal	
Postage & Handling	
Sales Tax	
Total	

Payable in U.S. funds only

Signature as on charge card_____